The Young Naturalist's Guide to Florida

Peggy Sias Lantz

Wendy A. Hale

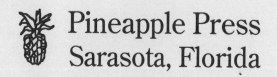
Pineapple Press
Sarasota, Florida

Some chapters in this book were originally sponsored by Walt
Disney World Co. Most of the chapters were published in the magazine of the Florida Audubon Society, *The Florida Naturalist.*

Inquiries should be addressed to:
Pineapple Press, Inc.
P.O. Drawer 16008
Southside Station
Sarasota, Florida 34239

Library of Congress Cataloging-in-Publication Data

Lantz, Peggy S., 1933–
    The young naturalist's guide to Florida/by Peggy S. Lantz and
Wendy Hale.
        p.   cm.
    Includes bibliographical references (p.   ) and index.
    ISBN 1-56164-051-4
    1. Natural history—Florida—Juvenile literature.   [1. Natural
history—Florida.]   I. Hale, Wendy, 1954– .   II. Title.
QH105.F6L36   1994   94-15485
508.759—dc20   CIP

Designed and composed by Octavo
Printed and bound by Rose Printing Company, Tallahassee, Florida

To my parents, Bill and Joanne, who taught
me to appreciate nature at an early age.

—Wendy A. Hale

To the memory of my father, Ralph Sias,
who loved Florida.

—Peggy Sias Lantz

Contents

Preface and Acknowledgments

Most of the chapters in this book originally appeared in *The Florida Naturalist,* a publication of the Florida Audubon Society, between 1985 and 1991, when Peggy Lantz was editor of the magazine.

Thanks to Walt Disney World Co. for sponsoring some of the original chapters in the magazine.

Thanks to the many people who helped us get our facts right, especially botanist Richard Wunderlin, who reviewed all the material about plants more than once. Also, Robert Gore, taxonomist David Hall, James Henry, Susan Jewell, ornithologists Herbert Kale and David Maehr, Gil Nelson, herpetologist Peter Pritchard, astronomer Gerald Reed, Doug Stamm, and Peter Stiling. If the authors have made errors in spite of all this help, we accept responsibility for them.

Thanks to Neta Villalobos-Bell, Valerie Gohlke, Marjory Bartlett Sanger, and Molly Wylly for their assistance with some of the writing for the original series.

And thanks especially to the artists who offered their time and talents to richly illustrate the articles when they first appeared in *The Florida Naturalist* and again in this book. Their names, a short biography, and the title of the chapter(s) they illustrated appear in a special section.

Introduction for the Young Naturalist

"The world is so full of a number of things,
I'm sure we should all be as happy as kings."

—Robert Louis Stevenson

When Robert Louis Stevenson wrote this, he was sickly and bedridden and unable to spend much time out-of-doors. How much more opportunity most of us have than he did to enjoy the great number of wonders the natural world has to offer!

Florida, especially, has a splendid variety of wildlife that should make us all as happy as kings. Plants, birds, insects, and reptiles, as well as mammals, enrich the lives of those who are observant. We hope that if you know something about Florida's natural places, you will feel an affinity with nature that will encourage you to take good care of Florida and Planet Earth.

Remember when reading this book that "animals" refers to all species within the animal kingdom, not just furry, four-legged mammals. We have taken the direction of the American Ornithologist's Union and capitalized the full species name of all plants and animals. In this way readers can understand the difference between, for example, the Florida Black Bear and a bear that is black, or that Yellow Jessamine is the full name of a plant and not just its flower color. We have elected not to use scientific names except in Chapter 14: "What's in a Name?"

The word "species" is used many times. It refers to a specific kind of plant or animal. The word is both singular and plural. Be sure you understand this word.

Most of the species included in these chapters are not common, everyday plants and animals. Many are included in the state's list of Endangered or Threatened Species or Species of Special Concern. Those listed species are marked with a superscript + the first time their names appear in each chapter.

A plant or animal listed as Endangered is in danger of extinction throughout all or a significant portion of its range (the area in which it lives). Extinction occurs when the last individual of a species dies and that plant or animal can never exist on earth again. A list of all of Florida's Endangered Species is found at the end of Chapter 25: "Extinction is Forever."

A species is Threatened when it is likely to become an endangered species within the foreseeable future throughout all or a significant portion of its range.

A category that applies to Florida animals only is Species of Special Concern. It is used to describe a species of animal in Florida that may become threatened if not protected and effectively managed.

Measurements are indicated first in metric—cm for centimeter, m for meter, km for kilometer, kg for kilogram, and l for liter (if not spelled out)—followed by the equivalent inches, feet, miles, pounds, or gallons in parentheses. Equivalents are approximate, or rounded off.

We hope the extensive glossary and appendix will be of benefit. All words that appear at the end of each chapter in the box under, "Do you know these words?" are in the glossary.

The authors hope that reading this book will make you more aware of the wonders of natural Florida, and that you will want to help in the efforts to protect what is left of Florida's wild lands.

Sabal Palm—Florida's state tree.

State seal

Chapter 1

Florida's Symbols

A symbol is something that stands for something else. Many states and nations have chosen symbols to represent something special or unique about their area, such as our country's national bird, the Bald Eagle, which is found only in North America. Did you know that Florida's state symbols, chosen by the state legislature over the years, include a bird, a tree, fish, mammals, and even rocks? Some Floridians can name the official state bird or state tree. Can you?

State Seal

Over 100 years ago, in 1868, the Florida legislature adopted a state seal (shown on page 6). It showed the sun's rays over a mountain in the distance, a steamboat on the water, an Indian woman scattering flowers, and a tree that was officially called a "cocoa" tree (but which was probably a Coconut Palm). Around the design were the words, "Great Seal of the State of Florida—In God We Trust." The unknown designer of this first seal could hardly have been very well acquainted with Florida, because Florida has no mountains, and Florida's Seminole Indian women didn't wear clothes like the woman depicted on the seal.

Changes were made over the years to correct several details of the seal. In 1970, the "cocoa" tree was redrawn as a Sabal Palm, the state tree of Florida. The most recent change was made in 1985. The official seal now appears as it is above, with no mountains, a Sabal Palm and Saw Palmetto, a steamboat that looks like ones that used to sail in Florida, and a Seminole Indian woman dropping Hibiscus flowers.

State Flag

The flag was adopted at the same time as the seal, in 1868, and it showed the seal on a white background. In 1889, the legislature added the diagonal red bars we see today, because people wanted the flag to have more color. Did you know that Florida law requires the flag of both the United States of America and the state of Florida to fly over every public school (weather permitting) each school day?

At least 16 different flags have flown over Florida or parts of Florida in its history, including those of five countries—Spain, France, England, the United States, and the Confederate States of America.

State Flower—the Orange Blossom

One of the most fragrant flowers of any tree—the Orange Blossom—is Florida's oldest symbol. It was declared the state flower in 1909. Millions of these white flowers perfume the air in central and south Florida during orange blossom time. Although a series of freezes in the 1980s killed many thousands of acres of citrus groves, trees have been replanted, and Florida is still the largest producer of citrus fruits in the United States.

Orange Blossom

3

Orange juice became the state's official beverage in 1967. People living in other parts of the country often think of Florida when they drink orange juice.

Northern Mockingbird

State Bird—the Northern Mockingbird

The Northern Mockingbird has been Florida's state bird since 1927. It is also the state bird of Arkansas, Mississippi, Tennessee, and Texas. The "northern" part of its name means it is a North American bird. Though its colors of gray and white are not as brilliant as those of some other songbirds, it lives year-round in Florida and its song is very special. During nesting season, the male mockingbird often sings continuously for hours, without repeating his tune. He can sing sitting on a branch or flying, during the day, or sometimes even in the moonlight!

State Tree—the Sabal Palm

The Sabal Palm, also called the Cabbage Palm or Palmetto, has been the state tree of Florida since 1953. It grows in all kinds of soil—sandy or loamy, wet or dry—and in states farther north, too. This tree was important in historical times, when early settlers used its leaf heart for food and its logs and fronds to build shelter.

Sabal Palm

State Shell—the Horse Conch, and State Stone—Agatized Coral

The Horse Conch (pronounced "conk") has been Florida's state shell since 1969. The word conch comes from a Greek word meaning "shell." The Horse Conch, found in the shallow ocean waters around Florida, is very large and is a beautiful pinkish orange color.

Coral is made of the skeletons of tiny ocean animals called polyps (pronounced POLL-lips) that grow together in colonies in warm tropical seas. When the polyps are alive, they combine carbon dioxide and minerals in the seawater to form a hard, limestonelike surface. After long periods of time, the coral becomes agatized when the silica, or sand, in the ocean replaces the coral with a hard quartzlike mineral. Agatized coral is found in Tampa Bay, the Econfina River, and the Withlacoochee and Suwannee riverbeds.

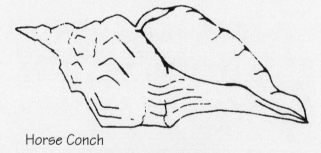
Horse Conch

State Nickname—The Sunshine State

Florida's beautiful sunny weather led many people to call it "The Sunshine State." The sun

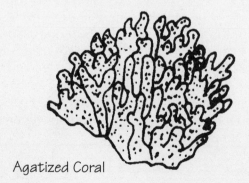
Agatized Coral

shines for at least part of almost every day of the year. The state nickname was made official in 1970.

State Gem—Moonstone

Humans first landed on the moon in July, 1969, on a space flight launched from Florida's Kennedy Space Center. Ten months later, Florida lawmakers memorialized this historic occasion by declaring the Moonstone the official state gem. The Moonstone is a gem found on earth, however, not one of the rocks brought back from the surface of the moon.

Symbols that Represent Florida's Waters

Several of Florida's symbols are water related, for one of Florida's most important assets is its water—springs, lakes, rivers, the Atlantic Ocean, and the Gulf of Mexico.

State Marine Mammal—the West Indian Manatee, and State Saltwater Mammal— the Porpoise

In 1975, Florida chose the West Indian Manatee to be the state's marine mammal, and the Porpoise to be the state's saltwater mammal.

The West Indian Manatee, which is an endangered species, swims in many Florida waterways, both fresh and salt, where it feeds on a variety of underwater plants. It is a large and slow-moving mammal that must come to the surface to breathe air. Boats often hit it, cutting its back with propellers. Slowing down speeding boaters, and research on where and how the manatee lives, are helping to bring public attention to the serious plight of this harmless, docile giant.

One species of porpoise, whose name is actually Bottle-nosed Dolphin, lives in Florida's coastal waters. Adding to the confusion of its name is an edible saltwater fish called Dolphin.

Porpoise

The state legislature, in adopting this marine mammal as a symbol, left open the issue of what to call the state saltwater mammal, designating the "porpoise, also commonly known as the dolphin." You can sometimes see a group of dolphins in the waves near the beach or swimming in the bow wake of large boats. Dolphins and porpoises have been a symbol of good luck to sailors around the world since ancient times. The Miami football team's logo and the trained animals at Marineland and Sea World are Bottle-nosed Dolphins.

State Freshwater Fish—the Largemouth Bass, and State Saltwater Fish—the Sailfish

No other state has designated two fish as state symbols. But in 1975, Florida named the Largemouth Bass, which lives in fresh water, and the Sailfish, which lives in salt water, as our state fish. Both are prized as game fish, and fishermen from all over the world come to Florida to try their luck at catching them.

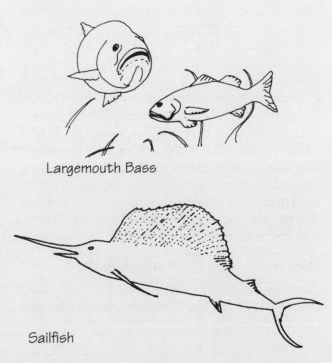

Largemouth Bass

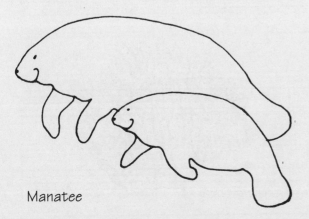

Manatee

Sailfish

Florida Panther

Where to learn more

See "Springs, Sinkholes, and Caves" for more on the West Indian Manatee.

See "Extinction Is Forever" for more on the Florida Panther.

See "Speaking of Trees" for more on the Sabal Palm.

Do you know these words?

Can you list them in alphabetical order?

symbol	coral
polyps	agatized
endangered	extinction
animal	agate
mammal	

State Mammal—the Florida Panther

The Florida Panther, the most endangered of all Florida's symbols, was chosen to be the state mammal in 1982 by a vote of Florida school students. This big, elusive cat needs many miles of wild land to hunt its main food, the White-tailed Deer. But much of Florida's wilderness is being cleared for farmland or houses, and the panther needs our help to make sure that it remains a living part of our unique wildlife community, instead of the first Florida symbol to become extinct.

State Song—"Swanee River"

Stephen Collins Foster, one of America's best-loved songwriters, wrote "Swanee River" (also called "Old Folks at Home") in 1851. Florida's Suwannee River (which Foster spelled Swanee to better fit the music) is a beautiful waterway that flows from the Okefenokee Swamp in Georgia to the Gulf of Mexico. "Swanee River" was chosen as the state song in 1935, and has become a symbol of love for home and family.

Can you play "Swanee River" on your piano at home, or on your school band instrument?

Swanee River

Words and Music by
Stephen C. Foster

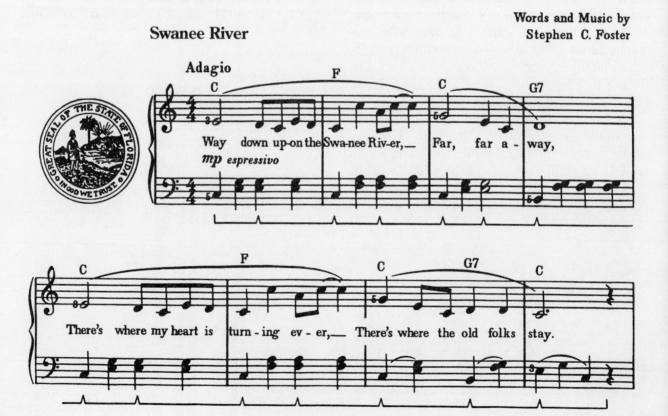

Chapter 2

Keeping a Nature Journal

My Journal

June 9—School is out! I plan to write in my notebook this summer about the weather, all the animals I see, and the flowers that bloom.

Today I walked down the lane, and the palmetto bloom smelled so wonderful. I stopped to look at it. Five different species of butterflies and some bees and beetles were enjoying it, too!

June 22—Today is a beautiful sunny day. It was cool when I got up, but now it's hot. I like it hot, but the difference in how it feels out in the sun and under the shade of the trees surprises me. I put a thermometer out in the open with just a box to shade it, and then I put it in the shade close to the big oak tree. It was 95°F in the sun, and 83°F in the shade—a difference of 12 degrees.

Holes for air

July 10—The Brown Thrasher sits at the top of the tree next door and sings all day long every day. He has as many different songs as the Mockingbird, but they're in short phrases instead of continuous. The Blue Jays are pretty, and they have a lot of different songs, too.

Blue Jay

I sat and watched a woodpecker hole in the stub of a dead tree for about an hour today. The woodpecker was a Red-bellied Woodpecker, and I saw it bringing food and going in the hole. I could hear chirps inside whenever it went in. It always landed on the side of the tree before going in. The woodpecker's tail always presses against the side of the tree when it lands, but the mockingbird almost always holds his up in the air.

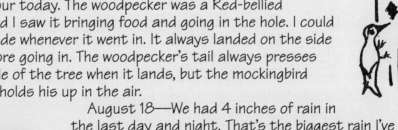

August 18—We had 4 inches of rain in the last day and night. That's the biggest rain I've measured all summer. I have a big can tied to a stake in an open space, and I measured the water in it with a ruler. Mom let me go out in the rain in my bathing suit. I watched the rain flow in tiny rivers through the grass.

Keep A Nature Journal

Writing about what you see in the world of nature around you will make you a better observer. Keep a journal for at least three months, and write down what you see and hear.

As you write, you may think of questions about what you saw, and next time you may look more closely. You may find yourself stopping to watch insects or lizards that you never even noticed before. You'll see the spots and stripes instead of just the overall color, because you want to be able to write it all down in your journal. Maybe you'll pay closer attention to how long it takes a blossom to bloom, or a leaf to unfold.

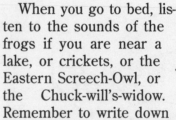

Green or brown

pink

You can buy a looseleaf notebook to write in, or use the leftover pages from a school notebook. You don't need to write in it every day, and you don't need to stop keeping your journal because you forgot to write in it for a few days, or went away on vacation. Just note in it whenever you see or hear or smell something that attracts your attention. Maybe you'll want to carry your notebook with you whenever you go outside.

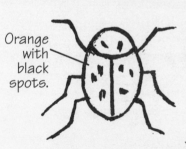

Orange with black spots.

Sometimes including drawings on your journal pages will help you remember better what you see. Even if you think you can't draw very well, a sketch of where the spots were on a beetle or butterfly with a note about its color can help identify it later. Drawing it will also help you look more closely and observe more scientifically.

Note the weather each day in your journal—is it sunny, cloudy, rainy, cool, warm, or hot? Keep a record of the thermometer readings each day at the same time, such as at noon and before you go to bed. Put out a rain gauge to measure the rainfall. You can buy rain gauges already marked with centimeters and inches, or you can use a can with straight sides (without ribs, which would alter your measurements).

Fasten your gauge or can to a stake planted in the ground so it can't be blown over or knocked over by a dog or other animal, and be sure it is at least 15 meters (50 feet) away from the nearest

tree or building, which would keep the rain from falling into it directly. Measure it with as thin a ruler as possible, so that standing the ruler in the water won't make the water rise very much. Then look where the ruler got wet.

Wake up early a few mornings, and listen to the birds outside your window. You may hear Northern Mockingbirds, Mourning Doves, Brown Thrashers, Rufous-sided Towhees, Carolina Wrens, Northern Cardinals, Northern Bobwhites, or Red-bel-

Brown Thrasher

lied Woodpeckers. If you don't recognize their songs, try to see who is singing, look them up in the bird guide, and then learn to identify them by sound.

When you go to bed, listen to the sounds of the frogs if you are near a lake, or crickets, or the Eastern Screech-Owl, or the Chuck-will's-widow. Remember to write down what you *hear* as well as what you see. Maybe you can pretend they are saying something to you and write down what the calls sound like. Some people claim that the Barred Owl says, "Who cooks for you, who cooks for you-*awll*!"

Remember to look for little things: lizards, beetles under leaves, spiders in the house or under the eaves, caterpillars and butterflies. If you have a magnifying glass, you may be able to look at some of these things up close. If you find a spider in a web, maybe you can keep watch in the evening or early in the morning, and see it at work.

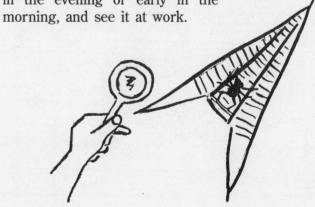

Write in your journal how the spider weaves its web.

Note what flowers are in bloom during the year. Look for the tiny flowers that bloom in the grass, or "weeds" that grow and bloom at the edge of the lawn. The trees have blooms, too. Look for them. Sometimes they look like catkins. Does the bloom smell good? What happens after the bloom dries up? Is there a seed? Lots of seeds? A fruit or nut? Can you figure out how the seeds are spread? Is it by blowing on the wind, or "catching" onto a passing animal or sock, or by being eaten and carried away by a bird? How does the sandspur get to a new place to grow?

Write and illustrate what you observe and what you think in your notebook.

If you have a pair of binoculars, you'll find that you can see birds and distant things easier. Learn how to adjust them for your eyes and focus them on objects. For some people it takes a little practice. If you have a camera, you can take

pictures of some of the things you see. Birds are very hard to photograph, but flowers and spiders could turn out to be good pictures.

Observe a nearby lake. The lake will rise and fall depending upon the rainfall, on how much is evaporating in the hot sun, and on how much people are watering their lawns. Put a stake or set a brick in the ground at the edge of the water, and use a yardstick or tape measure to keep track of how much the water's edge varies.

Or you can set a brick or concrete block where the lake is a foot or two deep so that the top of the brick is level with the sand at the bottom of the lake. Then you can set a yardstick on end on the brick to measure the change in the depth of the water. Measure the surface when the lake is calm, because ripples will make it harder to be accurate.

Compare your measurements with your records of the amount of rainfall, and record them in your journal.

Measure the height of the grass in the lawn at school or at home just after it's been mowed. Then measure it just before it gets mowed next time. How much does it grow in a week? Does it grow more in some places—such as sunny or shady locations, or where nobody walks—than in others? Do "weed" grasses grow more or less rapidly than the cultivated grasses?

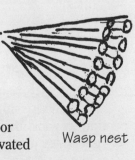
Wasp nest

If you see a wasp's nest being built—on the underside of a leaf, or on the outside wall of a building, or under the eaves of a shed—watch it instead of killing the insects (if it's not in a place that could be brushed by people). See how long it

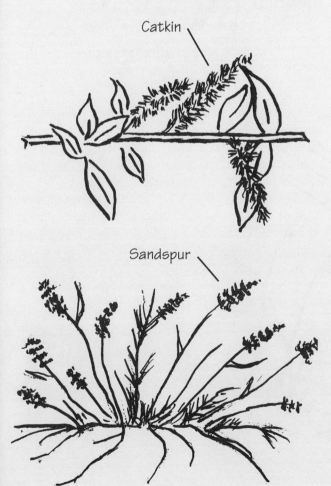
Catkin

Sandspur

takes them to build the cells that make their nest grow. Watch them watching *you!* (But don't annoy them!)

If you live near the beach, you can observe the tides. What time of day is the tide high and low, and how far up the beach does the water come? Learn to pace off a distance—stepping so that each stride is the same—then measure your stride. Then you can pace the distance between high tide and low tide without a long tape measure and someone to help you. Compare the tides to the stages of the moon. Write what you observe in your journal.

Look for crabs, try to identify shorebirds, see what a heavy storm and high winds do to the sand dunes, study the plants that grow on the dunes, make notes about the shells you find that wash in with the tides.

You may find that keeping a journal is exciting and fun. It may be you'll want to continue your journal throughout the year as interesting things happen in the world of nature around you.

And think of all the good material you'll have for writing English and science papers for school assignments!

Where to learn more

See "The Fun of Watching Birds" for more on how to identify birds.

See "Monitoring the Weather" for more on measuring a lake.

See "Discovering the Beach" for more on animals and plants of the shore.

See "A Little Botany Lesson" for more about plants.

See "Insects Are Not Just 'Bugs'!" for more about butterflies and spiders.

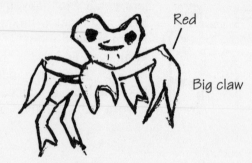

Red

Big claw

1½″ Fiddler Crab

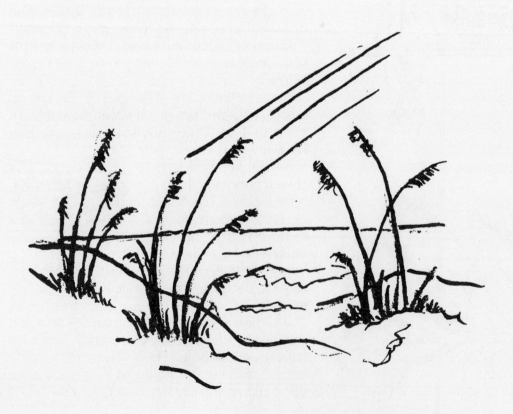

Florida's Special Places

Florida has some unique ecosystems—places with plant and animal species that are found nowhere else in the world. The Everglades is one of these. The Big Scrub is another. Both of these ecosystems occur only in Florida. Other habitats—while not completely unique to Florida—contain species that are found only here in all of the United States.

The discussion in each of these chapters includes information about species of plants and animals that live in each special place. Many of these plants and animals *require* this special place in order to live.

It is important to study the relationship of all the parts of an ecosystem in order to better understand the value of all life in our world. Animals cannot long survive outside of their natural systems. Young naturalists should think of animals and habitats together.

All of the special places included here are wonderful to know about and to visit. Some of you may be fortunate enough to live in or near one of them. The authors hope that this section will help you understand more about the special nature of Florida's wild places.

Historical area

Present area

Chapter 3

The Everglades

"Nothing anywhere else is like them: their vast, glittering openness, wider than the enormous visible round of the horizon, . . . under the dazzling blue heights of space."

— Marjory Stoneman Douglas in *Everglades: River of Grass*

Surrounded on three sides by the warm tropical seas of the Atlantic Ocean, Florida Bay, and the Gulf of Mexico, south Florida is truly different from Florida's other special places. Within this southern part of the state is a vast aquatic land known as the Everglades, unique in all the world.

Famous for its national park, the true Everglades covers much more than the park's 1.4 million acres. Before it was ditched, diked, and drained earlier in this century, the "Glades," as some people like to call it, extended from Lake Okeechobee south to the tip of the Florida peninsula, a distance of more than 160 kilometers (100 miles).

The Everglades is really a huge freshwater marsh dotted with tree islands, sawgrass prairies, and pine rocklands. Water in the marsh flows as a river system 80 kilometers (50 miles) wide but only about 15 centimeters (6 inches) deep. This "river of grass" creeps slowly southward, sloping only 6 to 9 centimeters (2 to 3 inches) to the mile, until it empties its fresh water supply into the shallow estuary of Florida Bay.

Receiving all of its fresh water from rain falling on big Lake Okeechobee and the Kissimmee River and its chain of lakes and wetlands farther to the north, the Everglades revolves around seasons of wet and dry. The rainy season begins in early summer, with frequent afternoon thundershowers and occasional hurricanes that fill the wetlands with life-giving water. Falling mainly between June and November, rainfall averages about 180 centimeters (60 inches) a year. This is a time of intense heat and high humidity, and mosquitoes are everywhere!

In late October the rains taper off and the surface of the land gradually begins to dry. In some years evaporation during the dry season may exceed the average annual rainfall, and the Everglades suffers from drought. Wintertime cold fronts from the north add to the drying effect and occasionally kill back some of the tropical plant life that cannot tolerate the colder temperatures.

Plants and animals that live here have learned to adapt to the extremes of temperature, moisture, and drought, and to the occasional fires and hurricanes that sweep through parts of the Everglades. Some complex ecological communities, or habitats, have evolved. Let's take a look at a few of them.

Pahayokee—"the grassy waters"

The heart of this unusual land is the "river of grass," or, as the Seminole Indians called it, Pahay-okee, the "grassy waters." The grassy prairie of the Glades extends as far as the eye can see, and this wide, green, open space that seems to stretch on forever is why later explorers called it the "ever-glades."

The dominant plant of the Everglades prairie is Sawgrass, not a true grass at all, but a sedge. (The small differences between grasses and sedges are not easily seen, but are important when studying them.) Sawgrass grows to eight feet tall, and has spiny leaf edges that can tear clothes and skin.

During the high water of summertime the Sawgrass marsh teems with life. Around the roots of the Sawgrass and other underwater plants

13

grow masses of a yellowish green algae called Periphyton (Pare-uh-FIE-tin). Microscopic plants and animals live in and feed upon the mats of Periphyton. Mosquito larvae, snails, tadpoles, and other small organisms feed upon these tiny plants and animals. Small animals are then eaten by fish, frogs, turtles, and birds. Eventually, they, in turn, may be fed upon by the "king" of the Everglades, the alligator. This feeding sequence is known as the food chain, and Periphyton is the beginning of the food chain for many animals in this freshwater marsh.

So important is the American Alligator[+] to the ecology of the Everglades that it is now protected by state and federal laws from uncontrolled hunting that reduced its numbers years ago. Alligators use their broad snouts and powerful tails to clear out vegetation and muck from large holes in the limestone, making a pond. In the dry season, as the water evaporates and the Sawgrass, Periphyton, and other aquatic plants begin to shrivel and wilt, these "'gator holes" provide a refuge for water-dependent creatures, such as frogs and fish, who move right in with their alligator host.

White-tailed Deer and the Florida Panther[+] come to drink, and River Otters and the rare Everglades Mink[+] search for crayfish and fish trapped in the 'gator holes as the water recedes. Long-legged wading birds—the Great Blue Heron, Little Blue Heron[+], and Tricolored Heron[+]; Snowy Egret[+] and Great Egret; Roseate Spoonbill[+] and Wood

Stork[+]—gather here and eat their fill. The dry season is also the time when many of these birds nest, because they can more easily gather food to feed their nestlings when prey becomes concentrated in small, shallow ponds.

Pine rocklands

Underlying most of the Everglades is a rocky bottom of porous limestone, made up largely of shells and coral, that was deposited ages ago when warm seas covered the southern part of the peninsula. In some places, marl (limy, organic mud) or peat (rich organic material resulting from years and years of compression of rotting plants) lies on top of the limestone, providing just an inch or two of shallow soil for plants to take root.

Sometimes the limerock juts up out of the thin soil or lies just below the surface. Pine trees grow here in abundance, finding a root-hold in the rock.

Pine rockland

"Pine rockland" is the term used to describe this distinctive habitat of south Florida.

As pine needles, palmetto fronds, and other plant detritus build up, weak acids leach out with each rainfall, eating away at the limerock below and creating a pitted, honeycombed surface. With such difficult footing underneath, hikers often find slow going over the rocky trails of the Everglades.

Slash Pines, Sabal Palms, and Saw Palmettos are the predominant plants growing in this habitat, which—though only a meter (three feet) above sea level—is some of the highest and driest land in south Florida. This habitat requires periodic fires, often caused by lightning strikes during summer thunderstorms, to maintain its existence. Without fire, hardwoods grow, eventually shading out young pines and creating tropical hardwood hammocks instead of pine rocklands.

Hardwood hammocks and tree islands

The flat, grassy expanse of the Everglades is frequently broken by scattered clumps of vegetation called "tree islands." Just a small increase in elevation allows soil to accumulate in limestone "pockets," providing nutrients for tropical hardwoods and palms to take root and grow.

Each tree island is a world of its own, with different plants and animals sharing these special habitats. A profusion of tropical hardwood trees, such as Mahogany, Gumbo Limbo, Poisonwood, and Strangler Fig, grow amidst palms and ferns, creating junglelike settings called "hammocks." Early Indian residents of the Everglades often lived, hunted, and grew their crops on these higher, shady spots. Some people say that "hammock" comes from an Indian word *hammocka*, meaning "garden place" or "shady place."

Many epiphytes (EP-uh-fites), or air plants, grow in the dimly lit environment of the hammocks. Epiphytes are plants that grow on other plants, getting their nourishment from dust and moisture in the air. One of the best known is Spanish Moss—not really a moss, but in the same family as pineapples, also known as bromeliads (bro-MEE-lee-ads). The giant Wildpine, growing on the sturdy limbs of Live Oak and other hammock trees, is another well-known Everglades bromeliad.

During the rainy season, bromeliads and other air plants collect rainwater in the base of their stiff, curled leaves. Tree frogs, spiders, mosquitoes, and other insects breed in these tiny reservoirs. During the dry season many arboreal (ar-BOR-ee-ul), or tree-dwelling, animals sip the life-sustaining dew that collects there.

Of all the air plants, the orchids are the most beautiful. Several species are rare, for over the years amateur botanists and commercial collectors have taken them by the thousands, and developers have destroyed many tropical hardwood hammocks that were important orchid habitats.

The largest orchid in the Everglades, called the Cowhorn Orchid, can grow to as much as 34 kilograms (75 pounds)! Unfortunately, only a few

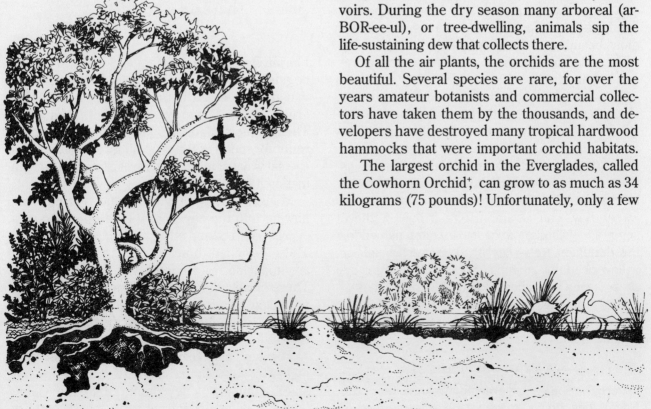

Hardwood hammock

Airplants

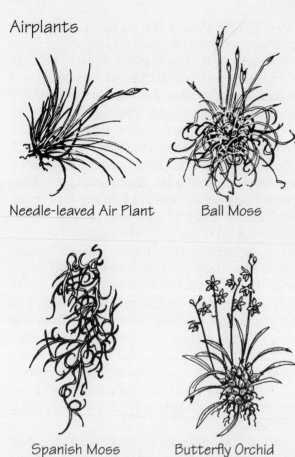

Needle-leaved Air Plant   Ball Moss

Spanish Moss   Butterfly Orchid

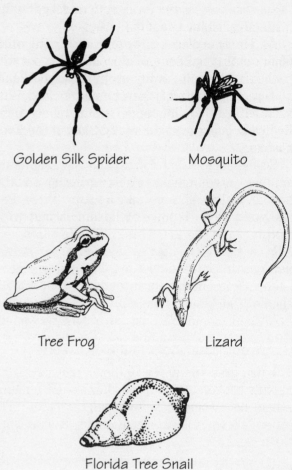

Golden Silk Spider   Mosquito

Tree Frog   Lizard

Florida Tree Snail

Animals that use air plants

large specimens remain, as poachers have practically eliminated this orchid from most areas.

A more widespread and fairly common species, the Night-blooming Epidendrum[+] is one of the most beautiful of the Everglades orchids, with white, spiderlike blossoms that are especially fragrant at night.

Besides the hammock tree islands, other clumps of trees, called "heads," grow in the Glades. Unlike the hammocks that grow on higher elevations, heads occupy depressions in the limestone bedrock—areas that remain as pools or wet places during the dry season. Water-loving plants, such as Cocoplum, Bald Cypress, Sweet Bay, and Swamp Holly, grow on these soggy tree islands, and heads are often named for the dominant tree—bay head, cypress head, or willow head, for example. Some of the larger cypress heads are called "domes." During times of drought, animals concentrate in and around these watery heads to search for fish, snails, and other aquatic life.

The Mangrove Estuary of Florida Bay

Where the southward-creeping fresh water of the Everglades finally reaches the salty waters of

Florida Bay, a transition zone of mangrove trees begins. Three kinds of broad-leaved, evergreen mangrove trees live in the Everglades—Red Mangrove, Black Mangrove, and White Mangrove. Though their roots are often submerged in salt water for much of the year, all three species have special ways of tolerating or resisting salt by eliminating it from their leaves.

Mangrove detritus adds to the rich nutrients flowing into the bay from the Sawgrass prairies, cypress domes, and other wetlands farther north. These enriched, brackish waters of the estuary are important as a nursery for fish and shrimp. These small animals spend their early lives in the protected mangrove creeks and rivers until they are large enough to swim into the open waters of the Gulf of Mexico.

The shy and secretive American Crocodile[+] makes its home in the salty waters of Florida Bay. Numbering just a few hundred in the United States, it is similar in size and appearance to its more common cousin, the American Alligator, but it has a narrower snout and a lighter, gray-green color. The Everglades is the one place in the world where both alligators and crocodiles are found.

Mangroves and other trees on the small islands of Florida Bay provide roosting and nesting sites for Bald Eagles[+], Ospreys, Roseate Spoonbills, Brown Pelicans[+], egrets, herons, and many other species. Many of these birds range far and wide to find food for themselves and their young—to the cypress domes and 'gator holes during the dry season, to the shallow mud flats in Florida Bay, and to the rivers and creeks of the mangrove forests.

More than 300 different species of birds have been recorded here, and the feathered denizens of the Everglades have attracted people's attention for hundreds of years. In 1832, John James Audubon came, searching for what he called the American Flamingo and other wading birds, and captured their beauty with his paint and brush.

Later on, others came with guns, hunting egrets and herons almost to extinction for their highly prized feathers. Today people come with binoculars and cameras, to admire and to study the remarkable bird life of the Everglades.

Endangered Everglades

All is not well in the Florida Everglades. Today, many of the fragile habitats have been severely disrupted by the actions of people.

In the early part of this century, developers began to drain the water from Everglades marshes, creating dry land for cities to be built and crops to be farmed. This effort was so successful that the southeast coast of Florida is now almost totally urban, and vast acres of former Everglades marshes have been converted to sugarcane fields, vegetable farms, and citrus groves. Agricultural chemicals and nutrients from farmlands have polluted Glades waters, causing water-quality changes that have been disastrous for fish and wildlife.

Canals and impoundments have altered the Everglades' seasons of wet and dry, sending too much or not enough water at unnatural times of the year. The flow of fresh water that should go to the Everglades has been reduced to a fraction of the historic flow in order to share the water with cities and farms, and when released from dammed impoundments, it floods the Everglades with too much at once. The Everglades and all of its plants and animals have suffered for over 50 years from this human-enforced cycle of flood and drought.

Though hurricanes can help the Everglades by replenishing its supplies of fresh water, Hurricane Andrew in 1992 wreaked havoc. The sturdy Sabal Palms survived well, but nearly 30 percent of south Florida's Slash Pines were uprooted or snapped off in the 325-kilometer-per-hour (200-mph) winds. Then Pine Bark Beetles attacked

Where to learn more

See "Speaking of Trees" for more on mangroves, pines, and palms.
See "Alligators, Snakes, and Other Reptiles" for more on the American Alligator.
See "The Keys" for more on the American Crocodile.
See "Florida's Native Plants" for more on Saw Palmetto.
See "Water and Wetlands" for more on the food chain.
See "Exotics—More than Just a Nuisance" for more on exotic plants.
See "Discovering the Beach," "The Keys," and "Extinction Is Forever" for more about egret feathers.
See "John James Audubon in Florida" for more about the flamingo.

Do you know these words?

algae	exotic
animal	food chain
annual	fronds
aquatic	habitats
arboreal	hammock
botanist	head
brackish	hurricane
bromeliad	impoundment
cold front	larvae
detritus	marl
dome	microscopic
drought	organic
communities	organism
epiphytes	peat
estuary	Periphyton
evaporation	tropical

many of the remaining stressed trees, and exotic vegetation replaced many of the native plants of the pine rocklands and hardwood hammocks.

It has taken people a long time to learn that the Everglades is a fragile and complex ecosystem, now on the verge of collapse. Scientists, developers, farmers, environmentalists, and government officials are working to find ways to protect the remaining Everglades. Only through better understanding of the unique subtropical world of Florida's Everglades, and by carefully applying protective and management practices, can we hope to restore some of the lost wonders of the Everglades.

Mangrove estuary

Chapter 4

Discovering the Beach

Sandy beaches

Florida's coastline is over a thousand miles long from north of Jacksonville all the way around the Keys to Pensacola in the Panhandle—the longest of any state except Alaska. The place where land meets the sea is sometimes mangrove forest, sometimes salt marsh; but the place that attracts the most people is Florida's broad, white sand beaches, thought by many to be the finest in the United States.

To get to these beaches, often you must drive across a long bridge or causeway to an island. Florida's coast includes 80 barrier islands—narrow strips of land that act as barriers to protect the bays behind them and the mainland from ocean waves and storms. Barrier islands are found on both the Atlantic coast, where the waves often crash ashore, and on the calmer Gulf coast. These coastal islands and beaches are constantly changing, their sands shifted by waves, currents, tides, and storms.

The beach is a wonderful place to see all kinds of living things, both in the water and on the shore. Gulls, pelicans, plovers, and sandpipers are nearly always there to be seen, but crabs, mice, and insects also live on the ocean strand, and in the summer, sea turtles lay their eggs in the sand.

Where do they live?

Marine creatures are found in all parts of the ocean environment. Many live far offshore in deep ocean waters; these are referred to as pelagic (puh-LAJ-ik) animals. Those that live closer to the shore are called neritic (nuh-RIT-ik) animals.

Some of the areas, or zones, where different plants and animals may be found are shown on the next page.

Pelagic zone. Pelagic sea life consists of plants and animals that live in deep ocean waters. Many creatures float and drift freely with the ocean currents; others are strong swimmers. Some birds dive to catch fish swimming near the surface.

Lower beach. The intertidal, or surf, zone is the area of breaking waves and churning sand where the surf sweeps in and out all day. Although it seems as though it would be a dangerous place to live, many organisms like it here. Some live in the water between grains of wet sand, others burrow

completely into the sand under the waves, and still others find someone else's empty shell to crawl into.

Middle beach. At low tide, the middle beach is exposed to the hot sun. At high tide, this part of the beach is under water. Most animals living here must keep from drying out by closing up their shells, or must keep from being washed away by burrowing into the sand. Other animals move up and down the beach with the tide, searching for food.

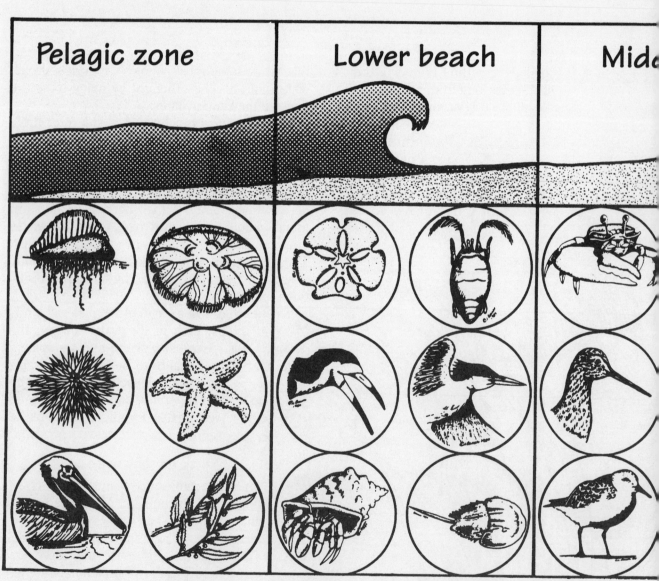

Portuguese Man-o'-war,
    12"
Atlantic Purple Sea
    Urchin, 2"
Brown Pelican, 45"–54"

Moon Jellyfish, 3"–9"
Common Seastar, 5"
Sargassum Seaweed, up
    to 2'

Sand Dollar, 6"
Black Skimmer, 18"
Hermit Crab, 1"–2"

Mole Crab (Sandbug), 15"
Royal Tern, 18"–21"
Horseshoe Crab, 24"

Fiddler Crab, 1"–2"
Willet, 14"–17"
Sanderling, 7"–8"

Upper beach. An endless drift line of debris—the refuse of plant and animal life in the sea—often marks the place where the highest tides have reached. Here, among the decaying seaweed, many insects breed and forage for food. They, in turn, provide food for other beach animals. Beautiful shells—once the home of some animal—are often hidden here, just waiting for you to discover them. (But remember, never take home a shell that contains a live animal.)

The dunes. Behind the beach rise the sand dunes, where waves reach only during heavy storms. Sea Oats, Sandspurs, and Beach Morning Glories grow here. Beach Mice[+] scurry under the plants, and sea turtles may crawl up and lay their eggs in holes dug in the sandy slope. You should not walk on the dunes, for you might loosen the roots of the plants that help hold the sand in place. Cross the dunes only on boardwalks.

When you go to the beach, look for plants and animals, and see if you can decide which zone they live in.

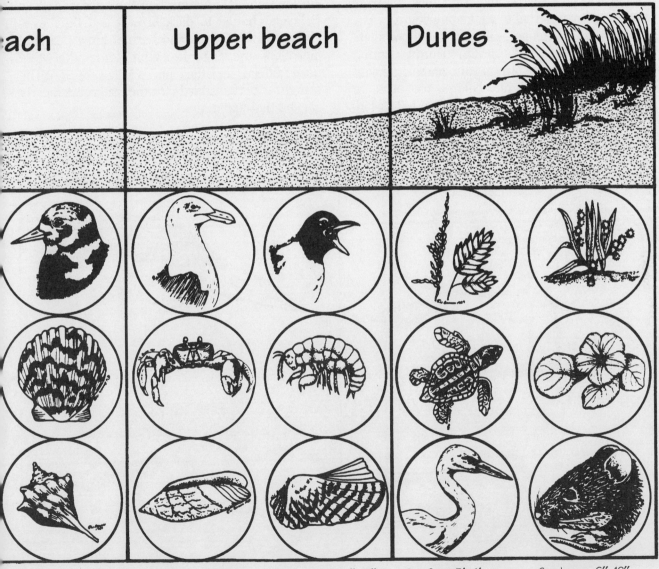

...ach	Upper beach	Dunes

Ruddy Turnstone, 8"–10"
Calico Scallop, 1"–2"
Whelk, 4"–16"

Herring Gull, 23"–26"
Ghost Crab, 2"
Lettered Olive, 2"

Laughing Gull, 15"–17"
Sandhopper (Beach flea), 0.5"
Turkey Wing, 3"

Sea Oats, 3'–4'
Hatchling Loggerhead Turtle, 2"
Great Egret, 37"–41"

Sandspurs, 6"–12"
Beach Morning Glory, flower 3"
Beach Mouse, 2"–3" (plus tail)

Bird wardrobe changes

Many birds seen on Florida's beaches change their plumage (feathers) at certain times of the year. One group—the gulls—can be very hard to tell apart. The Laughing Gull, named for its raucous call that sounds like laughter, is one of the most common gulls in Florida. Depending upon the time of year and the age of the bird, you might think you are seeing several different gulls when in fact all are Laughing Gulls. That's because the Laughing Gull takes three years to grow up and reach its first breeding plumage (the beautiful feathers it grows when ready to attract a mate). As the young bird grows, it molts (sheds its feathers and grows new ones), and each new plumage looks slightly different from the one before.

The adult Laughing Gull also has a complete molt every fall and spring. During spring breeding season, the bird is quite handsome with a black hood and brightly colored red beak. In winter it loses the black cap and bright bill and in-stead shows just a touch of dark gray on the nape (back of the head).

Terns are the graceful relatives of gulls, and can be recognized by their more pointed wings and bill, and by how they feed. Gulls swoop down and pick up food at the surface of the water; terns hover on rapidly beating wings and plunge-dive into the water after fish.

The Royal Tern is one of Florida's largest terns. It has a bright orange bill, and the adult has a white crown (top of the head) during most of the year, but sports a black cap during the springtime breeding season.

Other birds change "clothes" during breeding season, too. The feathers on the nape of Brown Pelicans change to dark brown, and their eyes change color. Egrets and herons grow beautiful aigrettes—the wispy breeding plumes that were used to decorate ladies' hats a long time ago. The slaughter of these birds for their aigrettes nearly caused their extinction.

Winter adult

Laughing gull

Breeding (summer) plumage

Breeding plumage

Royal Tern

Winter adult

Where to learn more

See "Alligators, Snakes, and other Reptiles" for more about sea turtles.

See "The Panhandle" for more about barrier islands.

See "The Everglades," "The Keys," and "Extinction is Forever" for more about egret feathers.

Do you know these words?

aigrettes	barrier islands
breeding plumage	crown
debris	dunes
extinction	forage
intertidal zone	molt
nape	organism
pelagic zone	plumage

Great Horned Owl

Chapter 5

The Big Scrub

Ocala Forest Big Scrub

Lake Wales Ridge Scrub

Scrub is something your parents might make you do to the kitchen floor or to your knees and elbows. How can it be a "special place" in Florida?

Scrub is a part of the state that many people think of as a wasteland, dry and hot with a few stunted trees. But others think of it as a unique and special place that exists nowhere else in the world but on a strand of high, sandy land in the heart of Florida.

The fine gray-white or yellowish sand of the middle ridge of the Scrub was actually the beach many thousands of years ago, when the Atlantic Ocean and the Gulf of Mexico submerged nearly all of Florida as the Ice Age glaciers melted. During this time, Florida was only a series of islands, and the limestone base was gradually covered by sand as tides and waves washed in.

Ice ages came again, and waters receded across Florida as glaciers froze in the far north. When the oceans finally stabilized, Florida was left covered with a sandy topsoil that appears forbidding to plants and animals. Yet somehow, seeds washed by water or carried by birds or wind came and sprouted in this sand-dune ridge in the middle of the peninsula. Trees and shrubby plants grew, and insects, birds, and small mammals moved in to live there. Scientists believe that the Scrub may include the oldest flora and fauna of Florida.

The Big Scrub

One of the best-known pieces of the Scrub is called the Big Scrub of the Ocala National Forest in north-central Florida.

The Big Scrub was described by Marjory Bartlett Sanger in her book *Forest in the Sand*: "The greatest stand of Sand Pine in the world spreads out in a unique plant community. It grows on leftover dunes over a hundred feet deep. The

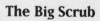

word 'scrub' is generally used to describe low, dwarf, bushy, stunted, or scrawny plants eking out an existence in poor soil. Actually the Ocala, with its high canopy of pines and understory of oak and Cabbage Palm, is a full-grown climax forest, one that renews itself automatically and protects itself from the invasion of alien species." A few pages later she says, "Then in many places there are no plants at all, simply dazzling snow-white sand where wandering lizards and mice have left a brief trail . . . and the starry footprints of birds are momentarily etched and blown away."

Ms. Sanger wrote, "Every forest has a story to tell—of its location, its soil and plants, of its inhabitants and its seasons, of its beginnings and evolution and how it grew old with the earth."

This is the story of the Ocala National Forest, nearly surrounded by the natural boundaries of the St. Johns River and the Oklawaha River. It is the oldest national forest east of the Mississippi River. The name Ocala comes from the Seminole Indians' word for "water's edge."

The Scrub is a thick Sand Pine woodland growing in fine white quartz sand. Sand Pines occur naturally nowhere else in the world. Under their thin canopy of pine needles grow Saw Palmettos, Sabal Palms, Scrub Oaks, and a collection of flowering shrubs. On the open spaces, lichens (LI-kins) and mosses lie barely tethered to the loose sand. Many of the common trees, such as Scrub Oak, Scrub Hickory, and Scrub Bay, are stunted and gnarled in the Scrub habitat.

"Dryness is the very essence of the Big Scrub," Ms. Sanger says, for the Scrub is dry most of the year. It is nearly a desert. During the winter and spring, Florida's dry season, brittle pine needles and oak leaves, shriveled ferns, and crisp Reindeer Moss crackle underfoot. Before the summer rains begin, the Scrub is so dry that it seems that predators—bobcats, snakes, and foxes—must find hunting difficult; and prey—mice, lizards, and Northern Bobwhites—must find it difficult to hide, for nearly every movement causes a rustle.

Yet in the Scrub grow colorful plants, with one kind or another in bloom nearly all year. Pygmy Fringe Trees and Scrub Plum bloom fragrant and white. Prickly Pear Cactus, Goldenrod, and Goldenaster have yellow blossoms. Fall Asters and Blazing Star are purple. Dayflowers are sky-blue and Spiderworts are lavender-blue. Tarflower bushes are covered with pinkish white blossoms.

Gray Squirrel

In the winter, hollies bear bright red berries and the Beauty Berry bush bears bright purple berries.

The Scrub is home to a diverse and unique variety of wildlife. Common mammals and birds live here, such as Raccoons, Opossums, and Gray Squirrels, Rufous-sided Towhees, Brown Thrashers, Carolina Wrens, Northern Mockingbirds, Red-shouldered Hawks, and Red-tailed Hawks. So do less common animals such as Gray Foxes, Florida Black Bears[+], Indigo Snakes[+], Diamondback Rattlesnakes, and Gopher Tortoises[+]. Eastern Screech-Owls, Barred Owls, Great Horned Owls, Pileated Woodpeckers, and Wild Turkeys live here year-round. Migrating songbirds and ducks travel through on their southward flight in late fall, and return northward in early spring.

Wild Turkey

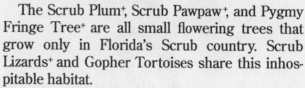

Turkey Vulture

Pileated
Woodpecker

Endangered Scrub Species

Some plant and animal species can live nowhere else but in this habitat. At least 20 plant species and several animals endemic (en-DEM-ik; restricted to a certain locality) to the Scrub are threatened or endangered.

Scrub Balm[+], a small shrub about half a meter (20 inches) tall, was first discovered in the Scrub in 1935. Since then, several other small plants in this genus have been discovered, one as recently as 1987! These little, fragrant, flowering plants have some unique properties that scientists are studying.

The Scrub Plum[+], Scrub Pawpaw[+], and Pygmy Fringe Tree[+] are all small flowering trees that grow only in Florida's Scrub country. Scrub Lizards[+] and Gopher Tortoises share this inhospitable habitat.

Florida Scrub Jay[+]

The animal that people seem to identify most with this habitat is the Florida Scrub Jay, a year-round resident of Scrub Oak areas. A bright blue, lively bird, it has a brownish shield across the back of its shoulders, but no crest nor white and black markings like the more common Blue Jay.

Scrub Jays mate for life and live in family groups, with younger generations helping their parents by defending the territory and feeding nestlings. They depend upon acorns for their main food, each jay burying nearly 8,000 acorns every fall for use during the winter when insects are scarce.

For both the Scrub Jay and many other Scrub species, fire is important. Scrub Jays need low-growing oak shrubs and open patches. When the oaks grow too tall or fill in the open places, the jays abandon the area. Without fire, the Scrub Rosemary dies out of old age when its seeds no longer have open sand in which to sprout. In the Scrub, however, it takes 10 to 40 years for enough dead leaves and branches to accumulate to support fire.

Refuge For Native Plants

The Ocala National Forest is not the only Scrub habitat in Florida. Some, called Coastal Scrubs, are found just inland of both the Atlantic and Gulf coasts. These are "newer" Scrub lands than those on the central ridge of the peninsula. Some

Florida Scrub Jay

Northern
Cardinal

little water and few nutrients, for water drains away rapidly through the fine sand. More endemic and endangered plants grow here than any other such limited area in the United States.

More than 80% of the Lake Wales Ridge was planted in citrus or built up in houses during the 40 years between 1950 and 1990. About 10,000 acres of the Scrub that now remain are slated to be included in the Refuge if they can be purchased in time.

Research on the Scrub Jay and other animal and plant inhabitants of the Lake Wales Ridge Scrub is carried on at Archbold Biological Station near Lake Placid.

Coastal Scrubs are treeless, with mostly Saw Palmettos growing there.

Another very important piece of Scrub land is a long narrow strip that originally extended down the center of Florida from west of Orlando to west of Lake Okeechobee. The federal government plans to purchase part of this Scrub and designate it as the Lake Wales Ridge National Wildlife Refuge. The state of Florida has already purchased 3,000 acres near Lake Placid. This is the first refuge in the United States to be set aside for the preservation of endangered plants.

The soil is white "sugar" sand and supports only those plants and animals that can survive on

---

Where to learn more

See "Alligators, Snakes, and other Reptiles" for more about the Scrub Lizard and the Gopher Tortoise.

See "What Is a Bird of Prey?" for more about Great Horned Owls.

See "The Mysteries of Bird Migration" for more about migrating birds.

See "Florida's Native Plants" for more about Scrub plants.

Do you know these words?

Can you list these words in alphabetical order?

canopy	lichen
predator	prey
endangered	endemic
habitat	species
germinate	flora
fauna	refuge

Chapter 6

Underwater Treasures: Coral Reefs

Coral reefs

Beneath the brilliant blue-green waters surrounding the Florida Keys lie some of our country's most valuable treasures—no, not sunken pirate ships full of gold doubloons, but underwater gardens called coral reefs. Some of the most colorful and varied forms of life of any place on earth are found here among the communities of plants and animals of the coral reef.

Coral reefs are found in tropical waters where the seas are clear, fairly shallow, and warm (22° to 28°C; 72° to 82°F). These waters often occur along the eastern shores of tropical land areas (such as the southern tip of Florida, Central America, and Australia) and around tropical islands (such as Hawaii, many Pacific islands, and the Bahamas). Reef-building corals also need lots of sunlight, calm wave action, and a constant salinity in order to grow (salinity is the amount of salt in the water; the ocean is usually about 35 parts salt per thousand parts [ppt] water).

The coral reefs off the Florida Keys are visited by millions of people every year who come to dive and fish in the clear waters, for Florida is the only state on the continent to have long reef formations near its coast. Approximately 6,000 coral reefs are found between Key Biscayne and the Dry Tortugas, and this stretch of nearly 320 kilometers (200 miles) of corals is sometimes called the Florida reef tract.

Coral polyps

The architects, or builders, of the reefs are billions of tiny organisms called coral polyps (POLL-lips), some no larger than the head of a pin. Coral polyps are animals—not plants or rocks—and are related to jellyfish and anemones (uh-NEM-uh-nees). Their soft bodies look like sacks with tentacles (or feelers) surrounding the mouth. Polyps use their tentacles to capture food, such as tiny shrimp, fish, and larval forms of other animals that drift or swim by. Special stinging cells on the tentacles stun the prey long enough for it to be passed into the polyp's mouth.

Elkhorn Coral

Each polyp lives inside its own cuplike skeleton. It forms this hard cup by secreting a substance called calcium carbonate from special cells in its body. This is the same substance that helps to form our bones and teeth as well as the shells of many sea creatures. Corals start to take shape when the polyp skeletons begin to grow and join or cement themselves together, building new cup skeletons on top of old ones. Corals grow very slowly, from one to ten or more centimeters (1/2 inch to several inches) a year, depending on the kind of coral, so you can see that it has taken many thousands of years for Florida's coral reefs to grow.

Algae

Corals are helped by tiny plants called algae (AL-jee) that live in the tissues of each polyp. Algae turn the energy from sunlight into food energy, as most plants do, and produce oxygen that the coral polyps use. Algae also give the corals their many beautiful colors of red, yellow, orange, purple, and blue—indeed, all the colors of the rainbow.

A waste product given off by the polyp—carbon dioxide—is used by the algae. This mutually beneficial coral polyp/algae relationship is called symbiosis ("living together"), a relationship that is very important to the health of the reefs.

Corals

Colonies of corals can form many different shapes. Nearly one hundred different kinds of Florida corals come in an amazing array of intricate patterns. Their names describe their shapes— Finger Coral, Rose Coral, Pillar, Brain, and Mountain Star Corals, Elkhorn and Staghorn Corals. These are called hard, or stony, corals because of their hard, rigid shape.

Pillar Coral

Parrotfish

Not all corals are hard, however. Some build more flexible skeletons that wave and sway in the warm ocean currents. They are called soft corals. Known as Sea Whips, Sea Plumes, and Sea Fans, they look like plants to many people, but if you look closely you can see the tiny polyps reaching out their tentacles to capture dinner as it drifts by.

The Amazing Parrotfishes!

As you float quietly above the colorful reef, peering down through your mask and breathing through your snorkel, you may be overwhelmed by the sights and sounds—yes, sounds!—below you.

One of the first creatures to attract your attention will surely be members of the parrotfish family, so named because their large jaws look like a parrot's beak. Some fourteen different species of parrotfish can be found in Atlantic coastal waters, and their

names—Bluelip, Emerald, Midnight, Rainbow, Greenblotch, and Stoplight parrotfishes, to name a few—describe their incredibly gaudy colors.

But if your eyes don't at first pick out a Parrotfish, your ears surely will. Parrotfish use their beaklike jaws to crunch corals and encrusted organisms such as algae, molluscs, and worms. The rasping sound they make as they eat can be heard easily by nearby swimmers. As parrotfish feed on corals and sift through sand for detritus and plant materials, they help to break down the corals and other sediments into smaller pieces, creating

sand particles that may eventually be deposited onto nearby beaches.

Some parrotfish are able to change colors, blending in with the environment around them. Still others go through some very unusual changes where certain females become males, called supermales, which are differently colored and twice the size of other parrotfish. Some species are able to enclose themselves inside a mucous cocoon that they secrete, apparently to protect themselves at night while they sleep.

You can observe many of these fascinating parrotfish behaviors when you visit a coral reef.

The value of Florida's coral reef

Coral reefs protect south Florida beaches and the Keys, slowing down strong ocean waves before they reach the shore. As the reefs break down, they also provide an important source of sand for nearby beaches.

Coral communities provide underwater housing for a dazzling array of marine life. The cracks and crevices formed by hard corals provide a safe home for young fishes and shelter for many animals such as lobsters, crabs, worms, sea urchins, snails, and clams. Some creatures such as sponges and anemones spend their entire lives anchored to corals, rarely moving from one spot. Reefs are feeding grounds for many creatures, including predators such as barracudas, grouper, and sharks that prowl the reef in search of food.

Coral reefs may soon become important to medical science. Researchers from the Harbor Branch Marine Institute of Sciences in Fort Pierce have recently found natural drugs in some

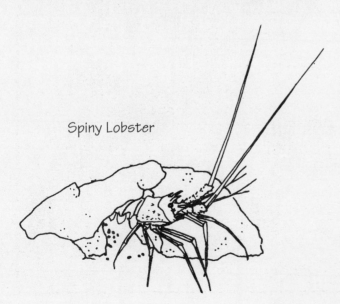

Spiny Lobster

sponges that may prove to shrink tumors and treat cancer. Others researchers are examining coral reef marine life for a possible treatment for AIDS.

Coral reefs contribute to the strong economy of the state, creating jobs in the fishing and diving industries and luring to the Keys millions of tourists who want to visit the reefs.

But most of all, coral reefs are places of beauty and wonder. This alone makes them important.

Our fragile coral reefs need your help!

Coral reefs are very important to us, yet we are not always good to them. Natural factors such as hurricanes and occasional increases in water temperature can severely damage corals and their inhabitants, but most of the dangers to coral reefs are caused by the actions of people.

Following are some of the ways we harm Florida's coral reefs and what we can do to help prevent it.

Boats. Big ships, such as tankers carrying oil, fertilizers, and other materials, have run aground on the reefs when blown off course by storm or while traveling too close to shore. These groundings cause great damage to the coral colonies.

But smaller boats actually do more damage because so many of them accidentally run onto the reefs when their captains fail to pay close enough attention to their navigating. Many recreational boats anchor near the reefs improperly, so that the anchor, with its rope and chain, slashes at the coral, breaking it into pieces.

If you go boating near coral reefs, help to care for them by urging your parents or the captain to tie up to mooring buoys that have been placed in some areas to protect the coral. If mooring buoys are not available, anchor only in a sandy area well away from the reef, and, if possible, have someone dive down to check on the placement of the anchor.

Souvenir hunters. Thoughtless souvenir hunters can cause great harm to coral. Few people realize that the living tissue of corals is only a thin layer made up of thousands of tiny polyps. When the "skin" of a coral is broken, a wound is created that is just as serious as a wound to your own skin, and infection can easily set in.

Snorkelers and divers who break off pieces of living corals, or take entire sea fans, are injuring the living coral reef. Some take sponges, or break apart the coral to collect tropical fish and crustaceans for home aquariums.

When you visit the reef, remember to leave Florida's coral gardens just as you find them. Never take anything home with you, and never stand on, or even touch, the fragile coral animals.

Fishing. Lost fishing nets, traps, and lines can seriously damage the reef by tangling and ensnaring corals and capturing fish, crabs, and other animals that can't escape. Catching too many fish and lobsters, either for the dinner table or the aquarium, can upset the balance of plants and animals on the reef.

Take home only as many fish as you can use, and always retrieve all your fishing lines, floats, sinkers, and other gear.

Pollution. Other dangers include sewage pollution from boats visiting the reefs and from houses on shore, silt and sand stirred up during coastal development, and oil spills from boats. Polluted water can smother corals by reducing the sunlight and oxygen they need to survive.

Sometimes too many nutrients from agricultural lands, lawns, and gardens can harm coral by making certain kinds of algae grow too fast. When these algae take over the reef, covering once-beautiful coral gardens with a greenish brown scum, they can create conditions for coral diseases to occur. In fact, scientists are now certain that nutrients invading the Florida reef tract from the Keys and surrounding waters are one of the worst problems facing this special place.

Remember that the residents in a coral community are dependent upon one another, just as people living in a town or city need their neighbors. When corals die, from whatever cause, other marine life must either move somewhere else or die, and the coral reef they have abandoned becomes a ghost town.

How to Visit the Reefs

Exploring new places on land is easy—just jump on your bike or go for a walk, and observe the world of nature all around.

But it is quite another thing to explore the sea. As soon as you enter the water you realize that there are obstacles to your exploration: you can't see as clearly, or breathe underwater, or move about as easily as on land. That's why mask, snorkel, and fins were invented—to give you greater freedom in and under water.

Snorkeling is swimming on the surface of the water with your face down and with a breathing

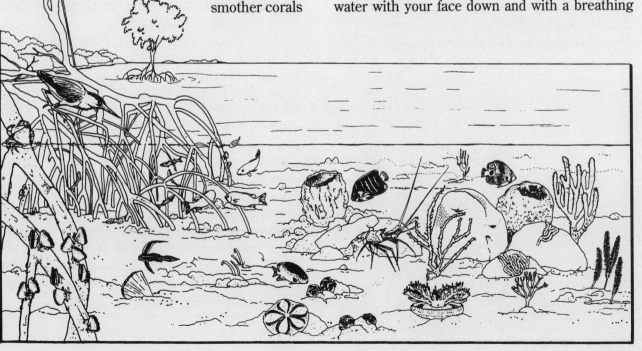

tube called a snorkel in your mouth. Once you learn how to do it, a whole new world will open up for you, for you will be able to see through your mask and breathe with your face underwater. Big fins on your feet make it easier to swim underwater without using your hands.

You can buy snorkeling equipment at most department stores, or you and your family can go to a store that specializes in diving equipment. If you wear glasses, you can even buy a mask with prescription lenses. You can also learn more about the sport of SCUBA (which is an acronym for Self-Contained Underwater Breathing Apparatus) and the classes you need to take before becoming a scuba diver. Once you are comfortable with your equipment, you'll be eager to visit the underwater world of the coral reefs.

In the Florida Keys several marine sanctuaries, or parks, have been set aside to protect the animals and plants living there. John Pennekamp Coral Reef State Park is famous as America's first undersea park. Here you can ride over the reef in a glass-bottomed boat, or float along using your snorkel gear. You can also visit an aquarium in the visitor center that holds 30,000 gallons of seawater and over 20 different species of fish and other creatures that live on the nearby reefs.

Other sanctuaries—such as Biscayne National Park, Key Largo National Marine Sanctuary, and Looe Key National Marine Sanctuary (pronounced "loo" and named after a ship that wrecked on the reef in 1744), and Fort Jefferson National Park in the Dry Tortugas—are also great places to snorkel and scuba dive. Can you find these places on your Florida map?

So important are these reefs—not only to Florida, but to the entire nation—that the government has designated the entire reef tract as the Florida Keys National Marine Sanctuary. Efforts are under way to study the best ways to manage this Keys sanctuary for the benefit of divers, fishermen, boaters, and, of course, all the sea creatures who call this area home. Let's hope this recognition, and everyone's efforts to help protect them, will assure that we can always enjoy Florida's living coral reefs.

Where to learn more

See "The Keys" for more on coral reefs.
See "Water and Wetlands" for more on the food chain.

Do you know these words?

algae	cocoon
community	coral polyps
coral reef	crustaceans
detritus	larva
marine	nutrients
organisms	pollution
predators	prey
salinity	sanctuary
scuba	snorkel
symbiosis	tentacles

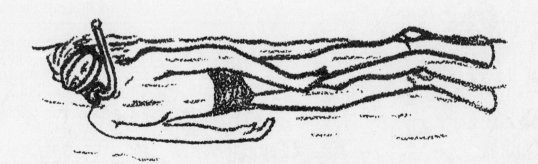

The Keys —

Chapter 7

The Keys

"Like pearls on a string, bound by bridges and a road, the islands of the Florida Keys curve from the Everglades to Key West."

So begins *World of the Great White Heron*, a beautiful book about the Keys by Marjory Bartlett Sanger. She writes that hurricanes and the Gulf Stream, coral reefs and mangrove trees, birds and fish, sun and sea—all contribute to the uniqueness of these islands.

"Something is lost," she writes, "if one surveys the landscape with its shimmering, multicolored and changeful beauty, and has not some conception of its teeming, and usually hidden, wildlife communities."

Florida's Keys were formed many thousands of years ago when the seas receded, leaving Florida and its string of island pearls above the water. The word "key" comes from the Spanish word *cayo*, meaning "little island." Some of them are too small to put up a tent; the biggest one is Key Largo—48 kilometers (30 miles) long and 0.8 km (.5 mile) wide. There are more than 800 of them, stretching over 290 kilometers (180 miles) from Biscayne Bay near Miami to Key West and on to the Dry Tortugas.

The islands are made up of limestone and coral rock covered with a layer of shell and sand. The natural plant life has had to adapt to this harsh soil. Where the mangrove trees and other vegetation have dropped their leaves for centuries, a layer of rich peat soil covers the limestone, and wonderful tangled communities called hardwood hammocks grow there, creating the only truly tropical area in the United States.

The only coral reefs in North America lie in shallow water just east of the Keys. Florida's coral reefs were

35

responsible for many of the shipwrecks of early explorers and still trap careless navigators whose ships cause great damage to the living organisms of the coral.

No natural water aquifer exists in the underground limestone of the Keys. Some successful wells have been dug into small pockets of underground water, which usually is too salty to drink but can be used to water plants. Most residents who live on the Keys now receive their water through a pipeline from the mainland near Miami. Their water bills are among the highest in the United States. If you drive on U.S. 1 through the Keys, you can see the pipe in some places running above the ground. Rainwater, held in surface pockets or in the stiff, cup-shaped leaves of bromeliads and other tropical plants until it evaporates, is the only supply for wildlife.

Hurricanes have dominated much of the life of the Florida Keys—not only human life, but animal and plant life as well. Red Mangrove trees live at the edge of the sea, propped up on stiltlike roots that allow the ebb and flow of tides and storm waves to wash beneath them. Many birds nest during the winter and spring seasons when hurricanes are unlikely. Hurricanes have blown in seeds, birds, butterflies, and snails that formerly lived in other parts of the world.

Hurricanes, mosquitoes, summer heat, and lack of a road connecting the islands delayed the development of the Keys for decades. Not until 1912, when the railroad built by Henry Flagler was finished, could anyone reach Key West except by boat. The railroad was destroyed in the 1935 hurricane. Then the Overseas Highway, built on top of what was left of the railroad bed,

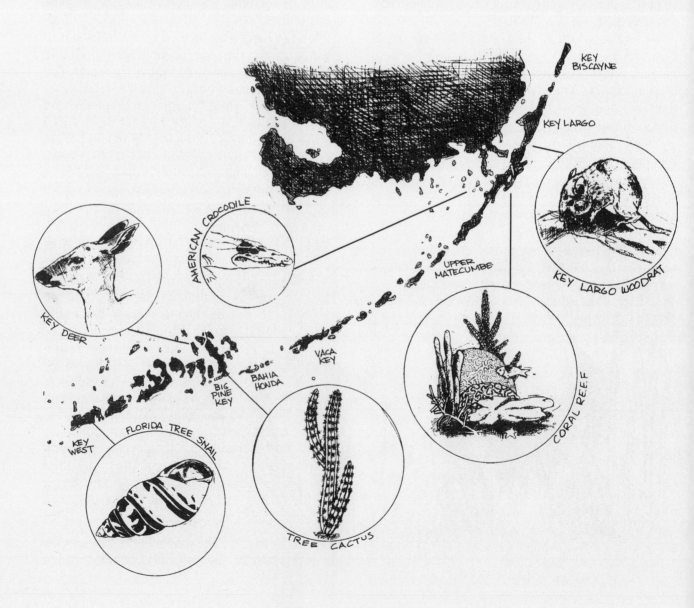

opened in 1938. The road, mosquito control, air conditioning, and a long period of years with no "killer" hurricanes have made the Keys an attractive place for people to live. Houses have been built on relatively few of the hundreds of Keys, but on those Keys connected by roads, developers are building houses in great numbers, destroying habitat for plants and animals that live nowhere else in the United States, and some that live nowhere else in the world.

Refuges

Parks and wildlife refuges have been set aside over the years in an effort to save some of these special species. The first one, in 1938, was the Great White Heron National Wildlife Refuge, a protected area accessible only by boat that provides roosting and nesting habitat for the many wading bird species that nearly died out in the "feathered hat" era nearly 100 years ago. When plume hunters killed the adult birds for their beautiful breeding feathers, their eggs and babies died, too. Great White Herons[+], Great Blue Herons, Snowy Egrets[+], Great Egrets, Roseate Spoonbills[+], and other wading birds dwindled in numbers from millions to hundreds. Fortunately, you can still see these birds and many other species in the Keys, including once-threatened Ospreys whose huge nests sit atop utility poles along the main highway. (Ospreys are still a Species of Special Concern in the Keys.)

Many of the wading birds that were so endangered at the turn of the century have increased in population so that they are no longer in peril of extinction, but their numbers will never again be what they were in the 1800s. Other special birds that can be seen in the Keys include the Roseate Tern[+], White-crowned Pigeon[+], Mangrove Cuckoo, and Black-whiskered Vireo.

The Key Deer[+], protected on the National Key Deer Refuge, is a tiny variety of the White-tailed Deer. It grows no taller than a big dog. It was nearly exterminated by hunting in the 1930s, but has been protected by the refuge on many islands around Big Pine Key since 1947. Today, the deer's worst enemies are cars, destruction of their habitat, and people illegally feeding them "junk food."

The American Crocodile[+] lives in mangrove swamps and saltwater bays of Everglades National Park and the islands of the northernmost Keys, and is the same species of crocodile that lives among the Caribbean islands. It receives special protection on and around Key Largo in Crocodile Lakes National Wildlife Refuge. The main threat to crocodiles, as well as many of the birds, is competition with people, boats, and jet skis for a quiet place to live.

Other species that are endangered or threatened in the Florida Keys include:

- Tree Snails[+]. Another park in the Keys provides a safe area for the beautiful Tree Snails that people collected almost to extinction for their particularly colorful shells. Stories are told of collectors so avid that they set fire to entire islands to prevent anyone else from ever finding snail shells like theirs.

  These snails are arboreal, living in the native hammock trees and feeding on lichens, fungi, and algae found on the bark and leaves. Snails with different color patterns live on different islands in the Keys. On some islands, more than one kind of Tree Snail live in different hammocks on the same island.

  Hurricane Andrew in 1992 devastated the habitat of the Tree Snails, but entomologists (EN-tuh-MALL-uh-jists; scientists who study insects) went to the Keys and rescued several hundred of them, replacing them after their habitat recovered.

  Clearing hammocks for development and spraying for mosquitoes put these beautiful snails on the Endangered list. The Stock Island Tree Snail[+] is one of the most endangered of the Tree Snail species.

- Atala Butterfly[+]. The caterpillar of this species feeds only on native Coontie plants, which

Schaus' Swallowtail

Key Largo Cotton Mouse

grow wild, and on imported cycad plants used in landscaping. It has been found recently only on Key Biscayne, except for those that people have caught and moved to the mainland coast to see if they will live again there.

- Schaus' Swallowtail[+] is also an endangered butterfly that lives only in the Keys.

- The Key Largo Woodrat[+], and the Key Largo Cotton Mouse[+]. They once lived on the entire island of Key Largo, but now they are found only on the northern third in the mature tropical hardwood hammocks. In 1970, in an effort to find a new place for them to live, woodrats were captured and moved onto Lignumvitae

Key (now a state park). Unfortunately, the colony all died out mysteriously, and there was no trace of them by the late 1980s.

- Over 30 plant species, whose existence is desperately threatened by development. These plants include many small trees such as the Tamarindillo[+], the Tree Cactus[+], ferns, shrubs, orchids, a palm, and a perennial flower.

The loss of any one of these creatures will diminish the uniqueness of the Keys of Florida. Who knows what the extinction of any of these species might mean to the world? It is important that we learn and care about the "string of pearls"—the Florida Keys.

Where to learn more

See "Underwater Treasures: Coral Reefs" for more on the reefs near the Keys.

See "Speaking of Trees" for more about mangrove trees.

See "The Air Around Us" for more about hurricanes.

See "Florida's Native Plants" for more about Coonties.

See "Insects Are Not Just 'Bugs'!" for more about butterflies.

See "Alligators, Snakes, and Other Reptiles" for more about the American Crocodile.

See "The Big Scrub" for more about Florida's geologic beginnings.

See "The Everglades" for more on tropical hardwood hammocks.

Do you know these words?

aquifer	coral
endangered	entomologist
evaporate	exterminate
extinction	hammock
hurricane	key
organism	peat
scuba	snorkeler
species	tropical
threatened	

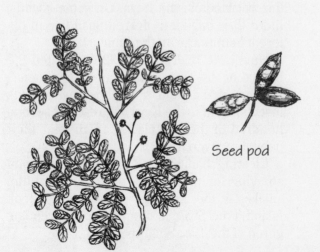

Seed pod

Tamarindillo

Chapter 8

Springs, Sinkholes, and Caves

Long known as "The Sunshine State," Florida could just as easily be called "the water state." People often think first of Florida's long coastline, for the state is rimmed with salt water.

But over 7,800 freshwater lakes dot the state (including Lake Okeechobee, the second largest freshwater lake wholly within the United States), and thousands of miles of freshwater streams and rivers wind across its surface. Lakes and rivers (and also water in the soil near the top of the ground) are referred to as surface water.

Just as important to the people who live in Florida is the water stored in huge natural underground reservoirs called aquifers. Most of the water we use comes from deep underground, with about 90% of all households depending on this supply, called groundwater, for drinking, bathing, and everyday use.

Several aquifers lie under the state, but by far the largest—known as "Florida's rain barrel"—is the Floridan aquifer. Aquifers fill up from the rainwater that filters down through sand and soil particles.

Eventually this water, cleansed by the sand, reaches a confining layer of limestone. There it is held in pockets, or hollow spaces, in the rock until a well is drilled to bring the water to the surface, or until it bubbles up through a natural hole and becomes a spring.

Springs

Florida has 320 known springs of flowing water—more, as far as is known, than any other state or country. The water that comes out is clear and refreshing, good to drink, and stays at a constant year-round temperature of about 22.2°C (72°F).

A spring that discharges more than 2,832 liters (747 gallons, or 100 cubic feet) of water per second is called a "first magnitude" spring. Florida has 27 first magnitude springs, including such famous ones as Silver Springs, Weeki Wachee, Alexander, Homosassa, and Wakulla. Can you locate these on a map of Florida?

Some small springs discharge less than half a liter (a pint) of water per minute. Your kitchen faucet probably discharges about 6 liters (1.5 gallons) a minute. Why don't you measure it and see?

Historically, Florida's springs were used by native Indians who caught fish, turtles, and shellfish in the spring run (the overflow stream) and gathered other foods nearby. They left the remains in middens, or garbage mounds, that you can see today near some springs.

In 1513, the Spaniard Juan Ponce de León searched for the "fountain of youth" in Florida. Nearly 250 years later, in 1774, the famous naturalist William Bartram described a large spring near the St. Johns River. He described it as an "enchanting and amazing crystal fountain . . . which threw up, from dark, rocky caverns below, tons of water every minute."

Soon after Bartram's travels in Florida, the beautiful springs began attracting tourists from the north and people with health problems who came to bathe in the water. Some of the springs contained sulphur water, which was thought to have healing properties. Today many Florida springs are major recreation areas that you may have visited or heard of.

Sinkholes

Sinkholes and caves are similar to springs in some ways, for they are all "holes in the ground." A sinkhole can be shallow—less than a meter (a few feet) deep—or it can be very deep.

Sinkholes can occur anytime, anywhere in Florida, but are more likely to happen when the water level in the aquifer drops because there is too little rainfall or too much water is pumped out, leaving a limestone hole without water to support its "roof." Then a crack begins to grow in the clay that lies under the sandy soil and above the limestone, perhaps caused by water seepage wearing away the clay and eroding the limestone beneath it. Eventually, the sand runs through the crack—like sand in an hourglass—into a hole in the limestone. When heavy rains add too much weight to the sandy soil above, the roof of the limestone hole may crash in. Then the ground above and everything on it—trees, and sometimes even roads and houses—fall into the hole.

Many of Florida's lakes are ancient sinkholes, and new sinkholes occur frequently. Central Florida officials received reports of 300 new sinkholes in a single recent year. During a cold spell, when farmers are pumping water to save their crops, 50 may occur in the Plant City area alone.

Sometimes you can read about them in the newspapers, such as the famous 1981 sinkhole in the central Florida city of Winter Park that swallowed cars, a house, and most of a large community swimming pool, and then half-filled with

Sinkholes are part of the natural process of erosion of limestone rock, and can happen anywhere in the state at any time of the year. Two types of sinkholes are generally formed in Florida.

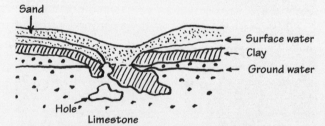

Solution Sinkhole—Solution sinkholes occur when the land surface gradually sinks into a cavity created by dissolving rock below. This bowl-shaped depression fills with sand, silt, and water, sometimes creating a marsh or shallow lake.

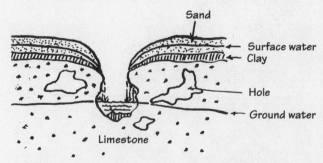

Collapse Sinkhole—Collapse sinkholes occur when an eroding cavity underground grows in size until the roof caves in. It usually happens suddenly, sometimes creating deep holes with overhanging walls (like the Winter Park sinkhole).

water. Other sinkholes remain dry, however, because the rain that falls into them flows quickly through to the aquifer.

Sinkholes vary in size from 1 meter (3 feet) to 18 meters (50 feet) or more in diameter, and 1 meter to 18 meters or more deep.

Inside sinkholes, the atmosphere is humid and fairly constant in temperature because the rim of the sinkhole shields it from sun and drying winds. Often, water seeps through the sand from the ground above and trickles down the inside walls. Many trees like the dampness, and they help to shelter special sinkhole plants. Ferns, mosses, and insectivorous (in-sek-TIV-uh-rus; insect-eating) plants—some of them endangered—like to grow in this small, almost enclosed atmosphere, called a microclimate.

There are two special sinkholes in Gainesville. One is a very old sinkhole called Devil's Millhopper, described by William Bartram in his *Travels*. The other, called the Squirrel Chimney Cave, on private land not open to the public, is the only place in the world that the Squirrel Chimney Cave Shrimp+ is known to live. This small, 3-cm-long (1-inch), transparent shrimp and several other very rare crustaceans live in the water at the bottom.

Caves

Caves may be springs that have dried up, or they may have been caused by underground water dripping through the ages, gradually eroding limestone in some places and building it up in others, making rooms and cave formations. Be-

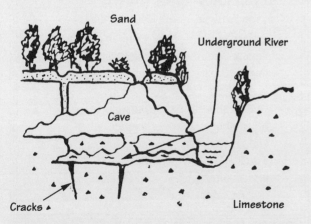

Underground Cave—If the roof does not collapse, erosion of the underground limestone can create a cave. Sometimes the rock dissolves sideways until it eventually reaches a river (like the Chipola).

cause the water table—the level of surface water in the soil—is usually high in Florida, most caves are flooded. In the Florida Panhandle, however, there are some beautiful caves with connecting rooms. Indians are thought to have hidden in them to escape soldiers in 1818. These caves are now part of Florida Caverns State Park. Bats live in the caves, and the Chipola River flows underground for 274 meters (900 feet) in the park before reappearing downstream.

A refuge for manatees

Water in Florida's springs maintains an even, year-round temperature of about 22.2°C (72°F) because it comes from deep in the ground where the air temperature does not affect it. In the winter, spring water can be much warmer than the temperature of the air and the ocean or rivers.

The endangered West Indian Manatee+ needs warm water to survive, for it becomes slow-moving and sluggish when the water temperature drops to around 18°C (60°F). Manatees stop feeding and, if the temperature stays cold for too long, they can become sick with symptoms similar to pneumonia.

Because of their low tolerance for cold water, manatees migrate to the warmer waters of springs in winter, usually staying in or near spring runs from about November through March.

In the summer, the West Indian Manatee occasionally travels as far north as Virginia on the Atlantic coast and west to Texas in the Gulf of Mexico, swimming in the ocean, estuaries, and rivers. They can live in salt water, brackish water, or fresh water. This same species also lives in the Caribbean and as far south as Brazil. Look on your globe or world map to find these places.

In the winter, those animals near the United States migrate back to Florida to search for warm water. Their winter refuges used to be only natural springs, but in the past 30 years or so, they have found other places to keep warm. Power plants and other industrial sites take water from a river, use it for cooling their equipment, and discharge it back into the river—warmer than it was before. Manatees sometimes congregate where this artificially warmed water pours back into the river. Unfortunately, if anything happens that causes the power plant to shut down, stopping the discharge of warm water, manatees may die.

Florida has more than 20 refuges for manatees

only on marked walkways or trails to keep from damaging delicate plants. Climbing the steep sides can cause erosion and gullies.

Never disturb bats or enter their caves during their hibernating or nursery periods. Human activity can disturb their sleep or cause them to abandon their offspring.

Don't pick ferns, mosses, or flowers in these microclimates. Leave them for others to see and for the plant to make seeds so there will be a new generation of plants.

Never take "souvenirs" or leave any trash—not even a gum wrapper. Do your part to keep the beautiful places in the world beautiful.

Never swim near manatees that sometimes enter springs. If you are boating in manatee areas, which are clearly posted, ask your parents to go slowly to give manatees time to get out of the way of your boat hull and its deadly propeller.

And don't forget to keep a record of your visit in your nature journal.

where you can go to see them. Five of the refuges are natural springs: Blue Spring in Volusia County where as many as 80 manatees may spend the winter; Crystal River and Homosassa Springs in Citrus County where more than 200 spend the winter, moving back and forth between the two places; Manatee Springs in Levy County where around 10 spend the winter; and Silver Glen Springs in the Ocala National Forest, where only a very few manatees congregate. Locate these springs on a map of Florida.

Most of the rest are found around power plants or other manmade sources of warm water, and, of course, scientists cannot account for all of them.

Manatees often return to the same warm springs each year, making it possible for scientists to keep records of the individual animals at each refuge. Because so many manatees have been struck by boat propellers that have left distinctive scars, over 900 of them are recognized and identified by the scar pattern. Scientists think that only about 1,800 manatees still exist in Florida waters.

Be a Conservationist

Springs, sinkholes, and caves are all fragile environments. When you visit any of these areas, walk

---

Where to learn more

See "What's in a Name?" for more about the manatee's name.

See "Extinction is Forever" and "Prairies—Wet and Dry" for more about insectivorous plants.

See "Florida's Native Plants" for more about William Bartram.

Do you know these words?

Can you list them in alphabetical order?

surface water	Floridan aquifer
aquifer	microclimate
midden	environment
water table	erosion
conservationist	nursery
hibernating	migrate
endangered	brackish
estuary	Species of Special
insectivorous	Concern
groundwater	

Chapter 9

Pine Flatwoods

Can you recognize the most common type of terrestrial (tuh-RES-tree-ul; dry land) habitat in Florida? Although you may see it often on your way to school, you might not realize that the everyday scenery of the pine flatwoods covers more than half of the state!

Early European visitors to Florida called these habitats flatwoods because of their characteristic flatness where pines, grasses, and shrubs grew. William Bartram referred to them as pine "barrens" when in 1791 he wrote about his travels through Florida on foot, in a sailboat, and on horseback. A few decades later, travelers and homesteaders settling this new state often called them piney woods and described them as being open enough to drive a horse and wagon through. It must have been difficult driving, though, as most pine flatwoods plants are typically found growing on loose, sandy soils.

In different parts of Florida, because of different soils, different plant communities grow. All flatwoods, however, include pine trees. The drier uplands may be covered mostly with

Sand Pines. In the wetter soils Pond Pines or Loblolly Pines grow. Slash Pines grow naturally in southernmost Florida—or wherever forest companies have planted them in what are referred to as pine plantations.

But the Longleaf Pine is the most distinctive feature of Florida's remaining natural pine flatwoods.

Longleaf Pine

Longleaf Pine flatwoods were once found throughout the state except for the very southern tip of the peninsula. Most of the native Longleaf Pine forests the early settlers traveled through at the turn of the century were tapped to provide "naval stores"—tar, pitch, rosin, and turpentine—made from the crude pine gum or sap, and then long ago were cleared for lumber. Longleaf Pine lumber, sometimes called yellow pine or pitch pine, is heavy, strong, and durable, and is still used for all kinds of building and construction. Only a few stands of native, old-growth Longleaf Pine can be seen today; most of these are growing in state or national forests or on small tracts of private land, mainly in north Florida.

The Longleaf Pine is an unusual tree. Its seedling remains for as long as six years or more in what is called the "grass stage." The bud of the seedling tree stays close to the ground, sometimes buried in sand, while a plume of long, dark green, shiny needles waves above it like a shaving brush. During this time the tree is sending its life-support system—its taproot—down several feet before beginning its above-ground growth.

This unusual growth pattern is a safety feature against the frequent lightning fires that often swept through Florida's pine flatwoods in earlier days. The long, moist needles of the grass stage protect the bud from heat.

When it finally starts to grow, the Longleaf Pine shoots up quickly, growing as much as a meter or more (3 to 4 feet) in a year, raising the bud out of reach of the next low-burning forest fire.

Mature Longleaf Pines can reach 500 years of age and have tall, straight trunks about half a meter or more in diameter (about 2 feet). The bark is thick, insulating the trunk from fire. The needles grow in clusters of three, from 25 to 51 centimeters (10–20 inches) long, the longest needles of any pine. Cones are large—sometimes 30 cm (a foot) long—and have thick scales with small, curved prickles. If the squirrels don't eat them while they're still green, they usually fall from the tree soon after the seeds, one tucked under each scale, ripen.

Flatwoods understory

Even the densest natural pine forests have thin canopies because of the nature of pine needles, which allows sunlight to reach the forest floor. Larger open spots, perhaps where a lightning strike felled an old tree or a fire raced through, provide breaks in the forest canopy that create opportunities for sun-loving plants to grow.

This understory—the shrub and grass layer growing beneath the forest canopy—includes many berry-producing plants such as Saw Palmetto, Gallberry, Dwarf Huckleberry, Wax Myrtle, Gopher Apple, and Fetterbush. All are important wildlife foods.

Grasses and herbs on the forest floor include Broom-sedge, Indian Grass, Beggarweed, Deer Tongue, Partridge Pea, and Rabbit Tobacco. One of the most characteristic species associated with the Longleaf Pine forest is Wiregrass.

From this brief list of some of the more common plants of the flatwoods community, can you name some of the animals likely to live here?

Flatwoods wildlife

Close to 30 species of reptiles and amphibians, including the Box Turtle and Eastern Diamondback Rattlesnake, live in the pine flatwoods understory. Some, however, such as the Pine Woods Tree Frog, the Oak Toad, and the Black Racer snake, climb higher into the canopy in search of insects or an occasional bird's egg.

Small mammals such as the Cotton Rat, Cotton Mouse, and Short-tailed Shrew provide food for nocturnal Great Horned Owls and Eastern Screech-Owls. Owls use the high limbs of the pines to roost on during the day and as a lookout to hunt from at night.

The Fox Squirrel[+] lives here, as does the Gray Fox and the White-tailed Deer. The Florida Black Bear[+] is surprisingly quiet and seldom seen as it shuffles through the understory, stuffing itself full of Huckleberries, Gallberries, and other fruits, as well as beetles and insect grubs that burrow in fallen and rotting logs.

Birds partial to the pinewoods community include the Pine Warbler, trilling high in the pine trees, and the Brown-headed Nuthatch, spiraling down the rough bark headfirst looking for insects

Red-cockaded Woodpecker

as well as feeding on pine seeds from the opened cones. Several sparrow species, including Bachman's Sparrow[+] and Henslow's Sparrow, hide in the Wiregrass on the forest floor, making them difficult to see unless you accidently flush them out.

Red-cockaded Woodpecker[+]

Once a common bird of the pine flatwoods, the endangered Red-cockaded Woodpecker can now be found only in a few remaining old-growth pine forests of Florida and the southeastern United States.

Named for the rarely seen red ear patch, or cockade, of the adult male, this small woodpecker's best field marks (colors and markings that help identify an animal) are its white cheek patches and black and white "ladder"-striped back. Nasal-toned call notes help birdwatchers locate it as it noisily searches the pine trees for insect larvae, ants, spiders, and caterpillars.

The most distinctive feature of this interesting bird is not its physical appearance, however, but its choice of home sites. Although all seven of Florida's other woodpecker species peck cavities, or holes, in decaying tree trunks with their chisel-like beaks, the Red-cockaded is the only woodpecker to perform this construction activity almost exclusively in living pine trees.

Around each cavity it drills several holes from which sticky sap continually drips, helping to repel predators such as the climbing Black Racer and other snakes, or the Great Horned Owl. This flowing sap is whitish in color, making it easy for birders to spot cavity trees from a good distance away.

The Red-cockaded Woodpecker excavates cavities in several species of pines, though Longleaf Pine is most often selected. Each living tree, however, must be at least 60 years old before a Red-cockaded Woodpecker is able to use it for a homesite. A type of plant fungus called Red Heart often afflicts Longleaf Pines 60 years and older. While it does not kill the tree, Red Heart fungus weakens the heartwood of the tree, making cavity excavation easier. Unfortunately for the Red-cockaded Woodpecker, most forestry practices do not allow pine trees to grow to such an age; trees are cut for pulpwood, paper, and lumber in 20- to 40-year cycles.

Florida's national forests—Apalachicola, Ocala, and Osceola—and some state and private lands are now beginning to manage areas of pine forests to accommodate the special needs of this endangered woodpecker.

Fire and the importance of prescribed burning

Human settlement of Florida has dramatically changed natural habitats around the state, and today few native flatwood forests remain. Silviculture—the practice of planting and harvesting trees for paper, pulp, and lumber—has changed forever the way most pine forests grow throughout the southeast. Many of the pine flatwoods that people see on their travels today are really Slash Pine plantations that have been planted for timber and pulpwood production, replacing the natural Longleaf Pine flatwoods of long ago.

Botanists and wildlife ecologists have recognized that, while the planted Slash Pines are often injured by fire, natural Longleaf Pine forests *require* fire in order to flourish.

Fire, every five to ten years, burns the pine needles and leaves so that seeds have bare soil to sprout in. Saw Palmetto fronds and other plants of the understory burn back, and young oak trees that have begun to grow are killed. If the oaks continue to grow in the absence of fire, pine seedlings are shaded out, Wiregrass and other wildflowers fail to bloom, and pine flatwoods can become oak hammocks.

State parks and other state and federal lands conduct a program called prescribed burning in which a fire is deliberately set, carefully controlled, and allowed to burn in small areas to help maintain Longleaf Pine and other habitats dependent upon fire. Though burning may seem to be temporarily undesirable—because of smoke, blackened trees, and the displacement of some wildlife—it is only a few days before new sprouts appear on Saw Palmetto and Wiregrass, wildflowers bloom again, and wild animals—seldom harmed in their flight from the fire—return to feast on the fresh, green growth.

Where to learn more

See "Prairies—Wet and Dry" for more on prescribed burning.
See "Speaking of Trees" for more on pines.
See "What Is a Bird of Prey?" for more on owls.

Do you know these words?

Can you list them in alphabetical order?

understory	roost
nocturnal	field marks
old-growth	silviculture
cavities	ecologist
botanist	Species of Special
prescribed burn	Concern
canopy	

Chapter 10

Water and Wetlands

Water on the surface of the ground is called "surface water." "Ground water" is water deep in the ground.

Plants suck up water from the ground through their roots, and then give off water vapor through their leaves in a process called "transpiration."

"Evaporation" occurs when water vaporizes from surfaces such as lakes or the soil. Both of these processes are caused by the sun's warmth, and for convenience the two words are often run together to make "evapotranspiration."

"Water, water everywhere, nor any drop to drink," cried the Ancient Mariner in Samuel Coleridge's poem, as he sat on his becalmed sailing ship in the midst of the vast ocean.

Water covers almost three-quarters of the earth's surface, but most of it is salty ocean or glacial ice. The salt seas are not part of the fresh water that all life—humans, animals, and plants—must have to exist. Only 3% of the water on earth is fresh, and nearly 90% of that small amount is frozen in polar regions. The tiny amount that is left provides all living things with vital liquid.

Water over all the earth circles endlessly in a process called the hydrologic cycle—clouds, rain, water running and collecting on the ground, soaking into the soil, evaporating and transpiring back into the air, and gathering into clouds again.

This water must serve a thousand uses, but only the rain that falls on trees, grass, lakes, and wetlands can seep into soil, returning to the groundwater (underground water) supply from which 90% of the people living in Florida draw their drinking water. Water that falls on streets usually goes into sewer systems that filter it and then dump it into rivers and out to sea.

Wherever it goes in Florida, surface water provides a special place for plants and animals—whether swamp, or clear lake, or grassy pond, or slow river, or cold spring run, or estuary where fresh water meets the salt sea.

One of the important places for rain to fall is on Florida's wetlands. Wetlands is a word you may have heard a lot, but have you ever wondered exactly what "wetlands" are? Your first guess might be "land" that is "wet" and you'd be right—but it's not quite as simple as that!

Wetlands are some of Florida's most important natural resources. In fact, some 46,000 square kilometers (11.4 million acres) of our state is wetlands! Wetlands exist in many different forms—coastal and freshwater marshes, swamps, ponds, mudflats, and wet prairies—to name just a few. They are generally described as natural communities where the soil is covered with water for one or more months during the year. Bodies of water that are wet all year, such as streams, rivers, deep lakes, and bays, are not included when we talk about wetlands.

Most wetlands are saturated (or soaked) often enough to grow plants that have adapted for life in wet soil conditions. You probably know the names of many of those plants—mangrove trees, cypress trees with their knobby knees, Sawgrass in the Everglades, Cattails, and Water Lilies.

Wetland food chains

Wetlands are among the most productive natural areas in the world because many wetland plants form the beginning of the food chain, providing food for many plant-eating creatures.

Both terrestrial plants (tuh-RES-tree-ul; that grow on dry land) and aquatic plants (uh-KWAT-ik; that grow in the water) make their own food. The process plants use to make food is called pho-

Food Chain Matching Game

Can you match these names of wetland plants and animals with their pictures? Can you guess what each species eats? Look for the answers at the end of the chapter.

Raccoon, Turtle, Water Lily, Great Egret, Red Maple, Water Snake, Snail Kite, Dragonfly, Air Plant, Apple Snail, Tadpole, Cypress Tree, Fern, Marsh Grasses.

tosynthesis (fo-toe-SIN-thuh-sis), and sunlight is the energy source that begins this complex chemical reaction.

Carbon dioxide gas dissolved in the water is absorbed by underwater plants, much as terrestrial plants absorb it directly from the air. Plants combine sunlight with the carbon dioxide in their tissues—their leaves, stems, and roots—to produce their own food. A by-product—oxygen—is released into the surrounding environment. The oxygen released by plants is, of course, vital, because humans and almost all other animal life cannot exist without it.

No animal of any kind can make its own food. It must find it in the environment around it. Plants, therefore, are the lowest links in the food chain. The next links are the animals that eat plants, and the highest links are the animals that eat other animals.

As small animals feed upon plant tissues, they are nourished and can reproduce, and, in turn, become food themselves for larger animals. For example, mosquito larvae live on tiny microscopic plants in the water that make their own food by photosynthesis, a dragonfly eats the adult mosquito, a frog eats the dragonfly, a snake eats the frog, and an egret catches and eats the snake.

This way in which energy is passed from plants to animals is also called a food web.

What wetlands do

Wetlands provide habitat for many species of fish, birds, and mammals, offering food, shelter, and protected nesting grounds. About 50% of the animals and 28% of the plants that are threatened or endangered in the United States depend upon wetlands at some stage of their lives for survival.

Water moves very slowly through wetlands communities, and as it travels, silt and pollutants such as chemicals, fertilizers, and wastes are filtered out and absorbed by plants. As the water continues to trickle through the ground, it helps to refill our drinking water supply, which is held in underground limestone-rock reservoirs called aquifers.

During heavy rains or hurricanes, wetlands act like big sponges, temporarily storing flood waters that could damage homes and property. By absorbing the destructive energy of storm waves and slowing water currents, wetlands help protect the coast from erosion.

Wetlands also offer unspoiled, open spaces for enjoying nature through activities such as boating, fishing, birdwatching, photography, and hunting.

Where have the wetlands gone?

For a long time, people who wanted Florida to grow economically did not recognize the importance of wetlands to wildlife, plants, and people.

Many wetland areas were drained or filled in to create dry land for agriculture, industry, homes, and shopping centers. Filling the wetlands smothered plants, and food and shelter was lost for many species of wildlife.

Dredging channels or canals for boat traffic changed the way water flowed in wetlands, often leaving them dry year-round instead of wet part of the time. Pollution from nearby development ran off into wetlands and overburdened their ability to filter sediments. Water quality in wetland areas decreased, as did the quality of water that soaked into underground aquifers. The historic wetlands of Florida, which used to cover 50% of the state, were reduced by more than 60% by 1974, and are still being destroyed for development.

Today, most people realize that wetlands are important for Florida's future. Florida has passed laws that help to protect wetlands from destruction, but more needs to be done. Citizens, businesses, government agencies, and conservation groups are working to preserve Florida's remaining wetlands so that we and future generations will enjoy the benefits of these important natural resources.

Where to learn more

See "The Everglades" to read about Florida's largest wetland and more about the food chain.

See "Prairies—Wet and Dry" to read more about wetland plants.

See "A Little Botany Lesson" for more about photosynthesis.

Do you know these words?

aquifer	endangered
erosion	estuary
evaporate	evapotranspiration
food chain	groundwater
habitat	hurricane
hydrologic cycle	larvae
nutrients	photosynthesis
pollutants	saturated
species	surface water
threatened	transpirate
wetlands	

Answers   The Raccoon eats the Dragonfly, the Tadpole, and also many other things.

The Turtle eats the Water Lily, and also water insects.

The Great Egret eats the Dragonfly, the Tadpole, the snake, and also fish.

The Water Snake eats fish and frogs.

The Snail Kite eats only Apple Snails.

The Dragonfly eats mosquitoes and other insects.

The Apple Snails eat vegetation in the water.

The Tadpole eats mosquito larvae in the water.

The Air Plant receives nutrients from moisture and dust in the air.

The Ferns, Cypress trees, Red Maple trees, Water Lilies, and Marsh Grasses survive on nutrients in the mud and water.

Paynes Prairie

Kissimmee Prairie

Chapter 11

Prairies—
Wet and Dry

If you watch cowboy-western shows, you may think of prairies as huge expanses of grassland that were once the Great Plains. But prairies are found in Florida, and though they are smaller in size than the western prairies, they still have many of the same characteristics—grasses, wild-flowers, flatness, and—especially—treelessness.

Prairies in Florida cover large sections of the state and are important habitat for some special plants and animals. Their designation by biologists as "wet" or "dry" depends on the plant species that live there rather than on the actual wetness of the soil.

Wet prairie

The Everglades are the world's largest and best-known wet prairie. Other wet prairies may surround marshes and swamps or may exist inland of ocean or gulf estuaries. Spots of higher ground sometimes support trees within the prairie, similar to the tree islands in the Everglades.

Except for the Glades, wet prairies—surprisingly—are usually wet for only 50 to 100 days out of the year and become dry for months during the winter "dry season." In south Florida, where the dry season is often prolonged, a wet prairie may be wet only briefly. In the Panhandle, where wet

and dry seasons are less pronounced, it may be wet longer than three months.

When summer rains flood the prairie, tadpoles and insect larvae hatch in the shallow water and wading birds stalk them. Bladderworts—an insectivorous plant with leaves that float on the water and trap swimming insects—grow here. When it is dry, Wiregrass and other drier-land species bloom.

When canals have been dug in wet prairies to drain the surrounding land for farming or housing developments, the drop in the water level may change them forever. Much dry land along the Kissimmee River in central Florida used to be wet prairie before an ill-advised government project "straightened" the river to prevent flooding during heavy rains. It was thought that the straight channel would carry the water away more quickly. Unfortunately, it carried the water so fast that silt, topsoil, fertilizer, and other pollutants washed downstream with it, causing pollution and eutrophication of Lake Okeechobee.

Eutrophication (YEW-truh-fuh-KAY-shun) is the natural process of "aging" in a lake as organic sediments build up over thousands of years. The process is accelerated when nutrients and fertilizers from farms and lawns are discharged into lake waters or flow into lakes with storm run-off, causing plants to grow faster. As they die, the decaying aquatic plants also add to the nutrient overload and deposit a layer of sediment on the lake bottom. A healthy lake can be damaged in only in a few years.

Pitcher-plants[+]

Among the most unusual plants of wet prairies are the six species of insectivorous Pitcher-plants, found mostly in the Florida Panhandle. This tubular, hooded plant uses nectar and bright colors to attract insects to the lip of the tube. There the insects encounter a slippery rim, and when they fall into the tube, they are digested by plant enzymes. Some Pitcher-plants are a meter (3 feet) tall. The Hooded Pitcher-plant[+] grows in wet prairies throughout Florida, but is rare. Several other species are listed as Endangered.

Dry prairie

Dry prairies often are found between pine flatwoods and lakes, rivers, or other wet places. A dry prairie may be wet only during a heavy or prolonged rain. A few scientists think that dry prairies are pine flatwoods with all the trees logged out and then kept out by frequent fires or overgrazing by cattle. Others think that dry prairies are naturally treeless, but no one knows why.

Low-growing Saw Palmettos often grow here along with grasses and wildflowers such as Goldenrod and the purple Blazing Star.

Dry prairie is home to some special birds. The Burrowing Owl[+], a comical, small, rather long-legged bird (for an owl), lays its eggs underground in a burrow it digs itself. It hunts mostly on the ground for insect food. It is listed by the state as a Species of Special Concern. You might be able to spot a Burrowing Owl peeking its head out of a burrow or standing on a fencepost if you visit the dry prairie habitat near Lake Okeechobee.

The Crested Caracara[+], listed as Threatened in Florida, is another unusual bird that prefers dry prairie habitat. The Crested Caracara, like the Burrowing Owl, is a bird of prey. It is a member of the

Pitcher-plants

Crested Caracara

Falcon Family and eats snakes, birds, and mammals. It also feeds on carrion, sometimes sharing the carcass of a dead animal with vultures.

Paynes Prairie

Paynes Prairie State Preserve near Gainesville was described by William Bartram, the famous naturalist whose travels from 1773 to 1776 included a year in Florida just before the American Revolution. Bartram called the prairie Alachua Savannah (savannah is a synonym for prairie), and at that time it was dry except for small streams that drained it into a big sinkhole on one side of the prairie. Alachua, it is said, means "big jug," which describes the sinkhole.

But in the early 1800s the sinkhole collapsed, plugging up the hole, and the shallow, 130-square-kilometer (50-square-mile) bowl filled with water. Then the sinkhole fell again, this time opening up, and again the prairie dried out.

This happened several times between 1800 and 1873. Sometimes when the water drained out, millions of fish were left dying on the bottom of the basin. Then the basin filled with water and remained full for nearly 20 years. During this time, it was called Alachua Lake. Vegetables, cotton, and oranges were grown around its shores, and a steamship ferried passengers and produce across it.

In the fall of 1891, the sink opened again, draining Alachua Lake so suddenly that steamers were left stranded on the bottom.

In the 1930s, ranchers dug canals to keep the prairie dry so their cattle could graze on it. Only a small lake remained around the sink.

In 1970 the state of Florida bought 18,000 acres of the prairie as a preserve for the 800 species of plants and 350 species of animals that live there. People visit the preserve to see Sandhill Cranes[+], Burrowing Owls, and other wildlife. Beautiful wildflowers bloom in summer and fall. You can hike, camp, and ride horseback in the Preserve, and on some trails you can see sinkholes.

Burrowing Owls

The name "Paynes" comes from the name of an Oconee-Seminole Indian who was chief of the Alachua Indian settlements in 1812. He was known as King Payne by settlers. There was also a white landholder known as Dr. Payne who lived south of the prairie in the 1800s, but most people feel that naming the prairie for the Indian chief is more picturesque.

Sandhill Crane[+]

The Sandhill Crane is a bird that stands over a meter (4 feet) tall with a 2-meter (6 to 7 feet) wingspan. Its existence is threatened mainly because of the draining of Florida's prairies and marshes by farmers and cattlemen. When a Sandhill Crane finds no wet places in its prairie habitat, it fails to raise a family.

Florida has its own resident population of Sandhill Cranes that live year-round on the prairies. In winter, migratory Sandhill Cranes also come from the midwest to spend several months in Florida.

Sandhill Cranes usually build nests in patches of marshy vegetation. The shallow water offers their eggs and young some protection from predators. The nest is made of Pickerel Weed and prairie grasses, and sometimes it floats when rains raise the water level.

If an enemy approaches a nest while the crane is brooding her eggs, she will stretch her long neck out flat on the ground trying to hide in the

Sandhill Crane and chick

grasses. The male will often fly protectively overhead.

It is worth a visit to Paynes Prairie State Preserve or National Audubon Society's Kissimmee Prairie Sanctuary near Lake Okeechobee to see this huge bird with a raucous voice. In the winter months at dusk, you can stand on the edge of the prairie and see flocks of Sandhill Cranes, necks stretched out, flying in to roost for the night.

Whooping Crane[+]

A close relative of the Sandhill Crane is one of the nation's most well-known endangered species. Named for its loud, ringing call that can be heard for several miles, the stately Whooping Crane is native to Florida, although no birds had been seen here since the early 1900s—until 1993.

An important scientific experiment took place that year on prairie habitats in central Florida. Twelve Whooping Cranes were brought to the Kissimmee Prairie from the midwest where they had been raised in captivity at a special crane breeding and research facility. Out on the prairie, these young birds were initially confined in open-topped pens, with one wing restrained to prevent them from flying out while they looked over and adjusted to their new home.

After a few days the birds' wings were gently freed, and they discovered that they could fly out of the pens and explore their surroundings. Food was placed in the pens in case the cranes were unsuccessful in capturing frogs and insects, but they quickly established their own routines in the wild and no longer needed human assistance.

Unfortunately, over the next few months, several birds were preyed upon, mainly by Bobcats. Biologists had predicted that as many as 60% of the Whooping Cranes in the project might die, but they hope the surviving cranes will assist in teaching new ones to be alert for predators.

The experiment will continue for ten years with 20 Whooping Cranes introduced each year onto Florida's prairie lands. Biologists hope that the newly created flock will be nonmigratory, remaining year-round in Florida.

Fire

Scientists are not sure why prairies remain treeless, but they do know that one of the requirements for prairie habitat is fire. Fire keeps hardwood plants from growing and seems to help prairie grasses and flowers maintain their species vitality by burning the plant debris, leaving the soil bare so seeds can sprout.

Before Indians and ranchers found that starting fires kept prairie grasses healthy, natural fires were caused by lightning strikes. Since Florida's thunderstorms most often occurred during the summer rainy season, fires sometimes were stopped by water standing in the marshes, limiting the fires to small areas. On other occasions, miles of prairie might burn from a lightning-caused fire.

Ranchers, however, found that it was easier to burn the grasses for their cattle in the winter, because the air is cooler and the vegetation is dryer.

Then, as people crowded close together in towns and cities, and roads were cut through

---

Where to learn more

See "What Is a Bird of Prey?" for more about the Burrowing Owl and the Crested Caracara.

See "Extinction is Forever" for more information about Endangered and Threatened species and Species of Special Concern.

See "Springs, Sinkholes, and Caves" for more on sinkholes.

See "Pine Flatwoods" for more on fire-maintained habitat.

See "The Panhandle" for more on insectivorous plants.

See "Monitoring the Weather" for more on eutrophication.

See "The Mysteries of Bird Migration" for more on migration.

Do you know these words?

annuals	enzymes
estuaries	eutrophication
germination	habitat
insectivorous	pollutants
pollution	predators
prescribed burn	propagate
raptor	sanctuary
Species of Special Concern	threatened
	topsoil

prairies, fire became a hazard to humans. Most fires were put out as quickly as possible to protect people and their property.

But now biologists know that lack of fire during the summer interrupts the cycle of some plants and nesting birds. Without fire, Florida's prairies begin to decline, woody plants grow, and wildflowers fail to propagate. Prairie birds and mammals can no longer find their familiar habitat.

Now Florida wildlife managers set prescribed burns, trying to reconstruct the natural cycle with small, well-controlled fires in specific places. Within days after a fire, new green shoots appear in the blackened stubble, seeds burst their coats and begin their incredible germination process, and birds and small mammals return to glean the toasted seeds and nibble the fresh sprouts. Birds, especially the endangered Grasshopper Sparrow[+], come back in double the numbers, raising a second family and feasting on the grasshoppers, which, in turn, have come back to take advantage of the fresh vegetation. Because many of the flowers are annuals—blooming, going to seed, and dying in a single growing season—prairies thrive best when they are burned every one to five years.

Burrowing Owl

Chapter 12

The Salt Marshes

Salt marshes

Salt marshes are not among Florida's most beautiful scenic places, but they are some of Florida's most important natural communities. They often appear to be nothing more than wide swaths of plain, unadorned, wind-blown grasses. The land is low, with no rises or hilly places, and doesn't receive much wave action from the ocean. Shallow creeks sometimes wind through grasses and mud flats where inland freshwater rivers meet incoming ocean tides.

An estimated 1,550 square kilometers (383,000 acres) of salt marshes stretch along Florida's coastline. Salt marshes are more common in northeast Florida and from Tampa Bay northward around the bend and along the Panhandle. The Indian River salt marshes near the Space Coast are at a higher elevation above sea level than usual for this habitat and are called "high marsh."

The rest of Florida's coastline, around the southern shores, is mostly sandy beaches or mangrove forests, which cannot grow very far north because of colder temperatures.

Only plants that can live in brackish (somewhat salty) or saline (salty) conditions grow here. On the salt marshes of the east coast, the most common species is a wiry grass called Smooth Cordgrass. On the Gulf coast, hollow-stemmed Needlerushes are more common. A very few

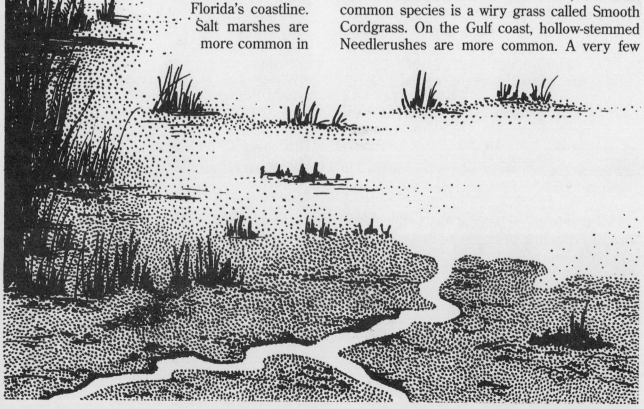

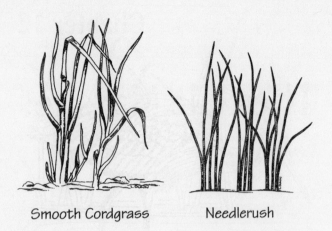

Smooth Cordgrass   Needlerush

Raccoon

trees, such as Sabal Palms and Black Mangroves, can grow where the land rises high enough for them to maintain a roothold. Sometimes a single tree will stand in a huge expanse of salt marsh.

But in spite of their flat, unchanging appearance, salt marshes are very important to fish, shellfish, birds, mammals, and even insects. Because of the harsh conditions for living in the salt marsh, not many *different* species of animals reside here, but many of those that do are abundant.

One of the most important ecological functions of the salt marsh is as a nursery for fish and shellfish. Many species of fish, crabs, shrimp, oysters, snails, and mussels begin their lives in saltmarsh estuaries, feeding on detritus washed in by ocean tides or washed out by slowly flowing freshwater creeks. As they grow, many move into deeper water, eventually traveling through Florida's inlets to spend most of their adult lives in the ocean. Many others, though, are trapped in pools as the water ebbs, and become food for fish, birds, and mammals without ever reaching the sea.

Animals of the salt marsh

Few species of animals live all the time in the salt marsh, because the water level rises and falls with tides and rainfall. Many animals, however, come from farther inland to hunt for food in the marsh. Raccoons, Marsh Rabbits, Cotton Rats and Cotton Mice, Muskrats, Wood Storks[+], Roseate Spoonbills[+], herons and egrets, crows, hawks and owls, frogs, toads, and even alligators use the salt marshes for feeding. Sometimes West Indian Manatees[+] swim up the marsh creeks to feed on sea grasses.

Insects are important to the salt marsh, too. Nearly all of them are vegetarians, eating the juices and tissues of the grasses and rushes. Grasshoppers, planthoppers, spiders, and a large variety of wasps all help keep the grasses trimmed.

Many of the animals of the salt marsh, whether they live there year-round or come in only once in a while, are hard to see. Some have camouflage coloring and are able to safely hide among the tall, grayish green grass blades.

• The Rice Rat is a small mammal that nests in the tall grasses at about the same time (April through July) and near where Marsh Wrens and Seaside Sparrows nest. This makes it easy for the rat to eat the bird's eggs, after which it sometimes occupies the nest! The Rice Rat also eats

Rice Rat

grains and fly and moth larvae.

• The Saltmarsh Vole[+] is a relict species, left over from the Ice Age. Its nesting and feeding habits have only recently been researched. It is thought to eat seeds and insects, bird eggs, snails, and crabs. This little animal seems to be able to withstand wet and cold conditions, building its nest in a tight ball of grasses above the high-water mark. The Saltmarsh Vole is listed as Endangered.

• Diamondback Terrapins are turtles that used to be common along the Florida coast in estuaries, marshes, and mangrove-lined lagoons. People used to eat them, and much of their habitat has been developed, but, though their numbers have declined, they are not yet listed as Endangered. They are adapted to living in the salt water, and spend their days basking in the· sun or searching for snails, crabs, insects, and marsh plants to eat. At night they bury themselves completely in the mud. They climb up on a dry creek bank between April and July to lay their pinkish white eggs in shallow nests they dig in the sand.

Great Blue Heron

• The Salt Marsh Snake is secretive, nocturnal, and rarely seen. It is one of the few salt-tolerant snakes. They feed on small fish and bear their young live instead of laying eggs. The Atlantic Salt Marsh Snake[+] is Threatened.

alt Marsh Snake

• The little Fiddler Crabs are probably the most common and most often seen of the residents of the salt marsh. They are less than 4 centimeters wide (1.5 inches) and gather in large herds when the tide is out, feeding upon detritus and algae. When the tide comes in, they hide in their individual burrows, plugging the opening with mud, and when the tide goes out again, you can often see little balls of mud near their burrow openings. The male crab has one small claw and one large one that he often waves like a violinist's bow, giving the species its common name.

Three species of birds live exclusively in the salt marsh: Seaside Sparrows, Clapper Rails, and Marsh Wrens.

• The Dusky Seaside Sparrow that once lived on Merritt Island is now extinct, and the Smyrna Seaside Sparrow[+] may also be gone forever. Others of these small brownish birds live in the salt marshes, constructing nests of marsh grass, often with a "roof" over the top. They lay three or four eggs sometime between March and August, and eat snails, crabs, insects, and seeds. The Cape Sable Seaside Sparrow[+], found in the Everglades salt marshes, is endangered.

Fiddler Crab

Seaside Sparrow

Clapper Rail

• Clapper Rails are chicken-sized birds, long-billed and dull-colored. They lay six to a dozen eggs between March and July in nests built near the water's surface. The chicks are black and downy, and follow their parents away from the nest right after they hatch. They eat crabs, shrimp, and insects. The secretive Clapper Rails are more often heard than seen, and their call resounds from deep in the salt marsh.

• The Marsh Wren is a tiny bird, brown with white streaks, with a bubbly song that ends in a trill. It builds a large, globe-shaped nest of grasses attached to grass stems, and eats insects and spiders.

Humans in the salt marsh

One of Florida's longest-running battles with the environment has been with mosquitoes. The Salt-marsh Mosquito is one of the most numerous and most vicious of Florida's many mosquito species. Most of the Indian River salt marshes on Florida's east coast have been altered by impounding—building dikes to make the land either all wet or all dry to discourage mosquito breeding. All but 5% of the salt marshes in Brevard County were impounded by 1972. Some of the impoundments have been reopened because biologists began to recognize the value of salt marshes to wildlife. In fact, scientists realized—although too late—that these impoundments contributed to the extinction of the Dusky Seaside Sparrow.

Also, before the banning of the insecticide DDT, salt marshes were heavily sprayed to control mosquitoes, harming both plants and animals, and many marshes were (and some still are) used as dumps for sewage and solid waste from nearby cities.

The building of Kennedy Space Center on Merritt Island in the 1950s destroyed many thousands of acres of salt marsh, too.

The changing salinity of the water caused by the constant mixing of fresh and salt waters is vital to the species that live in these marshes. An impoundment that cuts off the flow of fresh water, or the dredging of a boat channel that alters the tidal flow, can kill salt marsh plants, fish, and other animals.

Some salt marshes have been dredged and filled to make dry land for houses and canals for boating. Fortunately, salt marshes are not good

Where to learn more

See "Extinction is Forever" for more about the Dusky Seaside Sparrow.

See "Alligators, Snakes, and Other Reptiles" for more about the Salt Marsh Snake.

Do you know these words?

algae	brackish
camouflage	detritus
ebbs	ecological
endangered	estuary
extinction	field guide
habitat	impounding
lagoon	nursery
relict	salt-tolerant

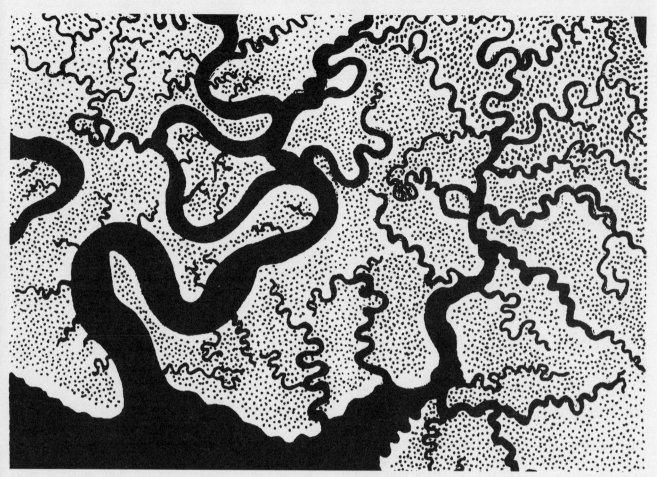

Salt marsh, aerial view

places to build cities and towns, and people today are beginning to recognize the importance of this special habitat. Salt marshes are protected on the Gulf coast in an almost unbroken line from St. Marks National Wildlife Refuge south to Chassahowitzka National Wildlife Refuge. This new attitude toward wetlands will help save important habitats for the plants and animals that live in Florida's salt marshes.

Where to visit salt marshes

If you ever have a chance to visit Kennedy Space Center, perhaps you can also visit Merritt Island National Wildlife Refuge near Titusville. Black Point Wildlife Drive is a long drive through the salt marshes along the dikes built to control mosquitoes. You can see many birds there, especially in the winter season. Take your binoculars and your field guide.

A little farther into the refuge is the Allan D. Cruickshank Wildlife Preserve, named for a famous bird photographer and naturalist who lived in Brevard County in the 1950s and 1960s. A walking trail winds through the marshes of the preserve.

Chapter 13

The Panhandle

Sometimes people think of the Florida Panhandle, the narrow projection on the northwest side of Florida, as almost another state. With its rolling hills and vegetation more typical of the temperate regions of the southern Appalachian Mountains farther north, it is indeed different from the flat, subtropical world of the Florida peninsula. The Panhandle has some interesting and special places to explore, and also offers a less-developed and less-hurried lifestyle than most other parts of the state.

The capital

Florida's capital city, Tallahassee (a Creek Indian word meaning "old field"), is located in the Panhandle. It's far from the Orlando area, which is now considered the center of the state, but in 1820, when the location was selected, Tallahassee was between the two centers of Florida's population. Most of the people lived in either Pensacola, near the western border, or St. Augustine on the east coast. William P. Duval, governor at that time, ordered that the capital site be chosen by having two travelers leave from St. Augustine and Pensacola on the same day. The one going west from St. Augustine traveled overland on horseback. The one going east from Pensacola traveled by boat, going up the St. Mark's River. Where they met became the site of the new capital, Tallahassee.

The highlands of western Florida are older than the coastal areas of the peninsula, because the receding ancient oceans left the land high and dry much earlier. The highest point in Florida—1,132 meters (345 feet) above sea level—is in Walton County in the Panhandle.

Some of the beaches in the Florida Panhandle are wild and primitive.

Florida's Panhandle has thirteen beautiful rivers.

Panhandle rivers

Thirteen wild and beautiful rivers cut across the narrow strip of Florida to the Gulf of Mexico, including three of Florida's largest: the Apalachicola (AP-uh-LACH-uh-KO-luh), Choctawhatchee (CHOK-tuh-HACH-ee), and Escambia (es-CAHM-be-uh). (Enjoy learning to pronounce these melodious Florida place names.) Most of these rivers are still natural, without dams or many houses or other manmade intrusions along them. All of them receive water from drainage areas in Alabama and Georgia, rather than from only rainfall or underground aquifers.

The Perdido (pair-DEE-doe) River begins in Alabama and forms the crooked state line between Florida and Alabama. *Perdido* is a Spanish word meaning "lost," maybe referring to the hidden nature of Perdido Bay.

The Aucilla River (aw-SILL-uh; the name is from the Timucuan [Tim-OO-kwan] Indian language) is a paleontologist's (PAY-lee-un-TALL-uh-jist) heaven—the river is one of the richest sites in Florida for prehistoric mammoth and mastodon bones.

Unusual places

Florida's only waterfall is near Chipley, protected by Falling Waters State Recreation Area. The waterfall is unusual, for it starts at ground level and drops about 30 meters (100 feet) into a deep, narrow, shady sinkhole; then the water disap-

pears and runs underground for about 275 meters (900 feet) through the park.

Near Marianna is Florida Caverns State Park, a natural phenomenon that the Indians knew about for centuries before the white man came. The Spaniards wrote about the caves in 1693. These caverns are similar to many of the underwater caverns created by springs and sinkholes. But these caves are dry, and you can walk through them and see the beautiful formations of stalactites and stalagmites. The endangered Gray Bat[+] lives here, as well as an extremely rare, white, eyeless cave crayfish and a sightless salamander.

The Steepheads—Florida's canyonlands

Among the most special places in the Panhandle are the steepheads—deep ravines where a person who is used to the flatness of Florida is surprised by the sudden drop-off of more than 30 meters (100 feet). If you stand on the edge of a steephead, you can look out over the treetops of tall Magnolia, Oak, and Hickory trees. The length of the ravines runs east and west, toward the Apalachicola River.

If you climb down the side of one of these ravines, it is so steep that you have to step carefully, holding onto whatever you can. You enter a cool valley with vegetation completely different from that growing higher up.

Some of Florida's rarest and most interesting plants grow here—the Florida Yew[+] and the Torreya Tree[+]. Neither grows naturally anywhere else on earth. A brook of clear water flows at your feet over clean white sand. The air is humid, and you can smell the dampness of the leaf litter. You are in a place that may be nearly the same as it was 100 million years ago. The crumbling leaves are inhabited by spiders, beetles, earthworms, and other creatures. Salamanders feed on them. The temperature of the brook water and the air at the bottom of these steepheads is almost constant year-round, providing a stable climate for the species that live here.

Steepheads have developed differently from most stream valleys. A river usually washes away the surface sands as it flows downhill to the sea, but steephead streams have undercut the sandy slope from the bottom up as the water seeps out from underground, continuously lengthening the valley.

The Apalachicola River

The Apalachicola River is the largest river in Florida in terms of total flow of water. It is the only river to actually receive snow melt from the mountains in northwest Georgia by way of the Chattahoochee River (chat-uh-HOO-chee). The Apalachicola River runs between steep bluffs, low banks, and broad marshes for 172 kilometers (107 miles) from Lake Seminole to Apalachicola Bay. Alum Bluff, 60 meters (200 feet) high, was considered for the site of a nuclear power plant years ago, but people became angry at the thought of spoiling the river and prevented it.

The floodplain may support more reptiles, mammals, and birds than any other area of comparable size in the world. The rare and beautiful Barbour's Map Turtle[+] lives only in the Apalachicola River and parts of its drainage basin.

Water Tupelo and Ogeechee Tupelo trees grow along this river. Tupelo honey, a light, pure, special-tasting honey, is made by bees from the flowers of the Ogeechee tree. Most tupelo trees grow in swamps throughout the eastern United States, but one species of tupelo is endemic, meaning that it grows only here.

A few years ago, one man claimed that an area of the Florida Panhandle near the Apalachicola River was the original biblical Garden of Eden, because the Torreya tree, which grows only here, is also known as Gopherwood. Gopherwood is mentioned in the Book of Genesis and is said to be the wood from which Noah's Ark was made.

Apalachicola Bay

When the river finally flows into Apalachicola Bay, evidence of the flow of nutrients and clay extends 260 kilometers (160 miles) out into the Gulf of Mexico. Apalachicola Bay is thought by some biologists to be one of the world's most productive estuaries, and some of the finest natural oyster beds and fish hatcheries in the world exist here.

Oyster fishermen use rakes to gather oysters.

In earlier times, the bay was a vital Gulf port. Logging companies cut trees from the banks and swamps, and sawmills made lumber to ship to other parts of the country. Now, many of the shipping and logging towns, so important in the past, are ghost towns, but shrimping and oystering in the bay still provide work for many people.

Barrier islands

The barrier islands of the Panhandle are important to the life of the bays and the mainland. Several long barrier islands help to create a huge basin, holding in the water flowing from the rivers

The floodplain and estuary of the Apalachicola River spreads over many miles.

Oyster

A shrimp boat spreads its nets to catch shrimp.

and holding out the water from the Gulf of Mexico. Nutrients in the salt and fresh waters held in the basin mingle into a soup that is perfect as a nursery for fish and shellfish. Barrier islands also protect the mainland from heavy storms and provide a safe haven for ships.

Some of these islands are wildlife refuges and national seashores, while others are being developed. Some, such as wild and primitive St. Vincent National Wildlife Refuge, can be reached only by boat. Others are connected to the mainland by bridges and causeways.

Lighthouses

Four lighthouses have protected shipping from the dangers of shallow waters of the Panhandle for many years: the Pensacola lighthouse, one on Cape San Blas, the Cape St. George lighthouse in Apalachicola Bay, and the St. Mark's lighthouse. None of these lighthouses has a lighthouse keeper any more; all are automatic.

Where to Learn More

See "The Big Scrub" for more about Florida's emergence from the sea in the Ice Age.

See "Springs, Sinkholes, and Caves" for more about Florida Caverns State Park.

See "The Salt Marshes" for more on estuaries.

See "Discovering the Beach" and "The Air Around Us" for more on barrier islands.

Do you know these words?

Can you list them in alphabetical order?

panhandle	peninsula
aquifer	paleontologist
steephead	floodplain
drainage basin	estuary
biologist	barrier island
prehistoric	stalactites
stalagmites	

Flora (Plants) and Fauna (Animals)

This section presents some of the natural history of Florida's wildlife—its trees, flowers, reptiles, insects, and especially its birds. Remember that "animals" refers to all members of the Animal Kingdom, not just mammals, and that species that are listed as Endangered, Threatened, or of Special Concern are marked with a superscript symbol.

Chapter 14

What's in a Name?

Centuries ago, when fewer people lived on earth and they gathered in small villages, one name was enough to identify anybody in town. Everybody knew John!

As the populations of towns grew, sometimes two people would have the same name. In order to know which "Bob" was being talked about, one might have to say, "Bob, John's son." As you can guess, Bob Johnson soon became a full name.

Now almost everybody in our country has a middle name, too. In Europe, four names are common, and in China, people sometimes have many names.

People had trouble knowing the names of plants and animals, too, because often the same plant or animal was called something different in every country or region.

In 1753, a Swedish botanist (plant scientist) named Carl von Linne began a system of classifying plants, and later birds, that we continue to use to this day. Since Latin has always been the language of science and knowledge, the system uses Latin words for names, and even calls Linne by his Latin name—Carolus Linnaeus. This makes it possible for scientists all over the world, whatever language they speak, to know the identity of the plant or animal under discussion.

Usually the name is made up of two words and is referred to as the scientific name, called a binomial (*bi* is Latin for "two" and *nomen* is Latin for "name").

The first word of the binomial is the genus—Latin for "birth" or "origin"—of the species. Any two individual plants or animals with the same first name, or genus, have something in common.

American Kestrel
Falco sparverius

Peregrine Falcon
Falco peregrinus

Falcons, for example, are streamlined birds of prey with pointed wings and long tails. The Latin name for this genus is *Falco*, which perhaps comes from a Latin word that means "furnished with scythes" referring to their extremely sharp, curved claws, like an old-fashioned hand-held scythe.

The second word of the binomial is the species, or "specific name," which tells that this particular kind of plant or animal has special characteristics about it that are different from any other kind. (Species, special, and specific are words that all come from the same Latin root, which means "kind of" or "appearance.")

Falco sparverius, the American Kestrel, for example, is a falcon the size of a Blue Jay with beautiful colors and markings. *Sparverius* means "sparrow," and the Kestrel is sometimes called a Sparrow Hawk because it often preys upon small birds such as sparrows.

Falco peregrinus, the Peregrine Falcon, is a bigger falcon—about the size of a Crow—with colors and markings different from *Falco sparverius*. *Peregrinus* means "wanderer," and the Peregrine Falcon is known as a world-wide traveler.

Sometimes a third name, called the Subspecies name (abbreviated "ssp.") is added to further identify a particular specimen, such as *Canis rufus niger*, the Red Wolf of Florida. When a third name is added to identify a plant, botanists can set it apart by Subspecies or by the word "variety," abbreviated "var." as in *Acer rubrum* var. *trilobum*, a variety of Florida's Red Maple tree.

The name is chosen by the scientist who first describes a new species, either the one who first discovers it in its natural habitat, or the one who studies it in the laboratory. The chosen name must be approved by an international commission on scientific names. Some names come from other languages such as Greek or Spanish, while some honor a person, or indicate the geographic location where the species was first found.

The scientific name of a pretty blue Florida wildflower, commonly called a Spiderwort, is *Tradescantia ohiensis*. *Tradescantia* was named for John Tradescant, who was a botanist and gardener to King Charles the First of England in the early 1600s. *Ohiensis* means "of Ohio" where it was first found. Linnaeus himself named this plant to honor John Tradescant.

When writing scientific names, the genus is always capitalized, and the species is never capitalized, even if it's the name of a person or a place, as in *ohiensis*. The words are always underlined or set in italic type, like this: <u>Tradescantia ohiensis</u>, or *Tradescantia ohiensis*.

Besides being identified by their binomials, species are also identified by their Family, their Order, their Class, their Phylum, and their Kingdom. These categories can be further divided by using the prefix *sub-*, meaning "under," as in Subphylum, Suborder, or Subspecies.

Let's choose Florida's state bird, the Northern Mockingbird, to illustrate how the complete identification system works.

The highest classification of all for the mockingbird is that it belongs to the Animal Kingdom, and is not a vegetable or mineral.

Phylum is a Greek word for "stock," "race," or "kind" of related living things. The mockingbird belongs to the Phylum Chordata, meaning it has a spinal chord, and the Subphylum Vertebrata, meaning it has a backbone to protect the spinal chord (the Phylum and Subphylum names end in "-ata").

It belongs to the Class Aves, Latin for "bird"—animals that have wings and feathers, and that fly (with the exception of a few such as the ostrich).

It belongs to the Order Passeriformes, or birds that perch instead of float on water or cling to trunks of trees (the Order name always ends with "-iformes").

It belongs in the Family Mimidae, or "mimic thrushes" (the Family name always ends with "-idae" for animals and "-aceae" or "-ae" for plants).

Spiderwort
Tradescantia ohiensis

The Linnaeus Classification System
for the Northern Mockingbird

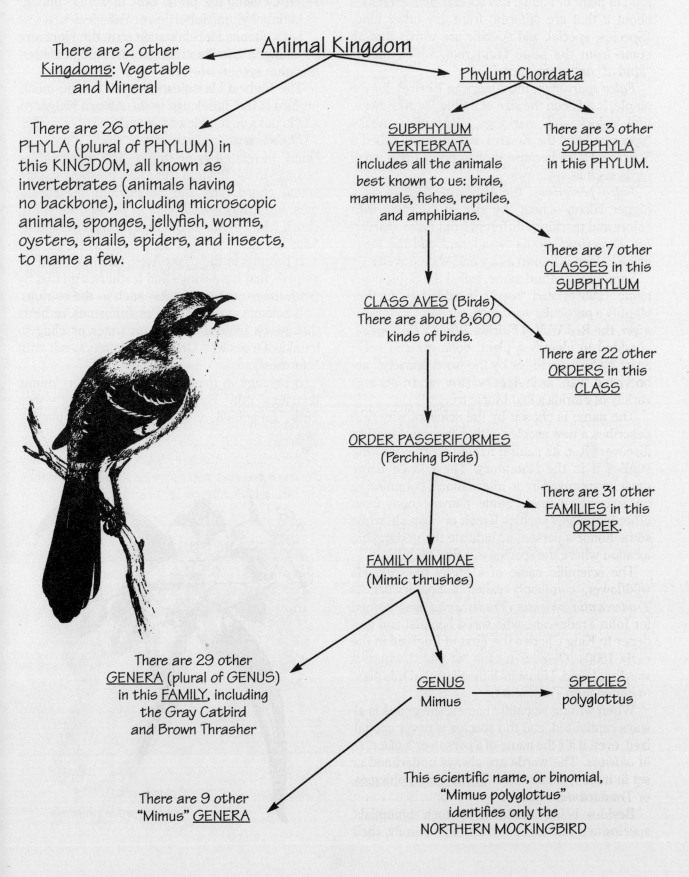

There are 2 other <u>Kingdoms</u>: Vegetable and Mineral

Animal Kingdom

Phylum Chordata

There are 26 other PHYLA (plural of PHYLUM) in this KINGDOM, all known as invertebrates (animals having no backbone), including microscopic animals, sponges, jellyfish, worms, oysters, snails, spiders, and insects, to name a few.

<u>SUBPHYLUM VERTEBRATA</u> includes all the animals best known to us: birds, mammals, fishes, reptiles, and amphibians.

There are 3 other <u>SUBPHYLA</u> in this PHYLUM.

There are 7 other <u>CLASSES</u> in this <u>SUBPHYLUM</u>

<u>CLASS AVES</u> (Birds) There are about 8,600 kinds of birds.

There are 22 other <u>ORDERS</u> in this <u>CLASS</u>

<u>ORDER PASSERIFORMES</u> (Perching Birds)

There are 31 other <u>FAMILIES</u> in this <u>ORDER</u>.

<u>FAMILY MIMIDAE</u> (Mimic thrushes)

There are 29 other <u>GENERA</u> (plural of GENUS) in this <u>FAMILY</u>, including the Gray Catbird and Brown Thrasher

<u>GENUS</u> Mimus

<u>SPECIES</u> polyglottus

There are 9 other "Mimus" <u>GENERA</u>

This scientific name, or binomial, "Mimus polyglottus" identifies only the NORTHERN MOCKINGBIRD

The Catbird and Brown Thrasher also belong in the Family Mimidae.

The mockingbird's binomial is *Mimus polyglottos.* In Latin, *mimus* means "mimic" and *polyglot* means "several languages." And if you've ever listened to the mockingbird, you know that it can copy the songs of many birds and even human whistling, so its name—both in English and in Latin—is a good one. (The "Northern" part of its English name tells us it is a North American bird.) There are no Subspecies of the Northern Mockingbird.

The science of naming and classifying all the species of life on earth is called taxonomy (tax-ON-uh-me) or systematics (SIS-tuh-MAT-iks). Even the word *taxonomy* is from the Latin, meaning "to name in order," or "to arrange by name" (*taxis* means "arrangement"; *nomen* means "name").

Taxonomists still have a lot of naming to do. Many bird and animal species already have been discovered and named, but thousands of plants and insects have never even been seen and described, let alone named and catalogued.

One term for each species

Some of the names we use for species are exact translations from the Latin, such as *Canis rufus.* *Canis* is the Latin word from which we take canine, meaning "dog." *Rufus* means "red." *Canis rufus* means "red dog," but since it's wild, we call it a red wolf. The Florida population of the Red Wolf is extinct, but when it existed here, it was dark in color instead of reddish, so scientists gave it a third name. It is called *Canis rufus niger,* or "black red-wolf." That seems strange, but scientists discovered that the two animals, though different in color, were really the same species—just as dogs of the same breed can come in different colors. Often when scientists discover a different-looking member of the same species, they will give it a third name, called a Subspecies, to identify it more accurately.

Let's look at some scientific and common names of plants and animals found here in Florida and see if we can tell why they were given the name they have today.

- A purple wildflower known as Bushy Aster is, scientifically, *Aster dumosus. Aster* is a Greek word for "star" and *dumosus* means "bushy." Find a Bushy Aster plant in bloom, or look it up in a wildflower guide. Does the flower look like a star? Is the plant bushy?

- The Latin name of the Gopher Tortoise is *Gopherus polyphemus.* You can see that its common name is taken directly from its Latin name. *Gopherus* comes from a French word meaning "honeycomb" and *polyphemus* was the name of a mythological one-eyed giant. Look at a Gopher Tortoise, or find a picture of it. Can you imagine why its discoverer named it *Gopherus polyphemus*?

- Alligator came from the Spanish words *el lagarto,* meaning "the lizard." The name gradually became pronounced "aligarto," and finally, alligator. The scientific name for the American Alligator is *Alligator mississippiensis.* What state do you think the naturalist was in when he or she first saw this animal?

- *Anhinga anhinga* is an example of the same word being used for both the genus and the species—and the common name, too. The Anhinga's name comes from the African name for this bird.

- From its common name, you might think our national bird, the Bald Eagle, has no feathers on its head, but the truth is that *bald* came from an Old English word meaning "white." Its scientific name is *Haliaeetus leucocephalus: leucocephalus* means "white head." (Another bird with white on its head is *Columba leuco-*

Red Wolf
Canis rufus

American Alligator
Alligator mississippiensis

cephala, the White-crowned Pigeon of the Florida Keys.)

- A fascinating group of birds called nightjars includes the Chuck-will's-widow. The call it makes sounds just like its name, and if you've ever tried to go to sleep while it's calling, you know that it certainly does "jar" the night! Its genus is *Caprimulgus* which means "milker of goats." Once there was an ancient myth that these birds sucked milk from goats, and today they are sometimes called goatsuckers.

- Biologists call the endangered Florida Panther *Felis concolor coryi. Felis* means "cat," *concolor* means "similar in color" referring to its being the same color all over, and Cory was the name of the person for whom the Florida Subspecies was named. Other *Felis concolor*s in western states are known as screamers, catamounts, mountain lions, cougars, pumas, and other common names, but the Florida Subspecies is always called a panther.

- *Trichechus manatus* is the West Indian Manatee. *Manatus* comes from a Caribbean Indian word, *manati*, meaning "woman's breast." Sailors at sea for a long time thought they were seeing mermaids when they first saw these animals swimming close to shore.

Who's who?

A scientist who generalizes in the study of living organisms is a biologist (bi-ALL-uh-jist). Biologists who specialize in studying certain aspects of the natural sciences can be further identified as follows:

Scientists who work with the classification of living things are called taxonomists (tax-ON-uh-mists) or systematists (SIS-tem-uh-tists), and they may specialize in taxonomy of plants, birds, mammals, insects, or fishes.

Plant specialists are called botanists (BOT-uh-nists).

Bird specialists are called ornithologists (OR-nith-ALL-uh-jists).

Animal specialists are called zoologists (zo-ALL-uh-jists), and mammalogists (mam-ALL-uh-jists) specialize in mammals.

Insect specialists are entomologists (en-to-MALL-uh-jists).

Fish specialists are ichthyologists (ik-thee-ALL-uh-jists).

Your turn to name one.

Would you like to name a species that no one has named yet? Suppose you were walking through the woods and you kicked over an old rotting log. Underneath, crawling in the moldy leaves and wood, was the imaginary creature you see in this picture. Would you name it for yourself or your best friend (you can add -us to the end of the name to make it like a Latin word)? Or the town you found it in? Maybe you'd like to give it a name related to its color, or where it lives in the soil. Or a name that describes its stra-a-ange appearance!

Where to learn more

See "Environmental Careers" for more on opportunities in scientific fields.

Do you know these words?

binomial	biologist
botanist	Class
entomologist	Family
Genus	ichthyologist
Kingdom	mammalogist
Order	ornithologist
Phylum	species
Subphylum	Subspecies
systematics	taxonomy
zoologist	

Chapter 15

A Little Botany Lesson

When we speak of wildlife, most people think only of animals, usually well-known mammals such as squirrels, panthers, or manatees. Or maybe they remember that birds, reptiles, and insects are wildlife, too.

We often forget that plants are part of the earth's wildlife communities. In fact, plants are such an important part that animals cannot live without them—not wild animals, not domestic animals, nor, for that matter, humans.

Plants benefit the earth by giving off water and oxygen, absorbing pollutants, softening rainfall impact, holding soil and preventing erosion, creating shade and microclimates (the temperature and moisture of a small area), and offering spectacular beauty.

What is a plant?

A plant is a living thing that does not have the ability to move from place to place under its own power. It can move only with the help of wind or waves, or by catching a ride with birds or other animals. Or people can transplant it (dig it up, move it, and plant it somewhere else).

Plants come in many different sizes and shapes, and have many different ways of growing. The biggest plants are trees, usually defined as having a single woody stalk called the trunk. Branches and foliage grow from the trunk above ground in a fairly definite shape, called the crown. Depending upon the species, a mature tree can be from 4 meters (12 feet) to 100 meters (over 300 feet) in height, and from 10 cm (4 inches) to more than 10 meters (32 feet) in diameter. One of the biggest trees is the Giant Sequoia of California. Trees can live from a few years to a thousand or more years.

Shrubs are shorter than most trees and have more than one woody stem instead of a main trunk. They usually live a few years at most.

Plants that are even smaller are called herbs (the "h" is silent), or are described as herbaceous (er-BAY-shus). They have soft, instead of woody, stems. The part that grows above the ground lasts for only one growing season. Some, called annuals (meaning "yearly"), live for only a year, forming seeds to propagate (reproduce, or increase) the species. Biennials (by-EN-ee-ul; *bi* means "two"), whose underground roots survive the winter, put out seeds in their second growing season before dying. Perennials (purr-EN-ee-ul, *per* means "through") live for several years, though their above-ground parts may die back each fall and sprout again the next spring.

All plants that reproduce by seeds have roots, stems, leaves, and flowers. Roots grow below ground, and serve to anchor the plant in place and absorb water and nutrients from the soil. Stems support the leaves and transfer water and nutrients to them. Leaves absorb light, using energy from the sun to change the water and carbon dioxide from the air into sugar that the plant needs to grow. As part of this process, called photosynthesis (fo-to-SIN-thuh-sis), oxygen is released into the air.

Flowers

Flowers are the most important part of the study of botany. Flowers are the reproductive parts of a plant, forming the seeds that will become new plants like the parents. Knowing flower parts and their contribution to the life of the plant is basic to botany.

Flower parts include petals and sepals, and stamens and pistils. The petals are the colorful rays of a flower that appear immediately above the green sepals. All of the petals together are called the corolla, and all of the sepals together

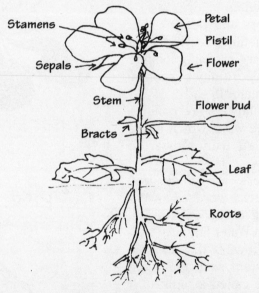

Flower Parts

Stamens — Petal
Pistil
Sepals — Flower
Stem — Flower bud
Bracts — Leaf
Roots

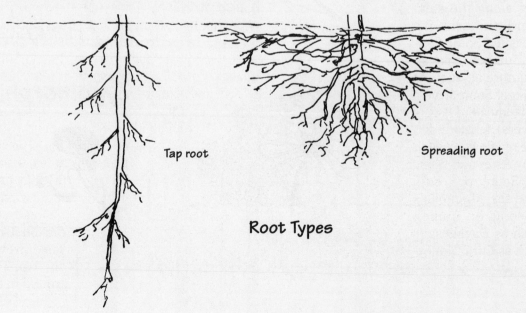

Tap root   Spreading root

Root Types

are called the calyx. The stamens contain pollen that is transferred to the pistils by wind or flying insects.

Flowers come in many colors and patterns, and many are fragrant. The colorful petals, unusual shapes, and odors attract bees, wasps, and other insects (and in some countries, bats) that are needed to pollinate the flowers. An insect brushes pollen from the stamen when it enters to sip the flower's nectar. Pollen is then transferred to the pistil, fertilizing the egg as the insect moves around inside the flower. The insect also carries pollen from flower to flower as it flies, pollinating other plants of the same type. Seeds grow from the fertilized eggs as a result of pollination.

Spiders and beetles that you sometimes see hiding in flowers are probably looking for an opportunity to capture the pollinator to eat!

Some flowers are pollinated by the wind, which blows the pollen from flower to flower.

Flowers are described with special words. Flowers standing alone on a stem, such as a Water Lily, are "solitary." Flowers that cluster along a stem, such as Blazing Star, are called a "spike." If each flower along the stem has its own little stem, it's called a "raceme." Some flowers grow in "umbels" like an inside-out umbrella, such as Butterfly Weed. Some have a tightly formed head of florets (small flowers) surrounded by petal-like ray flowers, such as the Bushy Aster and Daisy Fleabane. Some are cup-shaped, like the Magnolia's huge blossom; or funnel-shaped, such as Daylilies; or tubular, such as Coral Honey-

suckle or Trumpet Vine; or—how about this one?—zygomorphic (zye-guh-MORE-fik), which means that the flower is "two-lipped" and is symmetrical from side to side, but not top to bottom, as are the flowers of pea plants.

The language of botany

Many of the words you have been reading are unique to botany, the study of plants. Botanists are scientists who study plants.

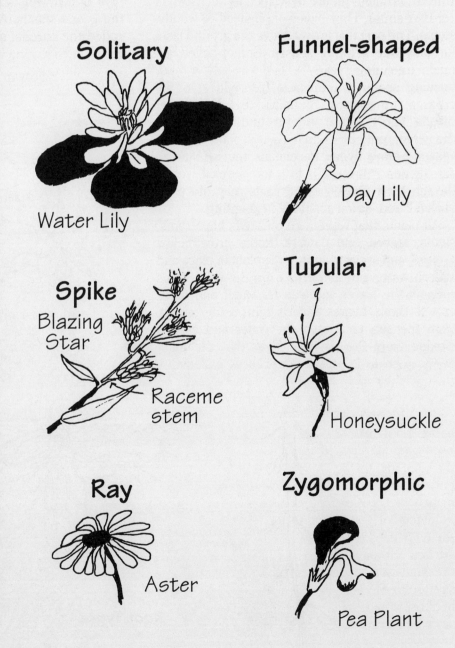

Solitary — Water Lily

Funnel-shaped — Day Lily

Spike — Blazing Star — Raceme stem

Tubular — Honeysuckle

Ray — Aster

Zygomorphic — Pea Plant

Fan Palm

All professions use their own special words to identify and describe features of their work in order to communicate accurately. Part of studying botany, or any science, is learning the words scientists use in that field. Much of the scientific vocabulary is based on the ancient Latin and Greek languages, and botanists around the world use Latin and Greek terms to identify plants and plant parts.

A leaf can be described quite accurately with one or two scientific words. So botanists describe a fuzzy leaf as pubescent (pew-BESS-unt), meaning "hairy," or glabrous (GLA-brus), meaning "hairless." Instead of saying "long and skinny," they say *linear.* Instead of "wide at the stem and pointed at the tip," they say *lanceolate* (LANCE-ee-oh-late). Instead of "pointed at the stem and wide at the tip," they say *obovate* (OB-oh-vate). A leaf is *palmate* if it looks somewhat like the palm and fingers of your hand.

Instead of saying "the edges are smooth (or the edges are saw-toothed)," a botanist would say "the leaf is *en-*tire (or *serrate*)." A leaf with deep dips in the edges is "lobed."

Leaves are *simple* when each one grows alone on a leaf stalk, or *compound* when two or more leaflets grow on a leaf stalk. Even a leaf stalk has its own special name: *petiole.*

Plant habitats

Botanists study plant communities, too. Different species of plants grow naturally together in a community called a habitat, or ecosystem. Many wild animals—including birds, insects, and reptiles, as well as mammals—have particular needs and require specific habitats. Often the habitats are named or described by the major plants growing there, such as pine flatwoods, mangrove forest, or Sand Pine scrub.

Linear
Cattails

Lanceolate
Chestnut

Obovate

Chapman Oak

Palmate

Serrate & Simple
Mulberry

Entire & Simple
Sea Grape

Compound
Walnut

Are these plants, too?

Botany includes the study of unusual—even strange—plants, such as seaweeds, ferns, mosses, algae (AL-jee; plural of alga, which is pronounced AL-guh), lichens (LI-kunz), and fungi (FUN-jye; plural of fungus), which include plants such as mushrooms, molds, mildews, and yeasts. These plants have different ways of growing, and propagate without flowers or seeds.

Some plants have been found to be specifically useful to humans, such as yeasts that make bread rise, and penicillin, one of the first antibiotic drugs, which is extracted from certain mold plants.

Botanists are able to discover much about living things by experimenting with the inherited traits of plants. Genetics is the study of how characteristics are passed from parents to their offspring, in humans and all other animals, as well as plants. Botanical research in this field has resulted in new food plants that are better able to withstand drought or cold, or that taste better, or are disease or rot resistant.

Botanists are very much concerned about the extinction of plants that have not yet been studied. Some undiscovered plants may prove to contain life-saving chemicals. Plants are the basis of the food chain for all animals. Scientists have said that the extinction of any one species may cause the extinction of many dependent species. If that happened, the wonderful diversity of plants and animals would be reduced, and our world would be poorer.

Where to learn more

See "Environmental Careers" for more about botanists.

See "Underwater Treasures: Coral Reefs" and "The Everglades" for more about algae.

See "Extinction is Forever" for more about endangered species.

See "Springs, Sinkholes, and Caves" for more information about microclimate habitats.

See "Water and Wetlands" for more information on photosynthesis.

See "What's in a Name?" for more about scientific names.

Do you know these words?

algae	annuals
biennials	botanical
botanists	botany
calyx	compound
corolla	crown
diversity	ecosystem
entire	erosion
extinction	florets
foliage	fungus
genetics	glabrous
habitat	herbaceous
herbs	lanceolate
linear	microclimates
nutrients	obovate
palmate	perennials
petals	petiole
photosynthesis	pistil
pollinate	pollutants
propagate	pubescent
raceme	reproductive
sepals	serrate
simple	solitary
species	spike
stamen	umbel
wildlife	zygomorphic

Have fun with what you know!

Plants lend themselves to a variety of experiments because they grow rapidly and respond quickly to outside influences.

- Place a potted plant on the windowsill and watch it grow toward the light. Turn the pot to see the plant bend again toward the light.

- Can you find flowers that illustrate some of the botanical terms? Cut one flower from each type you can find and press it between the pages of an old telephone book, turning about 100 pages between samples. If you pick a flower, remember that its seeds will not mature. Make only one or two pressed specimens of the same species, so that other flowers will be left in the yard to make seeds. You can also collect seed samples and press them.

- Find leaves on trees and shrubs to illustrate some botanical terms. Make a notebook with each leaf on a separate page. Identify the plant it came from with its common name and its scientific name. Use scientific words to describe the shape and features of the leaf.

Leaves of Florida's Red Maple

Chapter 16

Florida's Native Plants

The world is so full of such an incredible variety of trees, flowers, and shrubs that many of them are still unnamed and unrecorded, especially in the tropical rain forests around the world. Scientists think that about 250,000 different species of plants grow on the earth.

Botanists have been working for years to catalog all the world's flowering plants, including those in Florida, but new species are found almost daily. In one six-month period in the 1980s, 40 new native plant species were identified in Florida alone!

What is a "native"?

A native is someone who was born in a particular place. A native Floridian was born in Florida. We call American Indians "Native Americans" because they were here before Europeans such as the English and Spanish came to this country.

An oak hammock—one of Florida's important native plant habitats.

When we talk about plants and animals being native to Florida, we're not speaking of a particular individual, as in "native Floridian," but of the species as a whole, as in "Native American."

What is a native plant?

Botanists are still discussing where to draw the line between a plant native to Florida and a plant that came from another area of the United States or another continent (called an exotic, or introduced, plant). Most botanists agree that a "native" plant was one growing here in Florida when the Spaniards arrived in 1513. Unfortunately, it's hard to be sure what plants were here unless one of the early explorers in Florida wrote letters or kept a journal that described those he saw.

The renowned American naturalist William Bartram wrote a book, *Travels*, in 1791, in which he provided much information about what plants and animals, as well as Native Americans, were here in the early days of the European settlers. He traveled through Florida in 1774, describing and drawing hundreds of plants that he saw on his journey. We don't know for sure that some of these weren't brought over by the Spaniards, or brought in from the Caribbean islands or Central America, but at least they are plants that we know have been growing in Florida for over 200 years.

Florida has a greater assortment of native plants than any other state in the United States except Texas and California. Florida native plant species total about 2,500, but 6,000 or more plants are growing here, most of which are "exotic." Some exotics that have been here for a very long time, and which can survive without fertilizer, extra water, or care, are called "naturalized." About 1,000 exotic species have become naturalized in Florida.

Part of the reason for Florida's great diversity of plants is that more plants are able to live in a climate that is always warm than where the temperature drops below freezing for long periods. The southern tip of Florida is the only part of the U.S. that borders the tropics, that warmest part of the world on either side of the equator, and many plants can grow here that can grow nowhere else in our country. Some Florida native plants grow nowhere else in the world. These are called "endemic."

Other reasons for the many plants in Florida are:

- the rise and fall of the ocean over the peninsula during the past million years, depositing and forming the special soil.

- the abundant rainfall, at a latitude that in many other parts of the world is desert.

- the flatness of the land—water does not flow off quickly, allowing wetland habitats to develop in shallow depressions.

- the length of the state—its 644-kilometer length (400 miles) extends through many climatic zones (areas affected by the weather), from the tropical zone at the southern tip to the warm temperate zone in north Florida.

Different places in Florida are special for certain plants and animals. Some species won't live in a place if another species it needs to live with isn't there. The Hand Fern, for example, grows only in the boots (broken stubs of leaves) of the Sabal Palm, and needs a certain fungus (fungus is a family of plants that includes mildew and mold) in its habitat as well.

Scientists have named 15 different major habitat types in Florida, and many more smaller habitat types. Different native plant species are found growing in each one. Some habitats are near the ocean, some of them are on high, dry, sandy soils, and some of them are in low, wet places. Some habitats are in or near freshwater springs, lakes, and rivers. The most special habitat of all is the Everglades, a huge shallow bowl of land covered by a sheet of slowly flowing water, the only such place in the whole world.

Some of Florida's native plants

Very special endemic and endangered plants. Many plants whose habitats are being changed by development, or by cattle grazing, or by ditching to drain the water away, can no longer survive, and become endangered. Some examples are the Scrub Plum[+], the Gulfcoast Lupine[+], and the Big Pine Partridge Pea[+].

- The Scrub Plum is a little thorny bush with zigzag branches and white flowers that is endemic to the sandy scrub of central Florida.

- The Gulfcoast Lupine grows only on the dunes of the Gulf coast of Florida. Other kinds of lupines, however, with their clumps of beautiful blue or pink flowers, grow in sandy places from south Florida north to the Carolinas, and some varieties also grow in the New England states.

- The Big Pine Partridge Pea is endemic to the Florida Keys and is known to exist on only three islands. It is a small shrub that has yellow flowers and pea-shaped seed pods, usually found at the edges of hammocks and pinelands.

Common native plants. Florida also has some very common native plants that you see every day.

- The Saw Palmetto may be the most common native plant of all in Florida. You see it almost anywhere the bulldozers haven't come through—in the woods, along the roads you drive, on the sand dunes at the beach, and breaking the flatness of grassy prairies. Its name comes from the sawtooth edges on its stems. It should be left in the landscape when new homes are built, for it is evergreen, has a sweet-smelling blossom, and can survive almost anything—insects, disease, fire, and hurricanes. Saw palmetto grows as far north as the Carolinas.

- Sawgrass is another Florida native with sawtooth edges. This tall, broad-leaved, grasslike sedge is the main thing you see when looking across the Everglades in south Florida. It likes living in its watery world, not only in the Everglades, but marshy places west to Texas and north to Virginia.

- Sea Oats, a tall, graceful grass, grows on the sand dunes of Florida's coast. It is protected by law, because its roots help to keep the sand dunes from blowing and washing away. For a while it was endangered, but forbidding its destruction has helped to bring it back.

- The white Water Lily and the purple Pickerel Weed, while not limited to Florida, are native to the state. They grow in freshwater rivers and lakes. The Water Hyacinth, on the other hand, is a purple water plant that is exotic and troublesome because it can completely cover the surface of a body of water.

- Wax Myrtle is a thick, dark green tree or shrub that grows in many kinds of soils, and is a favorite shelter and food source of birds and small mammals. It helps to stabilize the

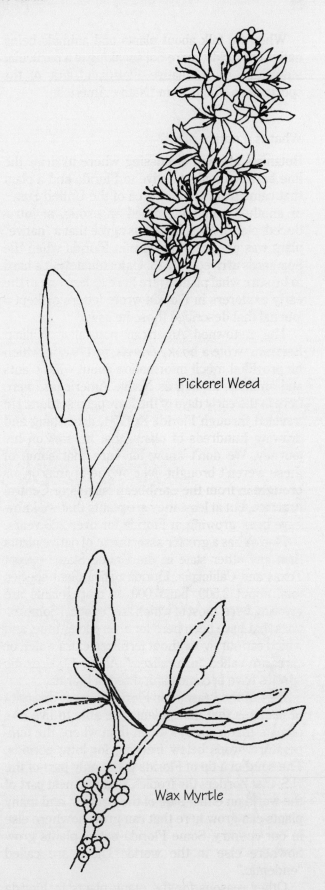

Pickerel Weed

Wax Myrtle

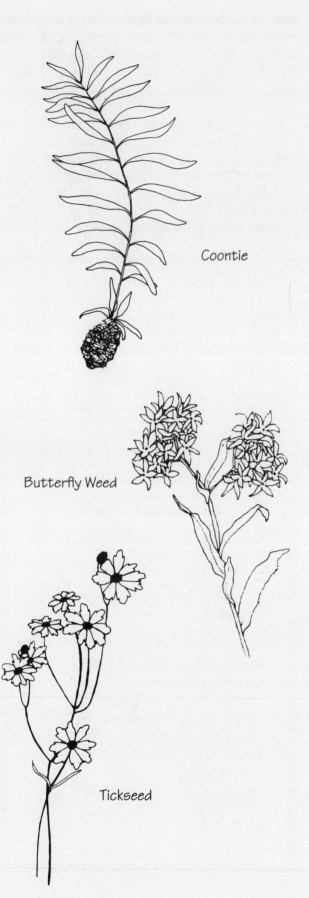

Coontie

Butterfly Weed

Tickseed

shores of rivers and lakes, filters pollutants from air and water (as all plants do), and produces gray waxy berries that can be used to make bayberry candles.

Other plants of interest. Some of Florida's native plants are neither very rare nor very common, but are important and beautiful species.

- The Coontie is such a plant. It is dark green and fernlike, and its large, rootlike, underground stem helped feed Florida's Seminole Indians and early settlers. Coontie would be beautiful planted in the dooryard of every Florida home.

- Spanish Moss is quite common, but it is neither Spanish nor a moss. It is an air plant that hangs from trees, but doesn't take any nourishment from them. It lives on moisture in the air and on dust and particles that the wind and moisture carry to it.

- Many of Florida's native plants are lovely small wildflowers, like the orange Butterfly Weed and the purple Blazing Star that like dry, sandy soils, and blue Dayflowers and lavender Spiderworts that brighten the woods whether they're wet or dry. The yellow flowers that you might see along the roadside may be either Goldenaster or Coreopsis, sometimes called Tickseed.

Try to learn what some of these plants look like, and look for them.

Go wild!

Discover what happens if a piece of land is left alone. Get your family to agree to let a small area of your yard—say, 3 meters (10 feet) square—"go wild." Or see if you can do this at your school. Don't mow it for a least a year. Don't water or fertilize or pull weeds.

Write in your journal about everything that happens there. In the beginning, if the area has been kept in a very neat lawn, it may be a while before new things enter your plot, but eventually the grasses that need care will thin out and the wild seeds will take hold and sprout. Try to find out the names of the things that now grow. The "weeds" may have beautiful flowers. Measure

Blazing Star

melt off the berries and float on top of the boiling water. Let it cool, then pour the water out from under the hardened wax. Remelt the wax, using very low heat to prevent fire, and pour it into a small, deep container, such as a clean soup can. Don't let the wax drip on the stove units.

Tie a washer or nail to a soft cotton string (or you can buy special wicks for making candles at a craft shop), and then begin dipping the string in and out of the wax. Each time the string passes through the wax, a new layer will cling to the string. Slowly, the wax will build up on the candle, dripping down the sides so that the bottom will become larger than the top. If you don't have much wax, you can put water in the can. The wax will float on top of the water and your wick will collect wax each time it passes through the layer of wax.

Aren't you glad bayberry candles aren't your only source of light at night as they were for some of Florida's early settlers?

how tall they grow. Do lizards and butterflies come to your plot? Do more birds visit there now, compared to when it was just lawn grass? Can you find a tree seedling? Can you find the source away from your plot where the seeds might have come from?

Making bayberry candles

If you have a Wax Myrtle near your home or school, maybe you would like to try making a candle from the waxy bayberries. The myrtle bears its fruits in the fall, and the time to pick them is when the berries turn gray with wax. You can hold a paper bag under the branches and pull the berries off the twigs easily when they are ripe. You'll need a lot—a grocery bagful or more—to make one candle.

Put the berries (a few twigs won't matter) in a big (preferably old) pot filled with water on the stove, and bring the water to a boil. The wax will

Where to Learn More

See "Speaking of Trees" for more about some of Florida's native trees.
See "The Big Scrub" for information about the first refuge for endangered plants.
See "What's in a Name?" for more on taxonomy.
See "Exotics—More than Just a Nuisance" for more on native plants.
See all chapters under "Florida's Special Places" for more about habitats, William Bartram, and descriptions of native plant species.

Do you know these words?

Can you list them in alphabetical order?

species	habitat
botanists	endangered
native plant	pollutants
exotic	fungus
naturalized	boots
aquifer	climatic zone
endemic	

Eating wild plants

Some of Florida's wild plants are good to eat. You might find it fun to try some wild eating. Be sure you know exactly what plants and what parts of them are good to eat before experimenting. Also, collect any wild foods away from roadsides or sprayed areas where pollutants may have contaminated them.

Most everyone knows the pine trees, however, and any pine species is safe for making tea. Here's a recipe for tea made from pine needles.

Pine Tea

Pick a handful of fresh green needles from the tip of a pine tree branch. Break the needles into a cup of boiling water and let them steep for about five minutes. More or fewer needles, and longer or shorter steeping time will change how strong the flavor is. Experiment to see how you like it best. Try it plain, then try it with some honey and slices of orange or lemon. It's not only good, it's good for you!

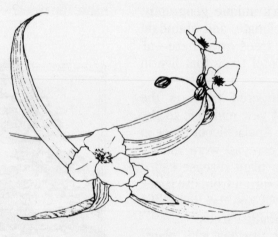

Spiderwort

Chapter 17

Speaking of Trees

Did you know that Florida has more kinds, or species, of trees than any other state in the United States? Because of Florida's unique geography, subtropical to temperate climate, and abundant rainfall, over 300 different trees grow here—almost half of all the species of trees that live in North America!

One of Florida's endangered trees is the Florida Torreya+, a type of yew endemic to the limestone bluffs along the Apalachicola River in the Florida Panhandle. Torreyas were almost completely destroyed by a plant disease called blight, but they continue to sprout from the roots, and botanists hope they will one day resist the blight and grow again into mature trees.

Can you think of other reasons why plants might become endangered?

Trees that lose their leaves in the winter are called deciduous (dee-SID-yew-us), and trees that keep their leaves year-round are called evergreen. Many people think that Florida doesn't have a fall season, with the beautiful gold, yellow, and red colors that are seen in other parts of the country as deciduous trees get ready to lose their leaves. But Florida's deciduous trees do change color, though often it doesn't happen until late November or December. Two of the prettiest are the Red Maple and the Sweetgum, which grow in wetland areas.

In the fall, watch the trees near where you live to see which ones are deciduous and which ones are evergreen. Do the leaves change color? Can you name the trees?

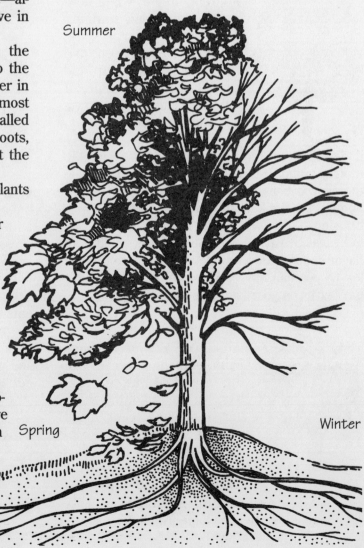

Summer

Fall

Spring

Winter

Flora and Fauna

Some of Florida's important trees

Pines. Seven different species of pines grow in Florida: Longleaf, Sand, Slash, Pond, Spruce, Loblolly, and Shortleaf. The southern pine forests have been and still are important to the economy of Florida. Slash and Longleaf Pines are the main species used for lumber. The Sand Pine is endemic to Florida's unique scrub habitat—it grows naturally nowhere else in the world. It is planted for paper pulp and Christmas trees.

Magnolias. One of the much-loved trees of the South is the Magnolia with its huge, fragrant, creamy-white flowers of spring and summer. The leaves are large, dark, shiny, and evergreen, and the tree grows big and spreading if it has room, or tall and slender if it is crowded by other trees.

Another species of magnolia is the Sweet Bay, or Silver Bay, that grows in moist ground. It is said that rain is coming when the wind causes the leaves to flash their silvery undersides. Look for this the next time a storm is brewing.

Leaves of bay trees can be used in cooking to flavor soups, stews, and sauces, just like the bay leaves you can buy in the store. See if you have bay leaves on your kitchen shelf.

Palms. Florida's state tree is the Sabal Palm, or Cabbage Palm, so named because of the large leaf bud or "cabbage" at the top of the trunk that is sometimes cooked and eaten as a vegetable (unfortunately, this kills the tree). Palm berries are food for many animals and were eaten by Indians many years ago. The Seminoles used the huge fronds for making

thatched roofs for their shelters, and some of the early pioneers made even the sides of their houses from palm fronds.

Some Sabal Palms retain their boots after the dead fronds break away, which then become a container for water and soil that plants can grow in and small animals such as frogs and insects can take refuge in. You can often see ferns growing in the boots high in a palm tree.

The Sabal Palm has the largest natural range of any of Florida's palms, growing as far north as North Carolina. Most species, however, are sensitive to cold and are found only in south Florida. Several species are rare or endangered.

Palms give Florida its unique tropical feel. Of 14 species of palm trees native to the United States, 11 can be found in Florida.

Cypress. One of the most unusual trees of the south is the Bald Cypress, a tree found in swamps and along stream banks and lakes. Bald Cypress trees can live longer than a thousand years and can grow to a huge size. They are deciduous, and are called "bald" because they lose their tiny leaves every autumn. These trees are unusual because their trunk spreads at the bottom to help support its great height, with knobby "knees" that stick out of the water. Scientists don't really understand the purpose of cypress knees.

Cypress was once plentiful throughout Florida, but almost all of the big trees were logged by the early 1900s. Encourage your school and your parents to use pine bark or chipped Melaleuca trees for mulch around plants instead of cypress. Pine bark is a common by-product of making lumber and paper, and Melaleuca is an exotic pest plant, but beautiful stands of cypress trees are often destroyed just to chip up for mulch.

Oaks. Over two dozen species of oaks grow in Florida, some of them merely shrubs. Oaks are very important to wildlife, for their acorns are a rich food, eaten by nearly all birds and mammals that eat plants.

The Live Oak, with its spreading top and gnarled branches hung with Spanish moss, is one of the most handsome trees in the south. As its name implies, it is evergreen. The wood is extremely difficult to saw and dry, but because of its great strength it was made into timbers and keels for wooden ships in the days of sailing vessels.

Mangroves. Mangroves are strange trees that can live in salty water. Three kinds of mangroves grow in Florida, and two—the Red Mangrove and the Black Mangrove—are found growing right at the water's edge. The White Mangrove usually grows inland of the other two. They grow along Florida's southern seacoasts, with one species, the Black Mangrove, found generally as far north as Cape Canaveral on the Atlantic and Cedar Key on the Gulf.

The word mangrove means "grove or stand of trees," and they often grow in forests so thick that a person can hardly get through them. They help protect Florida's coasts from being washed away by storms and hurricanes.

The Red Mangrove has arching prop roots and long, cigar-shaped seed pods. Black Mangrove can be recognized by its hundreds of breathing tubes, called pneumatophores (new-MAT-uh-fores), that stick up out of the mud like small thin pencils.

Mangrove forests are places where young fish, shrimp, and crabs begin their life, finding protection from predators among the tangled roots.

Trees are terrific!

Trees do wonderful things for us. They provide us with lumber to build houses. We make musical instruments out of them. Paper is made from trees. So are boats, furniture, and telephone poles. Think of some other things made from the wood of trees.

But trees do wonderful things even when we don't cut them down. They provide places for mockingbirds and squirrels to build homes. Their seeds and fruits provide food for us and for White-tailed Deer, Raccoons, Brown Thrashers, and dozens of other animals.

Trees shade the ground below, cooling it. If your house is shaded by a tree, your air conditioner won't need to work as hard. The leaves of trees give off oxygen and moisture into the air. They muffle noise, absorb pollutants, and filter dust and soot out of the air. They stop raindrops in their downward rush, which then drip slowly from the leaves, preventing erosion of the soil beneath.

Can you match the tree with its leaf? Write the name of the tree underneath each drawing.

1. _____

2. _____

3. _____

4. _____

5. _____

6. _____

Even dead trees are important! Woodpeckers find beetles and ants under the dead bark and peck nest cavities in them. When the woodpeckers have finished raising their young, other wildlife such as Eastern Screech-Owls, Barred Owls, and Opossums use the same holes. What other animals can you think of that need holes in dead trees?

When dead trees fall, mosses and mushrooms grow on them, insects such as ants and beetles live in them, and other insect larvae make tunnels in the wood. After a long time the wood finally decays and breaks down into particles small enough to become soil for a seed to sprout and start a new tree.

Answers to leaf quiz:
1. Live Oak, 2. Red Mangrove, 3. Longleaf Pine, 4. Bald Cypress, 5. Sabal Palm, 6. Magnolia. (Your answer is correct if you knew the italicized word.)

Where to learn more

See "Florida's Seasons" for more about fall trees.

See "Pine Flatwoods" for more about Longleaf Pine.

See "The Big Scrub" for more about Sand Pine.

See "Florida's Symbols" for more about Sabal Palm.

See "The Panhandle" for more about the Torreya tree.

See "The Everglades" for more about Mangroves.

Do you know these words?

blight	boots
decay	deciduous
endangered	endemic
evergreen	frond
mulch	pneumatophores
species	

Chapter 18

The Fun of Watching Birds

Watching birds is something you can do for a few fleeting moments as a Northern Cardinal flies by or as a hobby you can pursue for a lifetime. You can do it passively, by sitting comfortably inside your home looking out the window, or actively, by going outdoors with a pair of binoculars to see how many species you can find in a specific area. It can be casual, purely for enjoyment, or it can be scientific, serving a valuable purpose by gathering useful information.

People who see birds and hear their songs—in spite of the roar of traffic or the bustle of the day—take greater joy in the world around them. Birdwatchers, often called birders, are not preoccupied with just the humdrum activities of life, but see beauty in the tiny—as well as the magnificent—world of nature.

Learn to "see." Become a birder. Find out more about birds, and where and how they live. Buy a book called a field guide that will help you identify the birds you see, and look for different species of birds wherever you go.

Recognizing birds

Perhaps you have watched a flash of color streak past your eyes, land in a nearby tree, and begin to sing a beautiful melody. You probably wondered what kind of bird it was. You may have thought that you have to be an expert to identify birds, but birding can be enjoyed by anyone, year-round in Florida, wherever you are. The more you practice, the better you become!

So, how do you identify a bird you see if you have never seen one like it before?

Birders use many different methods to identify birds. Plumage characteristics are a bird's most distinctive mark. Feather color, spots or streaks on the breast, tail bands (bars of different colors on the tail), wing bars (thin stripes along the wing), and eye rings (circles around the eyes) are known as field marks. Field marks provide quick clues to a bird's identity, and they can be seen by a careful observer when a bird is perched or, on some species, when the bird is in flight.

Remember, however, that relying on only the color and pattern of a bird's plumage won't always make a positive identification. Young birds can be puzzling for months, because their colors may not be at all like those of their parents. In some species, males and females may wear different colors or appear different at certain times of the year.

Another helpful clue is a bird's size. Most of us are familiar with the House Sparrow (or English Sparrow), the American Robin, and the crow. Use these familiar species to compare the unknown bird with—is it smaller than a robin? bigger than a crow? Knowing the approximate size can help you identify the bird you have spotted.

After comparing the size, look at the shape, or silhouette. Sometimes the mere outline of the bird is all you need to see to confirm an identification. Is the body long and thin or short and stocky? If it is flying, are the wings rounded or pointed? Is the tail forked, pointed, or round?

Sometimes color, size, and shape will positively identify a bird. Other elements that perhaps cannot be seen so quickly provide further clues, such as the shape of a bird's bill. Cardinals, for example, have short, stout bills; egrets and herons have long, daggerlike bills; eagles and hawks have sharply hooked bills.

How is the bird acting? A bird's behavior—how it eats, flies, swims, and so on—is one of the best identification clues. Is the bird on the ground, hopping or running or scratching? Does it bob its tail up and down? Is it alone, or with a large flock of the same species of bird? Some experienced birders can identify a bird at a far distance simply by observing its flight pattern, without being able to see any color or pattern of feathers.

A more difficult clue for beginning birders is the sound a bird makes. You may not have to see the bird to identify it. Birding is not just a visual sport, for its joys can include hearing as well as seeing.

Learning bird songs and calls usually requires seeing the bird while it is singing or making other vocalizations. The association of sight and sound will stick in your mind and help you identify the bird next time you hear it. You can also get taped recordings of bird calls from a nature gift shop or the library to help you practice listening.

The final tool for identifying a bird is its habitat. Are you and the bird in a salt marsh, an open pasture, or the piney woods? Most species have particular habitat needs; you wouldn't be likely to find a woodpecker at the beach! Many parks have a checklist of the birds that have been seen there, and your bird guide usually describes the habitat for each species, as well as providing a picture of the bird.

Well, this seems like a lot of things to learn, but you don't need to know everything and every bird right away! As you practice, many of these concepts will become second nature and you will soon use them to identify birds without realizing which clue gave you the answer!

Some common Florida birds

The birds in your backyard and on your bird feeder are mostly songbirds. You'll see red Northern Cardinals and hear them singing, "What-cheer-cheer-cheer!" The gray and white Northern Mockingbird will sit in the tops of bushes and trees or on utility lines, singing an incredible variety of tunes, usually repeating each phrase two or more times. The Brown Thrasher may be seen scratching around under the shrubbery or, when the male is establishing his territory, he may be at the top of a tree. The Brown Thrasher will usually sing each song phrase twice before going on to a new one.

The gentle Mourning Doves will eat seeds off the ground under your feeder, and you can often hear them cooing softly from the trees. The Blue Jay, with his crest and his striking feathers of blue, gray, black, and white, sings a clear, two-note whistle, as well as several different harsh squawks.

Learning to recognize these backyard birds will be easy. Then you can start looking at the pictures in your field guide to learn others that may come to your backyard—the Carolina Wren, the Rufous-sided Towhee, the Tufted Titmouse, the Red-bellied Woodpecker, and others.

Learning new birds

If you see a large bird with long legs standing in shallow water, it's most likely a Great Egret or a Great Blue Heron. Is it white? Or is it grayish blue?

If it's smaller than these two big waders, but otherwise looks a lot like them, it may be a Little Blue Heron, or a Snowy Egret, or a Green Heron, depending on its colors. Look in the field guide for its field marks.

Is it a big bird soaring high overhead? Probably it's a Turkey Vulture with its dark body and silver wing linings. But it could be an eagle; if you see its white head and white tail, you'll know it's a mature Bald Eagle. Don't confuse the eagle with an Osprey, however, which looks mostly white from below, but doesn't have a white tail.

Other large birds that might fly overhead include the hawks—the Red-shouldered and Red-tailed hawks. Study your field guide to tell them apart.

If you're at the beach, you'll surely see the big Brown Pelicans flying overhead, often in a long line or vee formation, and sometimes diving head-first into the waves to catch fish.

The many different kinds of gulls are hard to tell apart. The Ring-billed Gull may be the easiest to identify if you can get close enough to see the dark ring near the tip of its bill. The Laughing Gull is the only gull that lives year-round in Florida. Its head is black in the summertime and gray in winter.

Along the edge of the waves could be long-legged Willets with their long bills and gray bodies. You'll see a flashing black and white wing pattern when they fly.

Smaller shorebirds, such as plovers with black breast bands, whitish Sanderlings, and brownish sandpipers, may be running along the beach, too. Some of these small shorebirds are hard to tell apart and are often called "peeps."

In the woods during the day, you can see wood-peckers climbing around on the trunks or branches of trees. The easiest one to identify is the very large, black and white Pileated (PIE-lee-ay-ted, or PILL-ee-ay-ted) Woodpecker with a big red crest.

At dusk, you might be lucky enough to see one of the owls—the Barred Owl, who calls "Hoo, hoo, hoo-hoo-aw," or the Great Horned Owl, who calls with a low-pitched hoot. Both of these owls are very large, and may sit on the branches of a big tree and watch you down below.

The Eastern Screech-Owl is a small, chunky bird. Its call isn't usually a screech, but sounds more like a soft trill.

You probably already can identify such common birds as the American Robins that fly through on their way north in the spring, the Red-winged Blackbirds in the cattails at the edge of the lake, and the big, black American Crows that "caw" and the slightly smaller Fish Crows that say "Uh-uh!" Try to learn what the brown-streaked female Red-winged Blackbird looks like, as well as her famous red-shouldered mate, and learn to tell the two species of crows apart by their calls.

Keep studying the pictures in your field guide, but also read the text so you'll know where they live, and when they might be here, and how they behave.

And have fun. Can you name all the birds in these pictures?

Dos and don'ts for birding

During the springtime, many birds are busy rais-ing families. While it is fun to watch birds and their nests of babies, you need to do several things to help make sure that the babies will grow up healthy and strong.

Be careful in choosing a place to watch nesting birds. Never climb a tree that a nest is in, or get so close that the adult birds become frightened. They'll tell you by their fluttering and squawking from the bushes nearby. They may even "dive-bomb" you. But worst of all, they might leave their babies unprotected. Exposure to a cold breeze, or the direct rays of the sun, can kill baby birds. You may not realize that your scent can attract predators such as Raccoons, Opossums—or even your cat!—to the nest.

Make as little noise as possible when you look for birds. You will see many more if you learn to move slowly and walk quietly without talking.

Baby birds often have a downy or fluffy appearance. If you see a bird that seems to have fallen from its nest, put it back if you can find the nest; otherwise leave it alone. It may have left the nest because it was already too big to stay in it, and even though you might not see them, the parents are close by and will continue to care for their fledgling. And remember that it is against Florida law to keep baby birds as pets!

Leave your dog at home when you go birding. Dogs love to run, and can disturb the birds you're trying to see. If you have a cat, keep it indoors all the time or put a bell on its collar so that birds can hear it when it comes near.

If your parents want to trim trees and shrubs around your yard, check to see if there are any nests before they begin. Better yet, wait until fall or winter, when fewer species are nesting, to trim trees. If a dead tree is not in danger of falling on your house or the traffic areas in your yard, leave it standing for the woodpeckers and other animals that need it for food and shelter. Or use a rope to secure it to something sturdy, such as a nearby healthy tree, so that it won't harm people or property.

If you want to look for birds on someone else's property, ask permission from the owner before you go there, and always leave it just like you found it. Don't beat on trees or bushes with a stick. Don't dig holes, or fill in holes. Don't try to push over dead trees, and don't ever be careless with matches. Don't be a litterbug—a careless person who leaves trash wherever you go. Litter can injure birds and animals that might eat it, or get entangled in it, or be cut by it.

Birds and conservation

Birds often tell us something about what's happening to the world we all live in. Songbirds have died because of poisons sprayed on the insects they eat, and wading birds have disappeared from some places because their wetland fishing grounds were drained or polluted. Shouldn't we be concerned about that?

The study of birds, called ornithology, helps us to understand some of the problems birds experience in their natural homes. Many amateur birders (that is, people who do it for fun, and not as a profession) have found out things that help scientists in their work with birds. You could help, too, by participating in any of these projects:

- Christmas Bird Counts take place during the Christmas season each year, when birders see how many birds they can count in a 24-hour period in a specific 24-kilometer (15-mile) circle. Most counters search from early morning to dark, but some people get up before daybreak to try to record owls that might be active during the night. Call the Florida Audubon Society to find out the name of a person in the Audubon chapter near you who could tell you how to participate.

- The Florida Breeding Bird Atlas was a six-year scientific project that located all the species of birds that nest in Florida and put the information into an atlas, or book of maps. The project involved hundreds of amateur birders who helped look for nesting birds and kept detailed record cards of what they saw. Follow-up surveys will be held to document future trends in breeding bird populations. You can help with these.

- Volunteer birders help take surveys of bird species in Florida parks. Local Audubon chapters are often involved in these activities.

- Most birders keep a "life list"—a checklist of all the bird species seen for the first time, in-

cluding the date and place and anything unusual, such as unusual weather. This information can be important to people studying birds.

So start your life list now. In years to come, you'll be glad you have a complete record of your observations. And who knows? You may be able to contribute information that will help ornithologists in their study of birds.

Where to learn more

See "Speaking of Trees" for more on the value of dead trees.

See "The Mysteries of Bird Migration" for information on bird banding.

See "John James Audubon in Florida" for more on bird bills.

See "What Is a Bird of Prey?" for more on bird beaks and owls.

See "Discovering the Beach" for more on bird plumage.

See "Directions for the Crew of Spaceship Earth" for more on helping wildlife.

Do you know these words?

amateur	atlas
birders	birdwatchers
crest	field guide
field mark	fledgling
life list	ornithology
plumage	polluted
predator	species

Chapter 19

What Is a Bird of Prey?

Birds of prey—powerful eagles, hawks, and owls—have very different lifestyles from Florida's backyard songbirds. Also known as raptors, they are predators, hunting and feeding on smaller animals (called prey) such as insects, mice, rabbits, fish, snakes, and even other birds. They often eat sick and weakened animals, sometimes even dead animals (called carrion), and they help to keep the population of rodents and insect pests in check.

Raptors have special adaptations for their predatory lifestyle. Their sharp, curved claws, called talons, help them seize and hold onto their prey. These talons are strong enough to pierce through a man's hand, and are especially useful to a bird such as the Osprey that must pluck a slippery, wiggling fish from the water and then carry it to a treetop perch.

All birds of prey have extremely good eyesight, and some, such as the Bald Eagle, can see the movement of a small animal from as far away as three kilometers (2 miles). Nocturnal owls rely upon keen eyesight as well as hearing to help them locate prey as they hunt during the night.

Beaks are hooked, curving downward to help raptors tear their prey into manageable pieces, much as we use a knife to cut meat at dinnertime.

Florida is home to over 30 different species of birds of prey and is a great place to go "hawk watching," partic-ularly during spring and fall migration. Some raptors are year-round residents, while others come at certain times of the year to raise a family or to spend the winter. Some raptors do not need to migrate in order to find food, as songbirds do, for the small animals in their diet rarely migrate.

Bald Eagles[+]

It is always a thrill to sight a Bald Eagle. Eagles can sometimes be spotted soaring on warm air currents, called thermals, high up in the sky. The Florida population of Bald Eagles increases in the fall and early winter months when birds

Bald Eagle

return from northern states to establish breeding territories.

One of our largest birds, the eagle has powerful wings that can span 2 to 2.5 meters (6.5 to 8 feet) from wing tip to wing tip. Adults are easily recognized by their white head and tail, but few people know that young birds in their first few years of life are all brown. Eagles feed mainly on fish, and they build their nests in tall pine or cypress trees.

Hawks

- Buteos are large, high-soaring hawks with broad, fanned tails and rounded wings. Red-tailed Hawks and Red-shouldered Hawks are the buteos you are most likely to see in Florida, but the well-named Broad-winged Hawk is often seen here during fall migration.

- Accipiters have short, rounded wings and long, rudderlike tails. Their shape enables them to fly rapidly through forested woodlands as they chase after prey. Their preferred diet of small birds also attracts them to backyard bird feeders! Florida's accipiters include the Sharp-shinned Hawk and the Cooper's Hawk.

Falcons

- Falcons are streamlined with pointed wings for rapid flight. They can be seen hunting for

American Kestrel

shorebirds or ducks along the coastal beaches and marshes, or searching for insects and mice in open country fields and grasslands. Peregrine Falcons[+], Merlins, and American Kestrels[+] can all be seen in Florida.

Vultures

Vultures used to be considered birds of prey, although they are scavengers, feeding primarily on carrion. Ornithologists now consider them to be more closely related to storks than to other raptors. The talons of vultures are not strong enough to kill a live animal. You can frequently see vultures (along with an occasional eagle!) soaring gracefully on thermals, or sometimes eating a road-killed animal along the highway. Their scavenging lifestyle helps to keep our highways, fields, and pasturelands clean of dead animal carcasses, and for this reason vultures often are called "nature's flying garbagemen."

The Turkey Vulture, with its red, featherless head and legs similar to a Wild Turkey's, and the Black Vulture, with a featherless black head, are the two vultures you can see in Florida. Some people incorrectly call vultures "buzzards."

Owls

Eagles, hawks, and vultures hunt during the day, so they are referred to as diurnal (die-URN-ul)

Red-shouldered Hawk

Screech-Owls

Barred Owl

birds. Owls, though, are nocturnal (nok-TURN-ul) birds, usually hunting at night. Often sharing the same habitats, diurnal and nocturnal birds make good neighbors. While one is sleeping the other is hunting. People get the benefit of round-the-clock pest protection when birds of prey are nearby.

An owl is a fascinating bird. Owls have binocular vision, which means they see an object with both eyes together, as humans do. The owl's eyes, however, face straight forward and cannot rotate or move in the eye sockets to look at an object to one side as people can. Instead, it must turn its whole head to follow moving objects, sometimes turning quickly to look behind, giving rise to the myth that they spin their heads all the way around.

Owls see very well in dim light, but they cannot see where there is no light at all. In the case of absolute darkness, owls such as the Barn Owl will utilize their acute sense of hearing to locate mice scurrying among the leaves on the forest floor.

Owls have been called "silent hunters of the night" because of the especially soft, fringed edges on their flight feathers. These feathers muffle the sound of air as it passes through the wing during flight, enabling an owl to silently capture its prey without the animal even knowing the raptor was nearby.

Owls in Florida include:

- Eastern Screech-Owls, Florida's smallest owl, are no bigger than 15 to 20 centimeters (6 to 8 inches). This common owl has feathers that look like ears, and it is more often heard than seen, its mournful call sounding like a trill rather than a "screech." Eastern Screech-Owls are cavity dwellers and will take readily to a nest box that is placed in a wooded backyard, as well as the woodpecker hole in the dead tree that was left standing.

- Barred Owls are large birds with smooth, rounded heads and brown and white stripes or "bars" on their breasts. Their "hoo, hoo, hoo-hoo-aw" call can be heard near wetlands, swamps, and river edges, where this bird hunts for reptiles, frogs, and even small fish.

- Great Horned Owls, Florida's largest owl, are fierce predators that can easily capture such large prey as rabbits, rats, and squirrels. This bird, with its feather tufts that resemble horns and its call of deep, booming hoots, is sometimes referred to as the hoot owl.

- Barn Owls have strange, heart-shaped faces. These raptors are true friends of the farmer because they eat primarily rodents. By roosting in farmer's barns and other buildings they have a steady supply of mice and rats that feed upon the farmer's grain.

- Burrowing Owls[+] are a Species of Special Concern in Florida because the open fields and pastures where they dig their underground homes are often turned into citrus groves or housing developments. They are unique among Florida's owls because of their occasional diurnal activities, which allow people to observe them more easily.

Other Florida raptors

- Ospreys, also called fish-hawks, plunge feet-first into the water for fish. They are commonly seen in Florida because of the abundance of rivers, lakes, and coastal areas that provide them with plenty of fish. Their huge nests of sticks can be seen on top of power poles along the highways and in the tops of tall cypress trees. Ospreys are also found on all continents except Antarctica.

Osprey

Kites are among the rare and endangered species of birds of prey. Kites got their name from their graceful pattern of flight, tipping and teetering in the wind.

- The elegant, black-and-white American Swallow-tailed Kite[+] returns to Florida every spring from Central and South America to make its nest of Spanish Moss high in cypress trees.

- The Snail Kite[+], which used to be called the Everglade Kite, lives only in southern and central Florida wetlands, where it hunts for a certain species of snail called the Apple Snail. Its slender, hooked beak is especially useful for cutting the snail's muscle loose from the shell before eating.

Snail Kite

Swallow-tailed Kite

Crested Caracaras+ eat carrion and are sometimes seen feeding together with vultures. This interesting member of the Falcon Family is also found in south Texas, Mexico, and Central America. It is the national bird of Mexico, where it is called the Mexican Eagle.

Where to learn more

See "What's in a Name?" for more about the Bald Eagle and falcons.

See "The Fun of Watching Birds" for more on identifying raptors.

See "Prairies—Wet and Dry" for more on the Crested Caracara and Burrowing Owl.

See "John James Audubon in Florida" for more on birds' beaks.

See "Water and Wetlands" for more on Apple Snails.

Do you know these words?

binocular vision	bird of prey
carrion	diurnal
flight feathers	migration
nocturnal	ornithologist
predator	prey
raptor	scavenger
species	talons
Species of Special Concern	thermals

Crested Caracaras

Chapter 20

The Mysteries of Bird Migration

Did you ever take a long journey with your family during your summer vacation? You probably planned ahead a long time for this special, once-in-a-lifetime trip. But can you imagine traveling this same journey each and every year for the rest of your life?

Millions of songbirds, ducks, hawks, and shorebirds do this every year, flying long distances between summer breeding grounds where they nest and raise their families, and other places where they spend the winter. This mass movement of birds, called migration (my-GRAY-shun), is an important part of the natural cycle of many species seen here in Florida. The word migration comes from the Latin word *migrare* (me-GRAHR-ray), which means to go from one place to another.

Fall and spring in Florida are great times to watch birds when they migrate to, or through, our state. Birds may be flying from Canada or northern states in the U.S. on their way to Caribbean islands or the tropical forests and other habitats of Central or South America. Some, how-

ever, end their southern journey in Florida, spending the winter in our marshes, estuaries, and forests. Others come north in the spring from the tropics to nest in Florida.

For centuries, people have tried to find out about the mysterious migration of birds. Why do they migrate, and where do they go? The ancient philosopher Aristotle thought that birds escaped from the winter by hibernating deep in the mud. Another early theory was that birds flew to the moon and spent the winter there.

From research, we now know that the coming of winter triggers the migration "urge" in birds. When temperatures begin to drop and the period of daylight shortens, birds move southward. Some species begin their fall migration as early as July.

Many shorebirds do not even wait for their fledglings (young birds just learning to fly) to grow up. The parents fly off, leaving their offspring to finish developing on their own and acquiring the instinctive urge that sends them on the same journey a few weeks later. The next year, the young birds that have survived will return to the same area where they were raised to begin their own families. How they find their way without any help from more experienced birds is still a mystery.

Migration Routes

Many birds follow the same pathway twice a year—south in the fall and north in the spring. One major migration route is along the Atlantic coastline southward to Florida—called the Atlantic flyway. Other flyways in North America are the Mississippi, Central, and Pacific flyways.

Some species travel each fall down the Florida peninsula and island-hop through the Bahamas, Cuba, and the West Indies to South America. These are called circum-Gulf (around the Gulf) migrants and include species such as the Yellow-billed Cuckoo, Indigo Bunting, American Redstart, Black-throated Blue Warbler, and the Common Yellowthroat. Others fly nonstop over the Gulf of Mexico to Central America, a journey of over 600 miles. These are called trans-Gulf (across the Gulf) migrants and include species such as the Scarlet Tanager, Rose-breasted Grosbeak, Black-throated Green Warbler, and Ruby-throated Hummingbird. These birds have stored up huge amounts of fat (for a bird!) to provide the energy to migrate these long distances, including the more than 15-hour flight across the Gulf without food, water, or even rest.

Usually the trans-Gulf migrants wait until sundown, leaving when winds from the north will help push them from behind. They are still over the water at daybreak, and must continue until they reach the Yucatan Peninsula of Mexico, or coastal areas farther south, before they are able to rest.

On the northward trip in the spring, when weather conditions are favorable, migrants may continue inland for more than 160 kilometers (100 miles) before landing. Small songbirds fly at speeds up to 48

Atlantic flyway, showing trans-Gulf and circum-Gulf routes.

km per hour (30 mph), while hawks fly 40 to 65 km per hour (30 to 40 mph), and ducks fly 65 to 97 km per hour (50 to 60 mph). They are usually flying at altitudes higher than 900 meters (3,000 feet), unfortunately far out of sight of bird watchers.

The Perils of Migration

Migration is a time full of danger for birds. Each year many thousands of them lose their lives during these perilous journeys.

Bad weather, the most obvious danger, is a powerful force for birds to cope with, particularly when they are crossing the Gulf of Mexico. Rain and strong gusty winds can force small birds into the water where they drown. Sometimes, if they're lucky, they can find a landing place on the deck of a ship, an oil drilling platform, or an island.

Birdwatchers like to be on the barrier islands off Florida's coastline, the Keys, and the islands of the Dry Tortugas when a "fallout" occurs, in which stormy weather forces hundreds of birds to drop to the first land mass they see. Usually this provides just a short rest and feeding stop, and when the weather improves, the birds continue on to their final destination.

Attacks by raptors (eagles, hawks, and owls) are another danger for small birds during migration. Many raptors, especially falcons such as Peregrines[+] and Merlins, travel the same routes as migrating songbirds and take advantage of this plentiful food source sharing the airways with them. Small birds are often not as alert as they are when on their summer nesting grounds, because all of their energy is consumed by the long journey. This makes them easy for predators to catch.

Tall structures, such as lighthouses, bridges, towers, and the cables that support them often kill birds when they're migrating. Even tall buildings, such as the Empire State Building in New York and the Washington Monument in Washington, D.C., have caused the deaths of many birds over the years.

During clear weather, few birds strike these obstacles, but on cloudy or foggy nights, birds fly lower and often are unable to see them, or, if the structure is lighted, birds may be attracted to the bright lights much like insects to a porch light. Bad weather, particularly when fog or mist distorts the light, seems to cause birds to fly headlong into the beam.

The Ponce de Leon Inlet lighthouse near Daytona Beach has also caused the death of many birds. On one sad occasion an observer gathered up a bushel-basketful of warblers, sparrows, and other songbirds that had struck the lighthouse during the night. A report in the Belize Audubon Society's October, 1988, newsletter (Belize is on the Gulf coast of Central America), told of 750 dead birds scattered on the ground below three tall towers. All species were birds that nest in North America and migrate to Belize to spend the winter.

The final danger, after birds have successfully completed their long migration, is finding that people have changed the natural environment so that birds can no longer live there. Tropical rain forests, where many birds spend the winter, are rapidly being cut down for farmlands. Woods in North America where birds nested last year may now be a shopping center. What would you do if you came home from your vacation and found your house had disappeared?

Bird Banding

How do scientists learn the answers to the questions and mysteries of migration?

The simplest and most effective method is by banding birds—attaching numbered metal or plastic bands around their legs. It may be done when the bird is still a baby in its nest, or when an adult is captured in a trap or net by a bird bander. Or it may be done when an injured bird is captured, healed, and returned to the wild.

When a bird is banded, several items of information are recorded: species name, the date and the place where the bird was banded, and, if known, the sex and age of the bird. Whenever a banded bird is seen or found again, the date and place information can be reported to the U.S. Fish and Wildlife Service in Maryland, and this is added to the records in a computer database. In 1993, nearly 46 million records of nearly 900 different species were in the computer, and a million more are being added each year.

A form of bird banding was used in Roman times, when colored threads were tied to the legs of swallows to carry news of victory in chariot races

Bird band

or battles. Peregrine Falcons often carried the royal mark of kings on their legs. The first documented scientific use of bird banding started in the 1740s in Germany when a piece of parchment was tied around the legs of swallows asking the finder to report where the birds lived in winter. John James Audubon was the first bird bander in America, placing silver rings on young phoebes nesting in his yard in Pennsylvania.

Now bird banding is done worldwide. About half the people who band birds are scientists; the other half are volunteers who receive training to do this special work.

The data on the movement of birds is helpful in getting laws passed to better protect birds. If scientists know where birds go, then environmentally sensitive areas that birds use before, during, and after migration perhaps can be protected.

You can help, too. Scientists rely on anyone who sees a bird with a band to send them the information. If you should see a banded bird, and can obtain the band number, or if the bird is color-banded, send the numbers, or the correct sequence of colors on each leg, to the Bird Banding Laboratory, U.S. Fish and Wildlife Service, Laurel, Maryland 20708. It will reach the Bird Banding Laboratory if it is addressed only to Washington, D.C. without zip code.

This is what you need to tell them:

1. The number on the band. Read it very carefully. There may be nine digits on a band small enough to fit around a wren's leg. Or, if the bird is dead, remove the band from the bird, flatten it, and tape it to your letter.

2. The date you found the bird.

3. The location, including how far it is to the nearest town.

4. The condition of the bird: alive? dead? injured? released (if so, the date and location of the release)?

5. A description of how or where the bird was found: at a picture window? brought in by a cat or dog? found by a roadside or on a beach? hit by a car?

6. Your name and address.

You do not need to identify the species if you do not know it. The numbers on the band will be in the Banding Laboratory's computer, and they will send you the information they have on the bird you have found.

If the bird is dead, and its body is in fair condition, it should be carefully wrapped and immediately stored in a freezer until it can be given, with a copy of the above information, to an educational institution. In Florida, the possession of live or dead birds without a permit is illegal, so take the bird to a museum, nature center, university, or other educational institution as quickly as possible. Even a damaged wing, the bones of a leg or a foot, or a skull can help students continue unraveling the mysteries of birds and their environment.

Where to learn more

See "John James Audubon in Florida" for more on the first bird bander.
See "Florida's Seasons" for more on changing daylight.

Do you know these words?

Can you list them in alphabetical order?

migration	trans-Gulf
circum-Gulf	estuaries
hibernate	fledgling
flyway	birdwatcher
barrier island	raptor
predator	species
birdbanding	instinctive

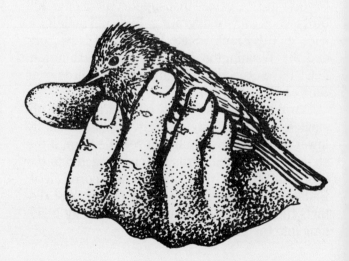

Chapter 21

John James Audubon in Florida

John James Audubon was an artist and naturalist who lived between 1785 and 1851. He was born in what is now Haiti in the Caribbean and spent his childhood years in France. He arrived in America when he was 18 and, even though he was still a young man, his life's ambition was to draw and paint every bird in North America.

Today, Audubon is famous for his paintings and writings about birds, and many conservation organizations all over the world bear his name.

His works were some of the first paintings anyone had ever done of hundreds of species of American birds, and his journal writings provided the first knowledge many people had that such creatures existed.

His work was done before the days of binoculars, cameras, or color printing presses. Travel was still by sailboat, horseback, and walking. There were no paved roads or telephones, and letters were hand-carried by anyone going in the right direction. Fulfilling his dream was not easy!

Audubon sketched and made notes about the birds he saw—where they lived and how they behaved—but the only way he had to study them up close was to shoot them and have them in his hand. In this way he was able to draw the feathers and bodies and beaks the way they really were, though he sometimes drew them in unnatural poses to display their plumage.

Flamingos

One of the birds Audubon wanted most to paint was the Flamingo—the flaming-pink wading bird that he had heard about but never seen. He traveled to the Florida Keys in search of them, and finally saw a flock on Indian Key. He wrote in his journal, "Ah! Reader, could you but know the emotions that then agitated my breast. I thought I had now reached the height of my expectations, for my voyage to the Floridas was undertaken in a great measure for the purpose of studying these lovely birds in their own beautiful islands."

Flamingos build an unusual nest out of mud on the ground, stacking it up like a miniature volcano. The female lays only one egg, setting on it to keep it warm and rarely leaving the nest during the 30-day incubation period (the incubation period is the length of time it takes for the eggs to hatch).

Flamingos prefer to live near shallow, saline ponds or lakes and are sometimes seen in Florida Bay and other coastal areas in Florida. The flamingo is now only a winter visitor from the tropics, and ornithologists are not certain that the flamingo ever actually nested in Florida.

The Greater Flamingo (the one Audubon called the American Flamingo) is the national bird of the Bahamas. One of the largest nesting colonies in the Caribbean is on the island of Great Inagua in the Bahamas.

Even though flamingos are a rare sight in Florida, they have often been used as a symbol of the state, decorating T-shirts, lawns, postcards, and the logo of the Florida lottery.

Pretty in Pink

The most striking and wonderful thing about flamingos is their beautiful pinkish red color. Two other wading birds—the Roseate Spoonbill[+] and the Scarlet Ibis—share this beautiful coloring. Flamingos are the largest waterbird of brilliant color in the world. They can be over one meter (4 feet) tall, and their wings can spread to two meters (6 feet). There are birds that are bigger than the flamingo, and birds that are more brilliantly colored than the flamingo, but no other large bird is so colorful.

There are five species of flamingos around the world, each with slight variations in coloring.

Bird bills

One of the characteristics that identifies an animal as a bird is the toothless, horny bill or beak (although birds are not the only animals that have beaks—turtles do, too!). Every bird's bill has two parts—an upper part and a lower part, called mandibles.

The many differences in the bills of birds are truly amazing. Birdwatchers look at the bill shape as a field mark, or clue, to identify birds and learn more about their habits.

Beaks of birds are important tools that help them capture and eat the food they need, but they serve in other important ways, too. Birds use their beaks to carry nesting material and to build intricate nests. They use them to preen—cleaning, smoothing, oiling, and combing their feathers. Beaks can be weapons for protection. Some birds clack their bills together to call with. Sometimes the bill changes color or shape during breeding season to attract a mate, or so that baby birds will recognize "mom" and "dad."

Let's take a close look at some bird beaks.

- No other bird has a bill quite like the thick, crooked beak of the adult flamingo, yet a baby flamingo's beak is straight for several weeks after it hatches.

  When flamingos feed, they turn their heads

Greater Flamingo

upside down as they swish their black-tipped bills through the water, collecting the tiny insects, shrimp, and snails they eat. Their enormous crooked bills serve as a soupbowl, and they have an unusually large, fleshy tongue to help them spoon the soup.

- Roseate Spoonbills are well-named birds. These rosy-colored birds have wide, spatulate (spoon-shaped) bills that make them easy to identify. They feed in shallow water, swinging their bills from side to side with their mandibles partly open to catch the small fish, insects, or shellfish they like to eat.

Roseate Spoonbill

Quiz!

Look in a field guide for pictures of some other birds you know. Do their beaks tell you something about their lifestyle? See if you can match the names of these birds with descriptions of their bill and its use. Write the bird's number next to the description. (Answers on next page.)

1. Cardinals and sparrows

2. Warblers

3. Nighthawks and Chuck-will's-widows

4. Hummingbirds

5. Hawks and eagles

6. Herons and Anhingas

7. Pelicans

8. Woodpeckers

9. Ducks and geese

___ have strong, sharp, curved beaks to tear meat.

___ have a pouch as part of their beaks to scoop fish.

___ have broad, flat bills to strain mud and water from their food.

___ have short, thick bills to crack seeds.

___ have very long, slender bills to probe flowers for nectar.

___ have thick, pointed beaks for drilling into trees for beetles and grubs.

___ have heavy, pointed beaks for spearing fish.

___ have wide mouths to catch insects in flight.

___ have slender, pointed bills to pick insects off leaves.

- Another pink bird with an unusual bill is the Scarlet Ibis, a rare, or "accidental," visitor to southern Florida. Its slender, down-curved bill is like the bill of the White Ibis[+], a Florida resident. Ibises feed on shallow beaches and mudflats, often in company with spoonbills and other wading birds. They use their long bill to probe and poke deep into the mud for insects, crabs, and snails.

Scarlet Ibis

Where to learn more

See "The Fun of Watching Birds" for more about field marks and field guides.

See "What Is a Bird of Prey?" for more about bird beaks.

See "The Mysteries of Bird Migration" for more about John James Audubon.

See "Keeping a Nature Journal" for more about journals.

Do you know these words?

Can you list them in alphabetical order?

incubation	ornithologists
mandibles	field marks
preen	spatulate
field guide	saline

Answers to quiz

1. Cardinals and sparrows have short, thick bills to crack seeds.
2. Warblers have slender, pointed bills to pick insects off leaves.
3. Nighthawks have wide mouths to catch insects in flight.
4. Hummingbirds have very long, slender bills to probe flowers for nectar.
5. Hawks and eagles have strong, sharp, curved beaks to tear meat.
6. Herons and Anhingas have heavy, pointed beaks for spearing fish.
7. Pelicans have a pouch as part of their beaks to scoop fish.
8. Woodpeckers have thick, pointed beaks for drilling into trees for beetles and grubs.
9. Ducks and geese have broad, flat bills to strain mud and water from their food.

Chapter 22

Insects Are Not Just "Bugs"!

Insects seem to create strong feelings in people. Some find them beautiful and fascinating to watch, while others can't stand the thought of "bugs" anywhere near them. Many people are even afraid of them. It is true that some of them can sting, some carry disease, and some destroy farm crops. But most of them are so necessary to the animals and plants that live on Planet Earth that we could not survive long without them.

Though some insects eat and can destroy plants, those same plants in most cases would not be able to set fruit or make a new plant without the help of insects that pollinate flowers. Pollen is the fertilizing dust of a flower that must be carried by wind or insects to another flower of the same kind of plant in order to grow seeds.

Bees are well-known pollinators. As they gather nectar from the centers of the flowers to make honey, their bodies brush against the pollen, and they transfer it to other flowers as they travel. Wasps, flies, butterflies, and moths also pollinate flowers. Vegetable farms and fruit trees must have pollinating insects to help produce the food we eat. Wildflowers and woodland trees must be pollinated by insects, too.

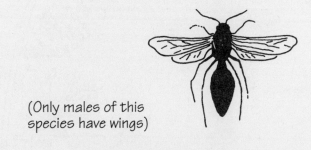

(Only males of this species have wings)

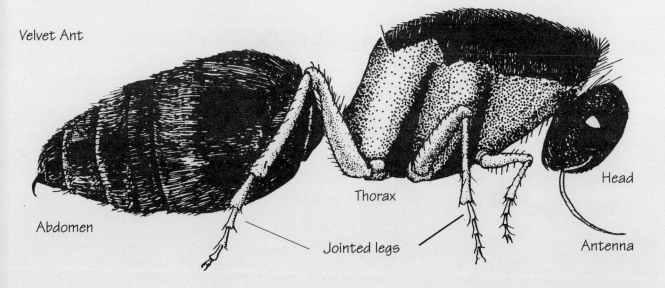

Velvet Ant

Abdomen

Thorax

Jointed legs

Head

Antenna

What is an insect?

Insects are invertebrates, meaning they have no backbone. They wear their "skeleton"—called an exoskeleton (*exo* means "outside")—as a shell on the outside of the soft parts of their bodies.

Black Swallowtail

Adult

Pupa
(Chrysalis)

Larva

The shell is made of chitin (pronounced KIE-tin)—a material similar to your fingernails.

Insects have jointed legs, and bodies that are usually divided, or segmented, into three parts: a head, a middle section called the thorax, and a rear section called the abdomen. The head has the mouth parts and a pair of antennae, or "feelers." Six legs are attached to the thorax—three on each side. The abdomen holds body fluids and the reproductive and egg-laying parts. Most insects have wings, attached to the thorax, during the adult part of their life cycle.

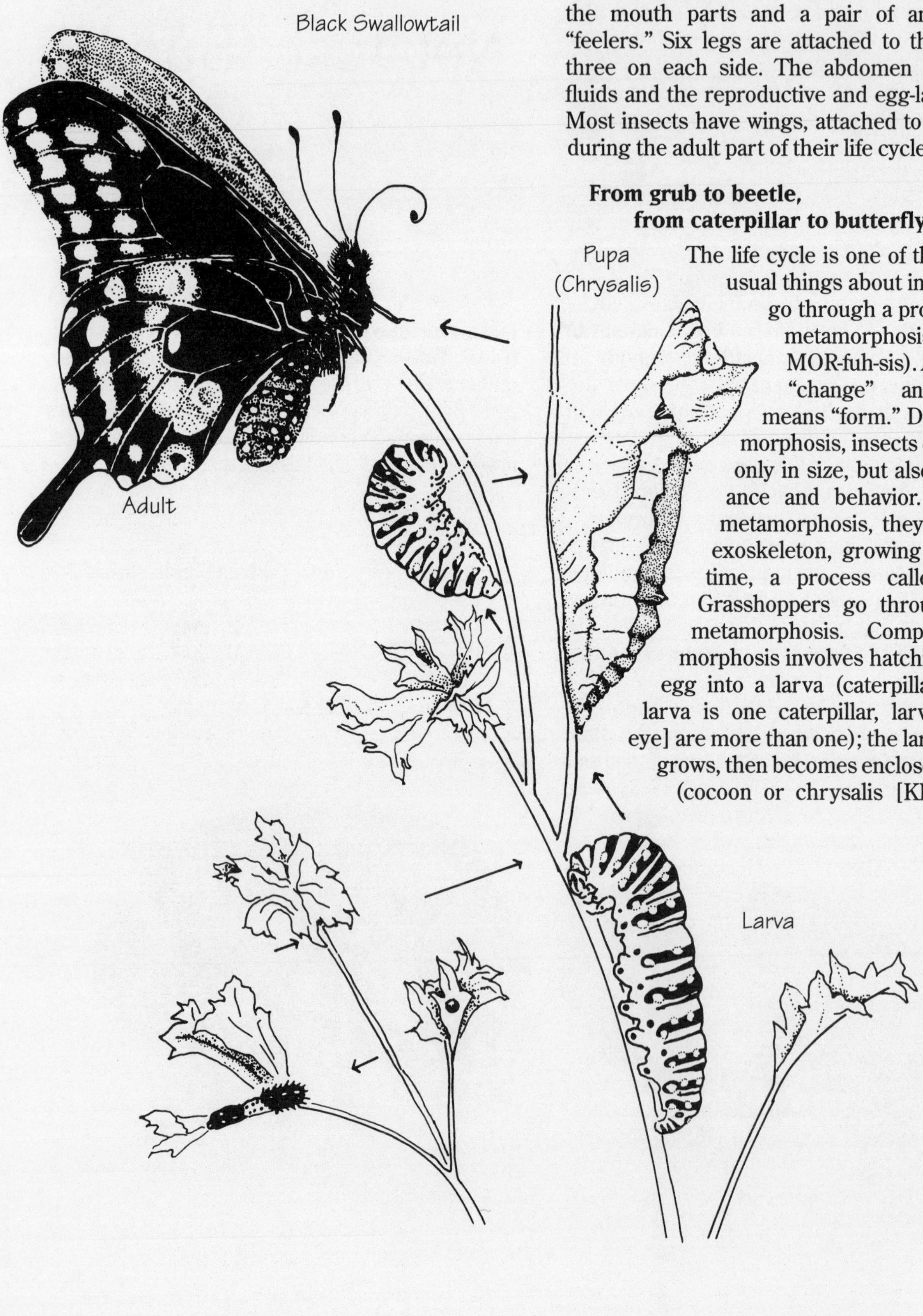

From grub to beetle, from caterpillar to butterfly

The life cycle is one of the most unusual things about insects. They go through a process called metamorphosis (met-uh-MOR-fuh-sis). *Meta* means "change" and *morpho* means "form." During metamorphosis, insects change, not only in size, but also in appearance and behavior. In simple metamorphosis, they shed their exoskeleton, growing larger each time, a process called a *molt*. Grasshoppers go through simple metamorphosis. Complete metamorphosis involves hatching from an egg into a larva (caterpillar or grub; larva is one caterpillar, larvae [LARV-eye] are more than one); the larva eats and grows, then becomes enclosed in a pupa (cocoon or chrysalis [KRIS-uh-lis]), and finally emerges as an adult insect with wings, such as a butterfly or beetle.

The female adult insect then lays her eggs, sometimes on a plant that the larvae can use for food, and the process continues.

Some insects (such as mayflies), after emerging from the pupa as an adult, do not eat at all, but live only long enough to mate and lay eggs, sometimes just a few hours. Other insects (such as 17-year cicadas) take years and years to complete their life cycles.

Some insects are endangered

Not even insects are safe from the changes people make to the environment. Some insect larvae can live on only one species of plant. If the wild plant they depend upon is bulldozed for roads or houses, the insect can no longer survive there.

Many birds, fish, and even other insects feed on insects. This is called natural control, and is nature's way of providing a species with food while reducing the numbers of insects. Dragonflies and Purple Martins eat great quantities of insects. Even ancient people knew that, and hung out gourd bird houses to entice the birds to live near them.

Using poisons called insecticides to kill insects that damage farm crops or animals, or that "bother" us, is called chemical control. Almost everyone in Florida is familiar with the efforts to control mosquitoes, fleas, and cockroaches with chemical sprays.

Many insecticides kill "good" insects that help the farmer as well as "bad" ones that eat crops. Killing insects also affects the birds and fish that feed on them, and may affect insects that do other "good" things, such as breaking down the wood of a dead tree to turn it back into soil.

Some insects that caused people harm have been exterminated in Florida, such as the mosquito that caused malaria (by chemical control with DDT) and the screwworm, the larva of a fly that caused the death of animals with wounds (exterminated by natural control).

One butterfly that used to be common in Florida, Schaus' Swallowtail Butterfly[+], is nearing extinction. Other insects, such as some species of mayflies, dragonflies, damselflies, katydids, moths, and beetles, and the Keys Scaly Cricket[+], are in trouble.

Millions of insects

Insects are remarkable. Just the incredible number of different kinds is astonishing. Over 840,000 species around the world have been identified and named, yet that number is perhaps only one-half to two-thirds of the total number of insects. That means there must be more than a million different kinds!

Hundreds of species of just ants live in North America. Entomologists who studied insects in the Florida Keys some time ago discovered seven species of ants new to that area alone. Sixty species of mosquitoes live in Florida. A scientist in Palm Bay a few years ago stood in one spot and found 25 insects in 30 minutes. Four of them were new to science.

Astonishing insect facts

Insects live everywhere. They are found in coldest Antarctica, in the driest deserts, in rivers, on top of the highest mountains, and on the surface of the ocean far from land. They can live in hot springs, in salt water, in crude oil, even in the tightest vacuum that humans can make with almost no air at all.

The smallest insects can be seen only with a microscope. The biggest ones are as big as a mouse. The Atlas Moth in India has wings that spread 36 cm (12 inches) from tip to tip.

Some insects escape their enemies by leaping, and some can leap incredible distances. A grasshopper can jump 30 times its length and a flea can jump 200 times its own length.

How much they can eat is astonishing. The caterpillar of the Polyphemus Moth, for example,

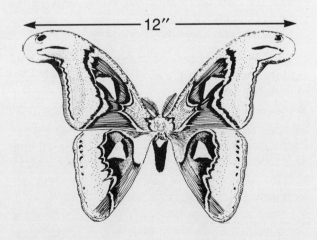

Atlas Moth

eats food that amounts to 86,000 times its birth weight in the first two days of its life. Insects of one kind or another eat nearly everything: wood, leaves, clothes, books, other insects, and animals, dead or alive.

Non-insects

Some "bugs" are not insects. Spiders and Daddy-long-legs are not, because they have no exo-skeleton. Ticks, centipedes, worms, and Pill Bugs are not because their bodies are not divided into three sections. Since insects can look so different during different periods of their lives, sometimes it is hard to tell if something you see is really an insect, not to mention what kind of insect it is.

Scarlet Wasp-Bodied Moth

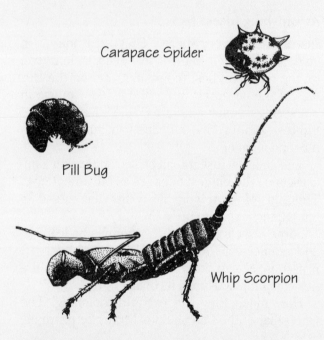

Carapace Spider

Pill Bug

Whip Scorpion

"Flowers that fly, twigs that walk, and thorns that climb stems"
(from Life Nature Library, *The Insects*, by Peter Farb)

Insects are masters of camouflage. They conceal themselves in many ways in an effort to prevent being eaten by a bird or frog or other insect. Some look like a twig or a thorn of the plant they live on. Some have big spots that look like eyes to frighten away predators. Some are colored to look like tree bark, or a green leaf or stem. Many species of moth larvae can hold onto a stem and lean outward to look like a twig.

Some insects are brightly colored or showy to warn birds that they will taste bad. The bad taste often comes from the plants they eat. Still others look like a flower or another insect that bird predators would not ordinarily eat.

Scientists have watched birds hopping all around camouflaged insect larvae that they normally would eat, but the birds could not see the insects unless they moved.

Ant Lions

Have you ever noticed small, funnel-shaped pits in dry, sandy soil and wondered what made them?

The larva of an insect called an Ant Lion carefully digs a pit and then buries itself at the bottom, waiting for ants and other small insects to fall into the trap. As the prey frantically tries to climb out, it dislodges sand that falls to the bottom, and often it slides back to the bottom on the tiny avalanche, alerting the Ant Lion that dinner is served! Sometimes the Ant Lion will flick sand at the ants to knock them to the bottom of the pit.

You can look for Ant Lions in the soil under window ledges, under a playground slide, or anywhere there's a patch of loose, dry sand. Drop an ant into the pit, and watch what happens! Or put a piece of grass into the pit and wait for the Ant Lion to bite it. Sometimes you can pull the grass blade out with the Ant Lion still holding on with its jaws!

When the Ant Lion metamorphoses from a larva, it becomes a flying insect similar to a damselfly.

What's in a name?

Insects belong to the Class Insecta, under the Phylum Invertebrata, and the Subphylum Arthro-

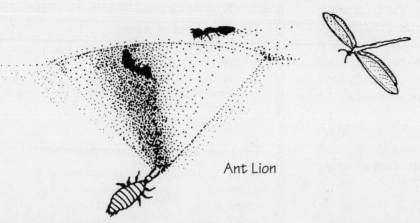

Ant Lion

poda. "Insect" comes from the Latin word *insectum,* meaning "notched." The scientific study of insects is called entomology from a Greek word *entomon,* meaning "insect."

You can be an entomologist.

Because insects are small and can be found almost anywhere, they are easy to study. A good place to look for them is around your porch light at night, or under rotting logs. Look for them on leaves, in your lake or pond, in the dust in the corner of a room, or even on your pet.

Don't destroy spiders you see in your home. They eat insects you may like even less than spiders. Spiders, in turn, are food for some birds and lizards. Catch a spider by putting a cup or bowl upside down over it, and sliding a piece of cardboard or paper between the glass and the

wall. Then carry your "captured" spider outside and release it.

Look down at the grass in the schoolyard or in your own lawn. Can you see any living things? Now get down on your hands and knees and spread the grass blades apart to look between them. Turn over the leaves of weeds to look on the underside. What do you see now? Can you see spiders and insects crawling around that were hidden before? Poke your finger in the soil between the grass blades. Are any beetles hiding in the soil? Use a magnifying glass to help you find and look at tiny insects.

If you are curious about insects, you can make an insect trap and try catching some to study. You can use tweezers to gently hold the tiny ones and a magnifying glass to look at them. Try not to harm them, and release them when you are through studying them.

Insects are interesting and there's no need to be afraid of them. Search them out and study them, and write about your observations in your nature journal.

Plant a butterfly garden

A small corner of your schoolyard or your yard at home can easily be turned into a butterfly garden. Certain species of native plants attract particular species of butterflies, and setting out these plants almost guarantees the arrival of beautiful "flying flowers." There have been reports of butterflies settling down on the flowers of plants that were still in their pots waiting to be put in the ground.

Plant a Purple Passionvine (also called Maypop) to attract yellow and black Zebra Longwings and orange Gulf Fritillaries. Plant Climbing Asters to attract the American Painted Lady Butterfly. In north Florida, plant a Spicebush to attract three

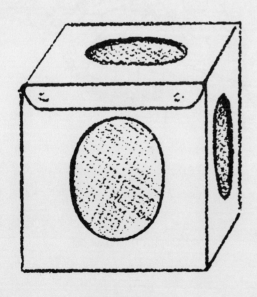

Insect trap

species of Swallowtail butterflies. Plant Butterfly Weed to attract Monarch and Queen butterflies. The list could go on and on, and much information is available through garden clubs and the Florida Native Plant Society. Some organizations have members that will assist schools in designing a butterfly garden.

Remember that a butterfly garden must have plants for both the caterpillar to eat and the adult to sip nectar from. And don't forget that spraying insecticides will kill your butterflies!

Where to learn more

See "A Little Botany Lesson" for more on pollination.
See "What's in a Name?" for more on taxonomy.
See "Environmental Careers" for more on entomology.
See "The Keys" for more on butterflies.

Do you know these words?

biological control	caterpillar
camouflage	chitin
chemical control	exoskeleton
entomologist	extinction
exterminate	invertebrate
insecticide	metamorphosis
larva, larvae	natural control
molt	pollinate
pollen	prey
predator	species
pupa, cocoon, chrysalis	taxonomist
Subphylum	
thorax	

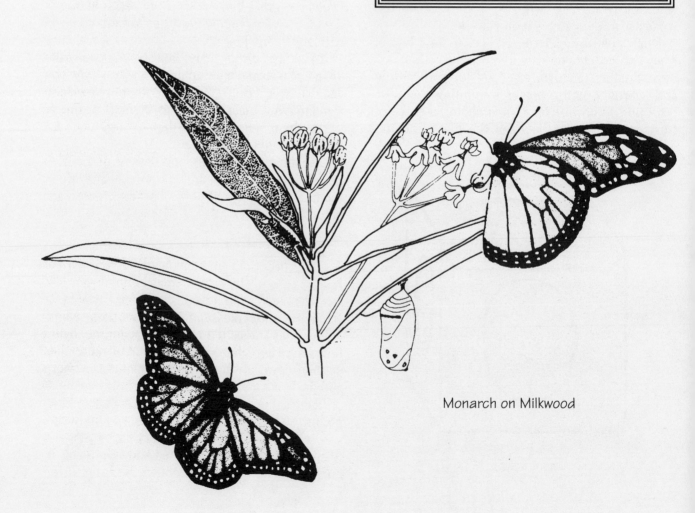

Monarch on Milkwood

Chapter 23

Alligators, Snakes, and Other Reptiles

Reptiles, like insects, either fascinate or horrify people. Coming across a snake in the wild makes your heart leap, and you are either attracted to peer at it or inclined to flee. But no one ignores these remarkable animals.

Reptiles include alligators and crocodiles, turtles, lizards, and snakes. They are vertebrate animals that crawl either on their bellies or on short legs; they usually have a protective covering of scales or bony plates, and breathe air.

Reptiles are cold-blooded, meaning that their body temperature is not regulated internally, but rather is affected by the temperature of the air, soil, water, and sunshine around them. They cannot move fast when cool, so they insolate, or absorb heat from the sunshine. When they get too cool, they either move into the sunshine, or lie on warm sand, or sleep. They can also get too hot. Then they search for shade, or go underwater or underground.

People who study reptiles and amphibians are called herpetologists (herp-uh-TALL-uh-jists). The word comes from the Greek word *herpeton*, which means "a creeping thing." Amphibians are animals that usually live in fresh water for the first part of their lives, and then change into animals that can live on land. Amphibians include frogs, toads, and salamanders.

The alligator and the crocodile

The American Alligator+ and the American Crocodile+ are the largest reptiles and the only members of the Crocodilian Family that live in Florida.

Crocodilians—22 species live in the world today—are the closest reptile descendants of the dinosaurs. (You may be surprised to know that birds—which have retained many reptilian characteristics, such as laying eggs, having scaly legs and beaks of hornlike material, and a similar arrangement of many internal structures—are more closely related to the dinosaurs than alligators are.)

117

Alligators and crocodiles have bony, armorlike scales on their backs, but the scales on their undersides are soft and smooth.

They are carnivores, which means they eat animal flesh. Their diet includes fish, snakes, birds, frogs, and turtles. Baby alligators and crocodiles eat snails, insects, and tadpoles.

Both species have three eyelids—the usual upper and lower ones that close to shut off their vision, and one that moves sideways and is transparent to protect their eyes underwater while permitting them to see and locate prey.

The alligator's snout is broad. The crocodile's snout is much narrower and tapering (although in other parts of the world there are species of crocodiles with broad snouts). Their many teeth are formidable, set in jaws that can clamp down with several hundred pounds of crushing force.

The adult alligator is black on the back with a creamy-white throat. Juvenile alligators have yellow markings across their backs. The crocodile is gray-green on its back and lighter colored on its underside and throat.

Alligators and crocodiles grow fast in their early lives—a foot a year or more—but with adulthood, growth slows markedly and eventually stops. The known record length for an alligator is about 6 meters (19 feet), but most are half that length or less. The American Crocodile on rare occasions may reach 4.5 meters (15 feet), though other species of crocodiles in other countries grow much larger.

Female alligators begin nesting in Florida in late June or July. The nest is a mound of vegetation that the female builds near the edge of a lake, river, or marsh. She lays 30 to 50 eggs with hard shells, each about 8 cm (3 inches) long. The heat of the decaying vegetation incubates the eggs, and the female stays nearby to guard the nest from predators such as raccoons. When the eggs are ready to hatch about 70 days later, the croaking of the babies attracts the female, who may help dig out the hatchlings and sometimes may carry them to the water in her mouth.

The crocodile builds a mound of soil, marl, or mud in April or May to serve as a nest. She lays anywhere from 20 to 80 eggs, which incubate for 100 days. The female crocodile helps dig out the young when they croak and, like the alligator, may assist them to the water.

The alligator lives in wetland areas throughout Florida and along the coastal areas to North Carolina and Texas. The only place in the United States that the American Crocodile lives is in the brackish and salt waters of the southern tip of Florida and the Florida Keys. This same species of crocodile is also found in the Caribbean and Central America, and as far south as Venezuela and Ecuador in South America.

Alligators and crocodiles are protected by law in the United States from people like the "hide hunters" of the early 1900s. They can be dangerous animals, although "attacks" by either species are rare. Nevertheless, never approach a nest mound or a group of young alligators or crocodiles, because the female may be on guard nearby.

Never feed them. Many animals that are a nuisance to humans became that way through our behavior, rather than through any fault of theirs. Feeding wild animals may cause them to lose their fear of people and to become habituated to our presence. Instead of fleeing when humans approach, they stand their ground or may even come nearer, expecting a handout. Then when the alligator becomes too "friendly," it is reported as a "dangerous nuisance" and is destroyed. People caused its fate, and people can prevent it.

Snakes

Florida is home to many different snakes—some large, some small, some colorful, some endangered. In fact, Florida has more species of snakes than any other state, yet little is really known about their behavior, especially in their natural habitat. The study of reptiles—and amphibians—is one science that needs more attention. If snakes and frogs, turtles or salamanders are interesting to you, your written observations about them could be useful. Make notes in your nature journal whenever you see them.

Snakes should not be killed without cause. Snakes are generally useful to people, eating insects and small mammals and rodents that can be harmful to farm crops.

There are no vegetarian snakes. With few exceptions, they all eat live animals, swallowing their prey whole. Their jaw hinges will separate and their skin will stretch to accommodate prey much wider or thicker than their bodies.

Only the underlying layer of skin will grow as a snake grows. The snake sheds the dead outer layer several times a year by loosening it around its mouth and crawling out of it, leaving the skin inside out. If you see a snake with cloudy eyes, it will shed soon. If you have time to watch it, you may get to see it crawl out of its skin. Sometimes you can find a shed skin wrapped around grasses that the snake used to help rub it off. Even the old eye cover is recognizable in the shed skin.

Some snakes are nocturnal, some are diurnal. Some live in or near water, some in trees, some underground. Most snakes lay eggs, but some bear their young live, such as the very common Garter Snake, many of the species of water snakes, and the poisonous Water Moccasins, Rattlesnakes, and Copperheads. Whether she lays eggs or bears her young live, the female snake does not "raise" the babies. They are on their own from the moment of birth or hatching.

Some of the most colorful snakes include:

- Florida Scarlet Snake and Scarlet Kingsnake, both red, black, and yellow like the poisonous Coral Snake.

- Red Rat Snake+ (or Corn Snake), with a beautiful mosaic of red and yellow, and Yellow Rat Snake (or Chicken Snake), yellow with brown stripes down its length. Both are farmer's helpers, for they eat rats that lurk in the barn or crop fields.

- Rainbow Snake, with dark gray and red stripes down its length, and a yellow underside.

- Rough Green Snake, slender and bright green for camouflage in shrubs.

The smallest snake in Florida is the Crowned Snake. It reaches a maximum length of only 23 cm (9 inches). Very little is known about this species.

The largest snakes are the Eastern Indigo Snake+, listed as Threatened, and the Eastern Coachwhip, both of which can reach 2.6 meters (over 100 inches, or 8.5 feet).

The ones you are most likely to see are:

- Southern Black Racer, a slender, glossy-black snake with a white chin, up to 1.8 meters (nearly 6 feet) long, but usually much smaller.

Racers are well-named, for they are fast-moving snakes.

- Eastern Garter Snake, gray-green with three yellowish stripes down its back, up to 1.2 meters (4 feet) long. It is common in the eastern U.S., often seen in backyards and schoolyards.

Since Florida is covered with so much water, it is not surprising that it is home to many water snakes. The Florida Water Snake, found in all wetland habitats, is one of the most common species of snakes in Florida. It can reach 1.5 meters (5 feet) in length, and is brown with dark bands across its back. It is often mistaken for a Water Moccasin, but the Florida Water Snake is not poisonous and should not be killed. Florida's

Indigo Snake (threatened)

Salt Marsh snakes are specially adapted to live in salt water.

These species are all listed as Threatened:

- Eastern Indigo Snake+, the largest nonpoisonous snake in North America, is glossy, iridescent blue-black with a rusty-red chin. It shares the burrow of the Gopher Tortoise, and the habitat of both of these animals is rapidly being developed. Overcollecting by herpetologists has also hastened the decline of these handsome, docile snakes.

- Rim Rock Crowned Snake+, the rarest snake in Florida, is found only in Dade County and the upper Keys.

- Atlantic Salt Marsh Snake+ is found only along the Atlantic coast from Volusia to Martin counties.

POISONOUS SNAKES

If you have moved to Florida from another state or country that has no poisonous snakes, you may be uncertain about the dangers of Florida wild places, for Florida does have several poisonous snakes. But knowing what to look for and how to avoid danger from them will prepare you for outdoor adventure.

The easiest poisonous snake to identify is the Coral Snake. It is circled with bright, shiny bands of red, yellow, and black. Two other snakes, however, that are similarly colored, are nonpoisonous. The Coral Snake's bands of red and yellow touch each other and the tip of the snout is black. On the Scarlet Snake and the Scarlet Kingsnake, the bands of red and black touch each other and the tip of the snout is red. All three of these colorful snakes are found throughout Florida.

An old rhyme helps you remember the difference between the poisonous Coral Snake and the nonpoisonous Scarlet and Scarlet King snakes: "Red touch yellow, kill a fellow; red touch black, all right, Jack."

Coral snakes are timid and will flee if given the chance, hiding under leaves or a log. They rarely bite unless stepped on or picked up. Their bite leaves a semicircular row of small teeth marks, and the venom affects the nervous system.

Three rattlesnakes occur in Florida: the Eastern Diamondback Rattlesnake and the Pygmy Rattlesnake are found all over the state except the Everglades, and the Timber, or Cane-

brake, Rattlesnake is a northern species found in Florida only in a few counties in the center of the Panhandle.

The Eastern Diamondback Rattlesnake can grow quite large—the record is 2.4 meters (8 feet)—and it can be easily identified by the clear diamond-shaped patterns on its thick body and the rattle at the end of its tail. When alarmed, its warning rattle can be heard 400 meters (.25 mile) away. It lives mostly in pine flatwoods or on the edge of wet prairies. Development has destroyed so much of its habitat that it is not common anywhere in Florida anymore.

Pygmy Rattlesnakes are small, usually only about 51 cm (20 inches) long. They can be identified by their dusky gray color with a row of alternate reddish and dark spots down their back. Their small rattle sometimes sounds like an insect buzzing.

The Canebrake Rattlesnake has zigzag dark markings across its back. Its bite can be serious, but fortunately the snake is mild-tempered.

The Cottonmouth Water Moccasin is the most feared, most common, and most dangerous of the poisonous snakes in Florida. It can be found in many watery habitats. Unfortunately, so are the harmless Brown Water Snakes that often are mistaken for water moccasins and killed. If you see a water snake and you are close enough, look for the elliptical eye pupil (like a cat's) to identify the moccasin (harmless water snakes have a round eye pupil). Also look for the broad, lance-shaped head, the dark band through the eye, and the light color below the band. The mottled dark back is not reliable as a comparison with harmless water snakes. The water moccasin does not always flee when approached, which makes it dangerous. If the water moccasin opens its mouth, the white lining, which gives it the "cottonmouth" name, is an identifying characteristic. But do not kill it unless it is a threat to you or your family. Even poisonous snakes have their important place in the grand scheme of nature.

The Copperhead, a dangerous poisonous snake in other states, is found in Florida in only a few counties in the Panhandle. It has alternating light brown and dark brown markings across its back. The Copperhead, like the Canebrake Rattler, is a docile snake, not striking unless disturbed.

Rattlesnake

If you should have the misfortune to be struck by a rattlesnake, a moccasin, or a copperhead, the result would be two fang marks and, to a degree depending upon the amount of venom injected, instant pain and swelling of tissue around the bite.

When hiking through wild areas, if you always look where you are going to put your foot or your hand, you are quite safe. Never walk carelessly through underbrush that is too thick to see your feet, or even weed your garden without looking. When boating or canoeing, never reach for an overhead tree without looking first.

If you are ever bitten by one of these poisonous snakes, you should realize that the chances of dying from the bite are very small. Most people receive quick medical assistance and fully recover from their experience.

Turtles and tortoises

A stranger animal than the turtle can scarcely be imagined! It carries its bony house around on its back, and can pull its head and legs inside. Some species, such as the box turtle, can "shut the door" by closing their hinged lower shells. The upper shell is called the carapace, and the lower shell is called the plastron. The bony tip of the upper jaw resembles a bird's bill and is called a beak.

All turtles lay eggs. They dig a hole in the ground with their hind legs, deposit the eggs in the hole, and then cover them up with sand. The eggs look like ping-pong balls, though they may be smaller if the turtles are small. Most turtle species lay leathery-covered eggs, but some lay hard-shelled eggs. Raccoons often dig them up and eat them.

Turtles may live a very long time. A few cases have been recorded of them living for a century.

Florida is home to five species of sea turtles, 30 aquatic turtles, and only two terrestrial turtles.

SEA TURTLES[+]

All of the world's eight species of marine turtles are threatened with extinction. These remarkable animals spend most of their lives swimming in the ocean, but when it is time to lay eggs, the female usually will return to a spot near where herself was hatched, to lay her eggs in the warm sand. So many of their nesting beaches along Florida's coast have been developed with hotels and houses that the turtles often find riprap (a wall of concrete pieces thrown together), bulkheads (retaining walls), and jetties (walls extending out into the water) instead of sand dunes when they come ashore to lay their eggs. Then, if the female does lay eggs, the hatchlings may find disaster when they dig out of the sand one night. Their instincts should lead them to the water by the gleam of moonlight on the ocean, but lights along the beaches from buildings and streetlights often confuse them, leading them instead to their death under the wheels of cars or by dehydration in the morning sun.

The Atlantic Leatherback[+] is the largest species of turtle. It can weigh over 600 kilograms (1,300 pounds) and its carapace from neck to tail can measure 1.8 meters (nearly 6 feet).

The Atlantic Green Turtle[+] can weigh as much as 200 kg (440 pounds), and the Atlantic Loggerhead can weigh up to 90 kg (200 pounds).

The Atlantic Ridley[+] and the Atlantic Hawksbill[+] are smaller, measuring less than a meter (3 feet). Ridleys weigh less than 45 kg (100 pounds); hawksbills may reach 65 kg (150 pounds).

If you have an opportunity to go on a nighttime beach walk to see these huge marine turtles nesting or their tiny offspring hatching, you'll find the experience fascinating and memorable. Always go with a leader who will help you find the huge tracks in the sand, and instruct you so that you will not cause the turtle to fail to lay her eggs, or prevent the baby turtles from finding their way to the ocean.

FRESHWATER TURTLES

Of all the pond and marsh and mud turtles, perhaps the most interesting are the Snapping Turtles. They can grow large—the Common Snapper to 22 kg (50 pounds) or more, the Alligator Snapper[+] occasionally over 90 kg (200 pounds).

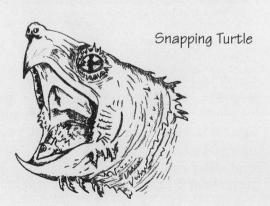

Snapping Turtle

Turtle

They have strong jaws, a ferocious bite, and rough ridges on the carapace and tail. The Common Snapper lives throughout Florida, but the Alligator Snapper lives only in north Florida and is protected by law.

Another strange-looking group is the Softshell Turtles. Their shells are flattened and flexible, and they have pointed, tubelike snouts.

The Florida Cooters, the Redbelly Turtle, and the Yellowbelly Slider are all common, colorful turtles in Florida's ponds, rivers, and marshes. Canoeists often see them sunning themselves on logs along the banks of rivers.

Barbour's Map Turtle+ is endangered, living only in the Apalachicola and Chipola rivers of the Panhandle. It is related to the Alabama Map Turtle, which in Florida lives in the extreme western part of the Panhandle.

TERRESTRIAL TURTLES

The Gopher Tortoise+ is a land turtle and is a protected species. The gopher lives in dry, sandy, upland habitats, only in Florida and the southern borders of Georgia, Alabama, and Mississippi, and just reaching Louisiana. It is renowned for digging deep, cool burrows that also provide shelter for many other species, including snakes, spiders, and rabbits.

Lizards

Lizards are today's miniature reminders of the dinosaurs (*dinosaur* from the Greek language means "terrible lizard"). About 3,000 species of lizards exist in the world today, on every continent except Antarctica. They range in size from 3- to 5-centimeter-long (1 to 2 inches) geckos to the 3-meter-long (9 feet) Komodo Dragon of Indonesia.

Florida has 22 species of lizards, divided into six Families. All are harmless; there are no poisonous lizards in the state. They are helpful to people; most of them eat insects. They are interesting to watch, and many of them are colorful and attractive.

Lizards and snakes differ in obvious ways—most lizards have legs, and most have eyelids, while snakes never have legs or eyelids.

Most lizards are diurnal, but some, especially among the geckos, are nocturnal. Nocturnal lizards have lower temperature ranges than diurnal lizards. Almost all the smaller species eat insects, and almost all lay eggs.

Many lizards have tails that break away from the body if grabbed by a person or by a predator, such as a snake or bird looking for a meal. While the tail thrashes about and distracts the predator, the lizard can make a fast getaway, and soon a new, slightly shorter tail will grow back.

SOME COMMON FLORIDA LIZARDS

The Green Anole (AN-ole) is the lizard often incorrectly called a chameleon (which is really an African lizard) because it can change color from green to brown to match the color of leaf or bark. It is common in all habitats in Florida, including gardens and borders around buildings. Sometimes you can see the male anole extend the bright red dewlap, or throat fan, under its chin to attract a female or scare away a trespassing male. Some south Florida anoles have a green dewlap. Anoles are diurnal, and can climb bushes and even walls while stalking spiders and insects. They are fun to watch.

A relative of the Green Anole that doesn't change color is the Brown Anole. You can recognize it by the light stripe down the middle of its back. It is not a native Florida species because it was accidentally introduced from the Caribbean, and it is taking over habitat and driving out the native Green Anole in some places.

Green Anole

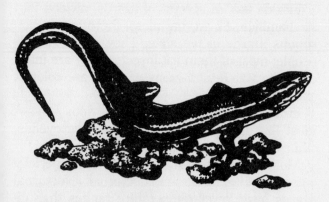

Southeastern Five-lined Skink

Skinks are lizards with a smooth round body and a long round tail. Florida has several species of skinks, including one called the Broadhead Skink that can grow to 33 cm (13 inches).

Most skinks in Florida are arboreal (ar-BOR-ee-ul), or tree-climbers, and you can often see them clinging to the bark of trees.

The Southeastern Five-lined Skink is named for the five yellow-white stripes along its brown back. During the spring breeding season, male Southeastern Five-lined Skinks have orange-red cheeks. With their stripes and blue tails, they are very colorful lizards.

The Six-lined Racerunner has the highest body temperature of Florida's lizards—over 42°C (100°F). It is brown with stripes, and the male is blue underneath. It eats insects, and will chase a pebble tossed near it to see if it is something for dinner!

One family of lizards, called Worm Lizards because they resemble earthworms, have no legs for burrowing, yet they live underground. The Florida Worm Lizard looks like a large, pinkish earthworm, but it can be 30 centimeters (nearly a foot) long. It doesn't like water and can't swim, so it lives in high, dry, pine and oak woods. Sometimes it comes to the surface after heavy rains. They eat ants and termites.

Three species of Glass Lizards live in Florida. Though many lizards shed their tails when captured by a predator, the tail of the Glass Lizard is very fragile, snapping off if the lizard even presses very hard with it in an effort to escape! They are tan in color with stripes, and can grow to over a meter (3 feet) long. They burrow in sandy places and eat spiders and insects.

Geckos are mostly nocturnal lizards that usually have large eyes, sticky pads under their toes, and round fleshy tails instead of the slender tails of most lizards. Their skin is soft, not scaly. They have a distinctive call (most lizards don't make any sound we can hear).

Florida's only native gecko, the Reef Gecko, is the smallest of the lizards in the state—no more than 5 centimeters (5 inches) long. The Reef Gecko is brown and lives only in south Florida. Exotic Geckos introduced from the Mediterranean, however, are found in other parts of Florida.

FLORIDA'S LIZARDS IN DANGER

Down the center of Florida's peninsula runs a string of ancient sand dunes that—many thousands of years ago when the ocean was higher—used to be the beach. Today these dry, sandy habitats are called Florida Scrub, home to many unique plants and animals found nowhere else in the world.

Unfortunately, much of this high land is being turned into shopping centers or citrus groves, and many Florida Scrub species—both plants and animals—are threatened or endangered.

One of these is the Florida Scrub Lizard[+], recognized—if you should ever be lucky enough to see one—by the sharp scales on its gray-brown body and the broad, dark-brown stripe along each side. It's about 12.5 centimeters (5 inches) long. If you frighten it, it will run across the ground instead of taking to the trees. (The Scrub Lizard is related to the Southern Fence Lizard, and they look very much alike except for the Scrub Lizard's brown side stripes.)

Florida Scrub Lizard

Another lizard that likes the hot, sandy scrub is the Florida Sand Skink[+], a secretive lizard that spends most of its time underground. Both its legs and eyes are very tiny, and its color is silvery gray, or tannish. The dry sand of the Florida Scrub is the perfect environment for this little 12-centimeter (5-inch) lizard. It is listed as a threatened species.

There are strangers in our midst, too!

The common Green Iguana has been introduced into south Florida from Central and South America. It can grow to 2 meters (6 feet) long, but most of that is its long, whiplike tail. Brought to Miami by the pet trade, some of them have escaped or been turned loose by owners who tired of taking care of them. These exotic species have caused many problems for Florida's native reptiles.

Where to learn more

See "What's in a Name?" for more about the Alligator and the Gopher Tortoise.

See "The Keys" for more about the Crocodile.

See "The Panhandle" for more about Barbour's Map Turtle.

See "Exotics–More than Just a Nuisance" for more about escaped species.

See "The Salt Marshes" for more about the Salt Marsh Snake and Diamondback Terrapin.

See "The Big Scrub" for more about Scrub Lizards and Gopher Tortoises.

Do you know these words?

amphibian	aquatic
arboreal	carapace
carnivore	cold-blooded
dewlap	diurnal
endangered	exotic
habitat	herpetologist
incubate	insolate
instinct	nocturnal
plastron	predator
reptile	species
terrestrial	vertebrate
wetland	

Green Iguana

Chapter 24

Exotics—More Than Just a Nuisance

Plants and animals that have come to Florida from other countries with the assistance of people are known as exotics. Some of them stay peacefully in cages, aquariums, or gardens, but others escape into wild places, sometimes becoming naturalized—able to live and propagate without human assistance such as feeding, watering, fertilizing, and other care. Some are acceptable "neighbors," but others become dreadful nuisances, spreading wildly and taking over habitat where native species used to live.

Many scientists say that the spread of unwanted exotic species is one of the biggest environmental problems in Florida.

What's wrong with exotics?

The Spaniards probably brought the first exotics to Florida when they settled St. Augustine in the late 1500s and early 1600s—including wild hogs and the seeds of orange trees. Orange trees need cultivating to survive, and rarely escape into the wild. Hogs, however, damage the environment by their rooting and feeding behavior, tearing out native plants which then can leave space for weedy exotic plants to grow.

Some of the earliest exotic pest species were brought home by travelers in the late 1800s (it is now illegal to do this without special permits). Some exotics are colorful flowering plants used for landscaping, others are brought in by the aquarium and pet trades. Some species—such as Centipede Grass and Camphor trees—were brought in so long ago that some botanists question whether we can still call them exotics. Instead, we call them "naturalized."

All goes well until the species escapes from the garden or cage, and finds that it can live quite well in Florida's comfortable wilds.

The biggest concern is the many species that were brought into this country that have no natural controls—such as disease, insects, cold or heat, drought or flood, or animals that use them for food—that helped to keep them from spreading

Wild Hog

125

too far and too fast in the country they came from. Sometimes, when natural controls are brought into this country to limit the spread of an exotic species, they don't seem to work here, or can even create problems of their own. Exotic animals—unusual deer species, monkeys, western cougars, and mice and rats—seem to thrive here.

Wild things, just like people, find Florida a wonderful place to live.

Some examples of "bad" exotics

Florida has the unfortunate distinction of being "home away from home" to more exotic species than any other state except Hawaii. About 925 exotic plants and 80 exotic animals are now living here, far from their original homes. Let's look at a few of the "bad" ones.

PLANTS

All of these plants are on Florida's Exotic Pest Plant List. It is forbidden by law to buy them, sell them, or transport them.

Cajeput Tree, Paper or Punk Tree, or Melaleuca. Some people think this tree with several names is absolutely the worst exotic species in Florida. This tree sucks up water like a sponge, and was brought to Florida in 1906 from Australia to help "dry up" the Everglades so people could farm and build houses there. According to plant experts, an acre of Melaleuca trees can slurp up 2,100 gallons of water every hour. Now we realize that water is the "life-blood" of the Everglades and we don't want to continue projects that dry up this impor-

tant ecosystem, though it may be too late to stop the spread of this terrible tree.

Australian Pine. Several species of this tall tree, which has long, slender, pine needlelike stems with scalelike leaves, were brought to Florida from Australia in the late 1800s.

One species was planted on beaches and along causeways near the coast to serve as a fast-growing, salt-tolerant windbreak. This species produces many tiny seeds.

A different species of Australian Pine was planted inland as windbreaks. It sends up new trees called suckers from roots near the surface and resprouts readily from the stump when it is cut down.

Both species litter the ground with dry "needles" that prevent most other plants from sprouting, and die back in freezes, leaving dead branches that can fall and be dangerous.

Australian Pine

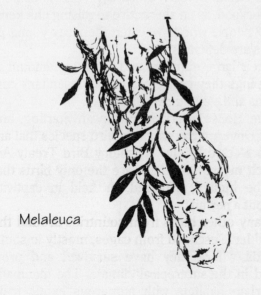

Melaleuca

Brazilian Pepper. This large shrub was brought to Florida in the late 1800s as an ornamental bush. Developers used them for landscaping houses they were selling. It is often called Florida Holly because of its evergreen leaves and bunches of small red berries produced in winter. Pepper bushes have escaped into many different habitats from wet to dry, and can resprout when they are cut down.

Brazilian Pepper

European Starlings

Water Hyacinth. This floating water plant with round leaves and beautiful purple flowers was brought from South America by a woman who admired it while traveling. It escaped from her home fish pond in the 1880s into Florida's St. Johns River and now strangles many lakes and inland waterways throughout the state.

Hyacinth can be either a floating plant with air sacs and dangling roots, or it can anchor its roots in the mud. It grows extremely fast, forming solid floating mats that boats cannot get through. The state of Florida has spent millions of dollars removing it and trying to eradicate it from rivers and lakes.

Hydrilla. An aquatic plant that arrived in the 1880s, Hydrilla probably was thrown into lakes when people tired of caring for their tropical fish aquariums. It can grow up to an inch a day in warm weather, and can completely fill in a lake. Plants are carried from lake to lake on fishing boat propellers and boat trailers. A tiny piece of the plant can start a new colony. Cities and counties have spent hundreds of thousands of dollars spraying Hydrilla with chemical poisons in efforts to kill it.

Chinese Tallow Tree. This tree has heart-shaped leaves that turn dark red in the fall and seeds that look like popcorn, making it attractive for homeowners to plant in their yards. But, it, too, is spreading rapidly without any natural enemies into the wild places of Florida.

BIRDS

English, or House, Sparrow. Brought from Europe, House Sparrows were released throughout eastern and midwestern North America in the late 1800s. This bird is now widespread all over North America and into northern South America, especially in cities. They can nest successfully before reaching a year old and at any time of year. According to one count, House Sparrows made up 45% of the residential bird population in St. Petersburg, Florida.

European Starling. Introduced from Europe into New York City's Central Park in 1890, Starlings have spread throughout North America. Their aggressive behavior displaces native birds, especially bluebirds and woodpeckers, from natural and manmade cavities. During the nesting season they eat many insects, but in fall and winter they gather in huge flocks and eat grain in farm fields.

Pigeons, Homing Pigeons, or Rock Doves, are the sociable but sometimes pesky birds familiar to all city dwellers. They were brought across the Atlantic Ocean by early European settlers as pets, and for food, as an alternative to raising chickens. Some people who have eaten them say young pigeons are delicious.

Their large numbers and the huge amount of droppings they create can cause unsanitary conditions and, sometimes, disease.

The House Sparrow, European Starling, and Rock Dove are the only wild bird species that are not protected by the Migratory Bird Treaty Act (which means that these are the only birds that can be hunted, captured, or held in captivity without a permit).

Many other birds from countries around the world have escaped from cages, mostly in south Florida where they have survived and prospered in the subtropical climate. The manmade suburban habitats with numerous exotic fruit-

Parrot

bearing tropical plants provide food and nesting places. These birds include Red-whiskered Bulbul, Spot-breasted Oriole, and several species of parrots and parakeets. Farther north in Florida, the Muscovy Duck, an exotic from Central America, has taken over lakes and ponds, driving out native Mallards and Wood Ducks.

OTHER EXOTICS

Armadillo. Nine-banded Armadillos are native to South and Central America, but didn't arrive in Florida until the 1920s when some of them escaped from a circus. Armadillos have also reached Florida on their own from Mexico through Texas in recent years. The armadillo is protected by nine armored bands on its back from some animals that might eat it, and—though it waddles slowly—it can dig a hole to hide in faster than a person with a shovel can dig it out.

Because it is food for the Florida Panther in south Florida, and eats fire ants, scorpions, and cockroaches, you might think we'd like having it for a neighbor, but it roots up wild lands and flower gardens alike when grubbing for food.

Fire ant. The Red Fire Ant, so named because its bite causes a burning sensation, originated in Brazil. It came to this country about 1940, first into Alabama, though nobody knows how. By 1957 it infested most of the southern states, including Florida. It spreads to areas that are cleared for development and agriculture.

The ants build high mounds of dirt for their nests that can damage mowers and other equipment, and their stings can kill cattle and cause pain in most people and occasionally death in people allergic to their poison. But they are not entirely bad. Fire ants feed on pest insects of several important agricultural crops, reducing the damage that the pest insects cause. Rainfall and moisture in the soil, as well as cold, limit the spread of fire ants.

Asian Tiger Mosquito. A species of mosquito, named the Asian Tiger Mosquito because of its striped markings, came to Florida in 1986 in a boatload of used tires from Japan or Taiwan. It can carry Eastern Equine Encephalitis (ee-kwine ensef-uh-LITE-us), a dangerous viral disease that attacks horses and humans.

Snail. Another very recent alien is a large, fist-sized snail imported from West Africa by pet stores. These snails eat every plant in sight, and could do enormous damage if they escaped into the wild. It is illegal to import them.

Walking Catfish. In south Florida, 12 species of exotic fish compete with native fish for food and shelter. The most successful of these, including the Walking Catfish, feed on plants and detritus in south Florida's many canals. This fish came from southeast Asia and can breathe air and slither along on wet grass, using its spiny fins. They became established in the wild in Florida when they "walked away" from a fish farm in 1967.

Competition for space is a way of life for all species, including humans. Even some native species find it hard to live together in harmony. The stronger, more aggressive individuals or species drive out those that are timid or less social. Some species are able to take over completely, allowing virtually nothing else to live there, resulting in the loss of what is called biological diversity, or

Fire Ant hill

biodiversity. Exotics often have an advantage over native species because their natural controls were left behind in the country they came from.

Ecologists know—and the public is beginning to understand—that the world needs a large diversity of plants and animals. The world would be poorer if the only animals in Florida were dogs and cats, armadillos and pigeons, and the only plants were lawn grass and Brazilian Pepper. Diversity in the natural world makes life interesting, healthy, and beautiful.

How you can help

People can help Florida's native plants and animals by leaving them room to live in and not intruding into their habitat with houses, businesses, and roads. This is why environmentalists are working hard to get the state to buy wild lands that can be protected from development.

Pet owners or aquarists (those with aquariums) should return unwanted pets or plants to the humane society or pet store. Remember, it is against the law to release any exotic species into the wild.

You can help by using no poisons such as insecticides and herbicides outside your house. Poisons become concentrated as they move up the food chain. If you kill insect larvae that eat plant leaves, you will not have butterflies or some of the other beneficial insects. And a poisoned insect may also poison a bird or lizard when the insect is eaten.

You can help by having less grass in your yard, because then you will use less fertilizer and water. Leave natural, wild areas around your home, with natural plants and fallen leaves that feed and protect shy birds and lizards. Plant native species that require less water, less fertilizer, and no pesticides. Landscaping in this way is called xeric (ZEER-ik) landscaping. Xeric means "dry," but xeric landscaping actually refers to using plants appropriate to the site, whether wet, dry, or halfway between.

You can help by pulling up, or getting your parents to help you pull up, any of the exotic nuisance plants you may have growing in your yard, near your lake, or around your school, and replacing them with a variety of native plants attractive to wildlife.

Florida is a unique state, with a natural treasure of plants and animals. Let's all do our best to keep it that way!

Where to learn more

See "Florida's Native Plants" for more on native plant species.

See "Water and Wetlands" and "The Everglades" for more on the food chain.

See "The Everglades" for more on exotic plants.

Do you know these words?

Can you list them in alphabetical order?

exotic	naturalized
propagate	species
environmental	controls
detritus	diversity
xeric	food chain
biodiversity	ecologist
introduced	

House Sparrows

Chapter 25

Extinction Is Forever

The last of the dinosaurs died out before human beings even lived on earth, and the Sabertoothed Tigers and Woolly Mammoths became extinct a long, long time ago because of some natural event.

Many other plants and animals, however, are gone forever because of the actions of people. The Dodo, a flightless bird that lived on an island in the Indian Ocean, was slaughtered for food until there were none left. It became extinct in 1681.

The Great Auk, a seabird of the North Atlantic, was also unable to fly and an easy target for hunters. Its population died out by 1844.

By 1914, two more birds—the Passenger Pigeon and the Carolina Parakeet—had disap-

peared forever, hunted to extinction for food and sport. Early in this century many of Florida's beautiful wading birds were killed for their feathers to decorate ladies' hats, and they came close to extinction.

One of the most recent extinctions in the United States was the black-and-white-streaked Dusky Seaside Sparrow. The last survivor died in captivity on June 16, 1987, at Walt Disney World's Discovery Island. These sparrows will never be seen again because people changed their habitat when the Space Center was built and left them nowhere to live where they could safely raise their families and have enough to eat.

The numbers of plants and birds and mammals and reptiles and insects that are nearing extinction—just in Florida—are astonishing. In 1993, 612 species were listed by the state.

Dusky Seaside Sparrow

Great Auk

These lists identify fish, animal, or plant species as "Endangered" if they are in danger of actual extinction throughout all or a significant portion of their range. A "Threatened" species is likely to become an Endangered species within the foreseeable future throughout all or a significant portion of its range. A category used only on Florida lists is "Species of Special Concern," which describes a species of animal that may become Threatened if it is not protected and effectively managed.

Many scientists think the official list contains far fewer species than are actually endangered. Some biologists think we may destroy 25% of the remaining variety of species on earth by the year 2000.

You have heard about many of these endangered animals: the Florida Panther[+], the West Indian Manatee[+], the Green Sea Turtle[+], the Right Whale[+], the Key Deer[+]. People still hunt some of them, though they should know that not many are left. For others, we simply continue taking away the places where they live.

Some can be saved by making a law that prohibits the sale of animal parts, as was done for alligators, which were killed for their hides. Because of that law, alligators have recovered to the point where managed hunting is now legal. Some can be helped by prohibiting the use of chemical poisons, such as those that affected the food chain and destroyed the eggshells of Brown Pelicans[+], Ospreys, and Bald Eagles[+]. But if people decide to build condominiums on every beach, where can sea turtles nest or the beach mice hide? And what can a plant do if the bulldozer comes along?

The big creatures that are endangered get more attention than smaller ones. But consider some of the tiny creatures: Schaus' Swallowtail Butterfly[+], the Stock Island Tree Snail[+], Pillar Coral[+], the Sinkhole Fern[+]. Who will help see that they don't disappear forever? Who will care enough?

Florida Panther[+]. This big, tawny-colored cat is perhaps the most en-

Wood Stork

dangered species in Florida. The males stand about 60 to 70 centimeters (24 to 28 inches) tall, measure over 2 meters (7 feet) from nose to tip of tail, and weigh 45 to 72 kilograms (100 to 160 pounds). Females are considerably smaller, weighing 30 to 45 kilograms (70 to 100 pounds).

Many large mammals have difficulty adapting to human-caused changes in the landscape because they often require extensive territories in which to travel. The Florida Panther, which once roamed throughout the southeastern United States, is now confined by cities, farms, and roads to remote swamps and hammocks in south Florida.

Florida Panthers are shy, solitary animals that prey upon White-tailed Deer, wild hogs, Armadillos, and other animals. A male panther's range can cover as much as 700 square kilometers (275 square miles) in his search for food, shelter, and a mate.

Because their territories are criss-crossed with highways, several panthers are killed each year by cars and trucks. The estimated 30 to 50 adult panthers that remain in southern Florida are mostly affected by the presence of more and more humans in and near their habitat.

Okaloosa Darter+. Few species of North American freshwater fish have ranges as small as Florida's Okaloosa Darter. Its name comes from the only place it is found—seven small streams that originate in Okaloosa County in Florida's Panhandle. These clear, shallow streams with sandy bottoms provide habitat for the fish, and for the midge and mayfly larvae that it feeds upon.

Because of its extremely small habitat, the entire population of this species could be destroyed by development along these streambanks, which could change the quality and quantity of the water. The Okaloosa Darter also has a rival for the available food and living space—the Brown Darter, introduced into this area by people in the 1960s.

Okaloosa Darter

Gray Bat

Gray Bat+. Some animals have such highly specialized requirements for homes that, if conditions are not right, the species has trouble existing.

The Gray Bat, named for its gray-colored fur, lives almost exclusively in caves found in northern Florida. There they hibernate during the winter and raise their young during the summer, using the same cave year after year. Each cave must have the proper air temperature for comfort, provide protection from predators, and be close to feeding areas.

Human explorers who visit the Gray Bats' caves during breeding times can cause bats to abandon their roosts and their young. Efforts to protect Gray Bats must include limiting human activities in caves during certain times of the year.

Schaus' Swallowtail Butterfly+. Schaus' Swallowtail Butterfly lives in the tropical hammocks of the northern Florida Keys where it can be seen flying low in the dappled sunlight. Only hammocks where the Torchwood tree grows provide a home for this butterfly, for that is the only plant on which it will deposit its eggs.

Much of this insect's habitat is sprayed for mosquitoes and is being bought by developers. Butterfly collectors also hurt the survival chances of Schaus' Swallowtail Butterfly.

Hurricane Andrew devastated its habitat in 1992. Many of the insects were in the pupa stage when the storm hit, and only two dozen of them survived the storm surge and tree destruction to emerge as adults. These were rescued, and the natural areas were restocked with their offspring after the Torchwood trees recovered.

Hand Fern

About three-quarters of the endangered species in Florida are plants. The only way they can "move" is by the scattering of their seeds or the slow spreading of their underground root systems.

The Hand Fern⁺ and two species of Pitcher-plants⁺. These plants are unusual. The Hand Fern lives only in the boots—the stubs of dead fronds—of Sabal Palms.

Pitcher-plants trap and digest insects in their long tubes for nourishment. These plants need moist, shady places to live, and draining these places to plant tree farms or build houses destroys them.

Where to learn more

See "Florida's Symbols" for more about the Florida Panther.

See "Insects are not just 'Bugs'!" for more about butterflies.

See "Springs, Sinkholes, and Caves" for more about bats.

See "The Panhandle" for more about Pitcher-plants.

See "The Keys" for more about tropical hardwood hammocks and butterflies.

See "The Salt Marshes" for more on Seaside Sparrows.

Do you know these words?

Can you list them in alphabetical order?

boots	extinct
hibernate	hammock
pupa	habitat
predators	prey
introduced	

Beach Mouse

Scrub Lizard

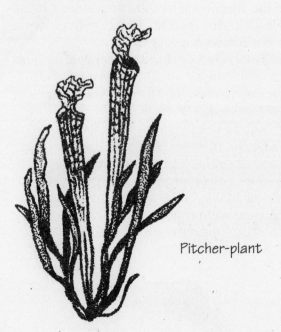

Pitcher-plant

These are the species listed as Endangered by the
State of Florida in 1994 (common name only):

Fish

Shortnose Sturgeon
Okaloosa Darter
Blackmouth Shiner

Reptiles

Atlantic Green Turtle
American Crocodile
Leatherback Turtle
Atlantic Hawksbill Turtle
Striped Mud Turtle
Atlantic Ridley Turtle

Birds

Cape Sable Seaside Sparrow
Florida Grasshopper Sparrow
Ivory-Billed Woodpecker
Kirtland's Warbler
Arctic Peregrine Falcon
Wood Stork
Snail Kite
Bachman's Warbler

Mammals

Right Whale
Sei Whale
Finback Whale
Florida Mastiff Bat
Florida Panther
Humpback Whale
Duke's Saltmarsh Vole
Gray Bat
Indiana Bat

Key Largo Woodrat
Key Deer
Silver Rice Rat
Key Largo Cotton Mouse
Choctawhatchee Beach Mouse
St. Andrews Beach Mouse

Ivory-billed
Woodpecker

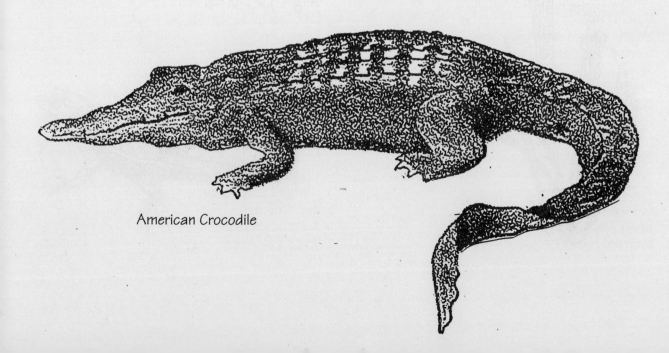

American Crocodile

Anastasia Island Beach Mouse
Perdido Key Beach Mouse
Sperm Whale
Lower Keys Marsh Rabbit
West Indian Manatee

Corals

Pillar Coral

Insects

Schaus' Swallowtail Butterfly

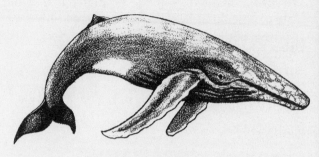

Humpback Whale

Molluscs

Stock Island Tree Snail

Plants

Tamarindillo
Golden Leather Fern
Fragrant Maidenhair Fern
Crenulate Lead Plant
Wild Columbine
Sicklepod
Blodgett's Wild-Mercury
Florida Three-Awned Grass
Curtiss' Milkweed
Green-Flowered Milkweed
Four-Petal Pawpaw
Auricled Spleenwort
Single Sorus Spleenwort
Dwarf Spleenwort
Bird's Nest Spleenwort
Aster (unnamed)
Nuttal's Rayless Goldenrod
Sinkhole Fern
Florida Bonamia
Little Strongback
Florida Brickell-Bush
Rattail Orchid
Fakahatchee Burmannia
Curtiss' Reedgrass
Robin's Bellflower
Leafless Orchid
Narrow Strap Fern
Baltzell's Sedge
Small-Flowered Lily-Thorn
Powdery Catopsis
Air Plant (unnamed)
Nodding Catopsis
Iguana Hackberry
Spiny Hackberry
Spurred Neottia

Fragrant Wool-Bearing Cereus
Aboriginal Prickly Apple
Simpson's Prickly Apple
Tree Cactus
Wedge Spurge
Wild Thyme Spurge
Garber's Spurge
Keys Hairy-Podded Spurge
Porter's Hairy-Podded Spurge
Porter's Broom Spurge
Southern Lip Fern
Pigmy Fringetree
Satinleaf
Florida Golden Aster
Cruise's Golden Aster
Balsam Apple (unnamed)
Large-Flowered Rosemary
Geiger Tree
Washington Thorn
Few-Flowered Croomia
Okeechobee Gourd
Cupania
Cowhorn Orchid
White Squirrel-Banana
Yellow Squirrel-Banana
Carolina Larkspur
Cuplet Fern
Long-Spurred Balm
Scrub Balm
Spotless-Petaled Balm
Shooting Star
Dollar Orchid
Dwarf Epidendrum
Acuna's Epidendrum
Trailing Arbutus
Wedge-Leaved Button Snakeroot
Red Stopper
Telephus Spurge
Small's Milkpea

Wiregrass Gentian
Wild Cotton
Lignum-Vitae Tree
Fuch's Bromeliad
Harper's Beauty
Mock Pennyroyal
Lakeside Sunflower
Liverleaf
Crested Coralroot
Green Violet
Highlands Scrub St. John's-Wort
Smooth-barked St. John's-Wort
Krug's Holly
Delicate Ionopsis
Wild Potato Morning Glory
Rocklands Morning Glory
Pineland Clustervine
Beach Clustervine
Cooley's Water Willow
Nodding Pinweed
Pine Pinweed
Harris' Tiny Orchid
Little People
Florida Gayfeather
Godfrey's Blazing Star
Licaria
Panhandle Lily
Sand Flax
Carter's Small-Flowered Flax
Carter's Large-Flowered Flax
McFarlin's Lupine
Hanging Club Moss
Curtiss' Loosestrife
White Birds-In-A-Nest
Hummingbird Flower
Ashe's Magnolia
Pyramidal Magnolia
Sea Lavender
Southern Barbara's Buttons
Alabama Milkweed
Anglepod (unnamed)
Florida Milkweed
Hidden Orchid
Pinesap (unnamed)
Pigmy-Pipes
Fall-Flowering Pleat-Leaf
Florida Beargrass
Scrub Beargrass
Burrowing Four-O'Clock
Dancing-Lady Orchid
Hand Adder's Tongue Fern

Semaphore Cactus
Giant Water Dropwart
Allegheny Spurge
Coastal Parnassia
Grass-Of-Parnassus
Paper-Like Nailwort
Everglades Peperomia
Cypress Peperomia
Pepper (unnamed)
Florida Peperomia
Pale-Green Peperomia
Spatulate Peperomia
Mahogany Mistletoe
Ninebark
Violet-Flowered Butterwort
Chapman's Butterwort
Panhandle Golden Aster
Everglades Poinsettia
Scrub Milkwort
Tiny Milkwort
Hairy Jointweed
Ghost Orchid
Scrub Plum
Buccaneer Palm
Beach Star
Snake Orchid
Small-Flowered Meadowbeauty

Key Deer

Mistletoe Cactus
Alabama Azalea
Orange Azalea
Chapman's Rhododendron
Miccosukee Gooseberry
Florida Royal Palm
St. John's-Susan
Bahama Sachsia
Heart-Leaved Willow
Bartram's Ixia
Nettle-Leaved Sage
White-Top Pitcherplant
Red-Flowered Pitcherplant
Tropical Curly-Grass Fern
American Chaffseed
Florida Skullcap
Fringed Campion
Gentian Pinkroot
Florida Pinkroot
Florida Keys Ladies' Tresses
Shade Betony
Narrow-Leaved Betony
Silky Camellia
Pride-of-Big-Pine

Bay Cedar
Florida Yew
Hattie Bauer Halberd Fern
Narrow-leaved Hoary Pea
Fuzzy-Wuzzy Air Plant
Florida Torreya
Florida Keys Noseburn
Lance-Leaved Wake-Robin
Young-Palm Orchid
Worm-Vine Orchid
Woods' False Hellebore
Coastal Vervain
Tampa Vervain
Ocala Vetch
Halberd-Leaved Yellow Violet
Clasping Warea
Carter's Mustard
Yellowroot
Karst Pond Yellow-Eyed Grass
Prickly Ash
Yellowheart
Simpson Zephyr Lily
Florida Jujube

Dodo

Florida's Skies

Florida has some of the most beautiful cloud formations and sunsets you'll ever see anywhere. The state also has some of the most devastating weather: lightning strikes here more often than anywhere else in the world; more hurricanes find landfall here than anywhere else in the world; tornadoes are frequent.

This section talks about some of the elements that cause Florida's weather and seasons, and ways anyone can use to predict the weather.

Chapter 26

The Air Around Us

The Wind
by Robert Louis Stevenson

I saw you toss the kites on high
And blow the birds about the sky;
And all around I heard you pass,
Like ladies' skirts across the grass—
O wind, a-blowing all day long,
O wind, that sings so loud a song!

I saw the different things you did,
But always you yourself you hid,
I felt you push, I heard you call,
I could not see yourself at all—
O wind, a-blowing all day long,
O wind, that sings so loud a song!

O you that are so strong and cold,
O blower, are you young or old?
Are you a beast of field and tree,
Or just a stronger child than me?
O wind, a-blowing all day long,
O wind, that sings so loud a song!

Surrounding Planet Earth is a huge blanket of air that we call atmosphere (AT-mus-feer; *atmo* means "vapor" and sphere refers to the globe of earth). It extends up more than 1,000 kilometers (621 miles) from the earth's surface. Air is held in by the gravity of the earth, getting thinner and thinner the farther out from earth it goes. This atmosphere protects earth from the intensity of the rays of the sun that could destroy life. Moisture, dust, and gases that are always in the air deflect or absorb most harmful rays before they reach the surface of the earth.

Air consists almost entirely of a constant mixture of 21% oxygen and 78% nitrogen. No matter whether the air is hot or cold, stormy or still, at sea level or in the upper atmosphere, the percentage of oxygen and nitrogen in the air remains the same.

The remaining one percent includes 0.9% argon, 0.03% carbon dioxide, and minute amounts of half a dozen other gases.

Oxygen is the odorless, colorless, and tasteless gas needed to keep all animals on earth—including humans—alive. Without it, all living things would die almost at once. Nitrogen combines with oxygen and other gases to form part of the tissues of all animal and plant matter.

People in Florida, where most of the land is close to sea level, are under constant pressure from the air of nearly 6.8 kilograms (15 pounds) per square inch. Our bodies are built to withstand this pressure, and even more, such as when we descend under water. In mountainous states, where people sometimes live 1.5 kilometers (a mile) higher than we do in Florida, the pressure is slightly less. Our bodies can adjust to the lighter atmosphere until we get up in an airplane about 3 kilometers (2 miles) high. Then airplanes need to pump in air to make it easier for passengers to breathe.

Earth's atmosphere provides enough lift for airplanes to fly and hot-air balloons to rise as high as about 19 kilometers (12 miles). Then the air becomes too thin for most of them to go any higher.

In Florida, almost all of the air density is in a layer about 11 kilometers (7 miles) thick, and virtually all "weather" occurs within this lowest layer of the atmosphere.

Air in Motion

Air in motion is called wind, but we often use many other names to describe it. Some—breeze, zephyr, or draft—tell of gentle, pleasant wind. Other names—gust, squall, blow, gale, tempest, tornado, cyclone, and hurricane—tell of wind moving in violent, dangerous ways.

Wind is caused by two main forces: the sun and the spinning motion of the earth. As the sun shines through the atmosphere, its rays warm the earth, and this heat is mostly radiated back into the atmosphere. Not all of the earth is heated the same—the area at the equator is warmer than the poles—so the radiated heat from the earth warms the air above it differently. Warm air rises, and the heavier cold air sinks. If the earth were stationary—if it didn't spin or move around the sun—the cold air at the poles would move continuously toward the equator, while the warm air at the equator would rise above the cold air and move toward the poles.

But the earth's rotation makes that pattern impossible. The spinning of the earth causes the air to move from east to west in some parts of the earth and from west to east in other parts.

The trade winds are the most constant. They are called trade winds because they were important in the days when trade and business between countries was done by sailing ships that depended upon constant winds to keep them on schedule. Trade winds occur in the tropics—the areas close to both sides of the equator—and they blow from the northeast in the Northern Hemisphere, and from the southeast in the Southern Hemisphere.

Many places on earth have their own peculiar winds that are not related to the overall pattern of winds around the earth. Mountains, for example, can cause local changes; cold air gathers on one side of a mountain range until it is pushed up and over the top and spills down into the valley on the other side with high-speed winds.

In the Northern Hemisphere, north of the easterly trade winds (where Florida is located), winds usually blow from the west, but they are not as steady as the trade winds are. They rise and swirl in constantly changing motion.

If you live near the coast, you may realize that during the day the beach becomes warmer than the ocean, which is so large and deep that its tem-

The storm surge is the most dangerous part of a hurricane.

perature remains more constant than the beach. Hot air over the beach rises, and cooler air moves in off the surface of the ocean to replace it, causing a cool breeze. At night, when the beach cools, the breeze blows off the land out over the ocean. The same thing can happen on a smaller scale near a lake.

Other factors that contribute to local weather conditions are natural areas with trees and developed areas with pavement and buildings. Black pavement and concrete buildings hold more heat than trees and woods, which affects surrounding air temperatures. The rising heat off pavement also causes winds and, if the air is moist, can precipitate rainfall as well.

Violent Weather

Florida is known for its frequent thunderstorms, lightning, tornadoes, and hurricanes.

Thunderstorms occur when warm air rises, sometimes to 20,000 meters, or 18 kilometers (60,000 feet, or more than 11 miles), causing the moisture in the air to condense into raindrops and fall. Or storms may occur when cold air from northern areas of the country moves southward in a "front" until it runs into warmer air, starting a rising and falling motion. Violent winds and lightning, and sometimes tornados, often accompany thunderstorms. Florida has more lightning strikes and deaths from lightning than any other state.

Tornadoes have the highest wind speeds of all wind storms—so strong, in fact, that meteorologists (mee-tee-yore-ALL-uh-jists), who study the weather, have never been able to measure their top speeds because the instruments are destroyed. Scientists think wind speeds may go higher than 645 km per hour (400 mph). Sometimes called twisters or cyclones, tornadoes are spirals of wind that drop down from a storm as hot air rises and cold air sinks.

Tornadoes can be a meter (a few feet) wide to half a kilometer (quarter of a mile) wide. They can move along the ground at about 65 km per hour (40 mph) and can scour the earth in a long path, or touch and skip. They usually last only a few minutes, but can cause tremendous destruction.

A hurricane, sometimes called a typhoon or tropical cyclone, needs both warm air and warm water to form. For this reason, hurricanes occur during the warmer months of summer and fall and always develop over the open ocean. A storm

Tornadoes cause great damage over a small path.

becomes a hurricane when it develops into a circular form caused by a combination of the rotation of the earth and a disturbance in the easterly trade winds, and when it reaches wind speeds of at least 45 kilometers per hour (74 mph). A hurricane always has an "eye" of still air in the center. Hurricanes in the Southern Hemisphere spin clockwise and in the Northern Hemisphere, counterclockwise. This kind of storm is called a typhoon when it develops in the western Pacific Ocean.

Hurricanes that affect Florida form over the south Atlantic Ocean, the Caribbean Sea, and the Gulf of Mexico. The Caribbean islands, Central America, Mexico, Texas, and, of course, Florida are where most of them strike land.

Hurricanes can reach wind speeds exceeding 325 km per hour (200 mph), and can cause flooding and wind damage over a 160-km-wide (100 miles) path. They move along the ground at about 16 to 19 km (10 to 12 miles) per hour. When they reach land, they begin to lose energy, which is why hurricanes rarely travel very far inland.

A hurricane usually drops 12 to 30 cm (5 to 12 inches) of rain, but sometimes rainfall can be as much as 38 cm (15 inches). The winds can strip trees bare or blow them down, take roofs off houses, or sweep cars from the roads. The greatest destruction from hurricanes, however, is caused by the "storm surge"—the wall of ocean that grows in front of the hurricane as it travels over the sea. The surge may be higher than 6 meters (20 feet) when it reaches the coast, causing great damage to houses and condominiums along the beach.

Tracking Hurricanes

The National Hurricane Center was set up in Miami in 1955. Before that, people were usually surprised by the big storms, not knowing when or where—or if—a hurricane was coming until it was nearly upon them. The National Hurricane Center locates the circling masses of air that could become a hurricane, and tracks them with airplanes, radar, and satellites. Since 1955, hurricanes have been given names in alphabetical order, with a new series of names selected each year. Before 1955, severe hurricanes were identified by the year in which they occurred, such as the terrible hurricanes of 1928 and 1935. Now we remember the bad ones by their names, such as "Hurricane Donna" in 1960 and "Hurricane Andrew" in 1992.

Many cities in Florida have plans for coping with a hurricane strike that include special routes for residents to use to leave the area, and storm shelters with blankets and food in sturdy, more inland buildings such as schools. Residents of ocean-front homes should always leave to wait out the storm in safer surroundings.

Barrier islands, off the mainland coast of Florida, are more likely than the mainland to be badly damaged by a hurricane. These barrier islands—actually just large sand bars that slow down the ocean surge—used to be a protection for the mainland. Storms would shift the sands of the islands, washing away parts of them and depositing sand in other places to make new islands. Now many of the islands themselves are covered with homes and hotels, and are dangerous places to be when a hurricane is approaching.

It still is impossible to tell exactly where a hurricane is going to go, but it is possible to warn residents of coastal and low-lying areas that a storm is on the way and could strike them. If a hurricane is coming your way, check your newspaper and listen to the TV or radio to find out what to do.

Air Pollution

Especially colorful sunsets are caused by the sun filtering through small particles of dust, smoke, and pollution suspended in the air. When the sun is overhead, it looks white or yellow because its rays are passing through much of the thinnest part of the atmosphere and only about 11 km (7 miles) of the lower atmosphere. When you watch the sun setting, you are looking at the sun through nearly 650 km (400 miles) of lower atmosphere! If the air contains much dust or smoke, the sun and the sky around it will look red.

Although sunsets are beautiful to look at, sometimes pollutants are present that can cause harm to plants and animals, including humans. All small particles of matter, whether natural or human-made, can be carried into the air by the wind. A small amount of dust and smoke is harmless, but a large amount is pollution.

Some natural particles are pollen from plants and light dust blown from the soil. Natural pollution can occur when forest fires or volcanoes blow large amounts of smoke or ash into the air. Some human-made particles, or pollutants, come from

Hurricanes spin counterclockwise in the Northern Hemisphere.

businesses such as coal- or oil-fired power plants, oil refineries, and paper mills. Exhaust from cars, buses, trucks, and airplanes, when combined with moisture, creates pollution called smog, a word that combines the two words, "smoke" and "fog." Fortunately for Florida, its cities have far less pollution than many other areas of the country because the constant breezes caused by the ocean blow it away.

A form of pollution that is invisible is carbon dioxide. In a natural balanced state, carbon dioxide is a by-product of people and other animals breathing in oxygen and exhaling carbon dioxide and other gases. The carbon dioxide is absorbed by plants, which then give off oxygen to be used again by animals.

When we clear the land of trees, however, we reduce the amount of vegetation that can use carbon dioxide. In addition, the burning of fuel—wood, oil, coal, or natural gas, for electricity, heating, powering automobiles, or even burning trash—causes more carbon dioxide to be released into the air. This extra carbon dioxide, with fewer trees to absorb it, adds to the increasing destruction of the ozone layer of the upper atmosphere. Ozone is an important gas that helps

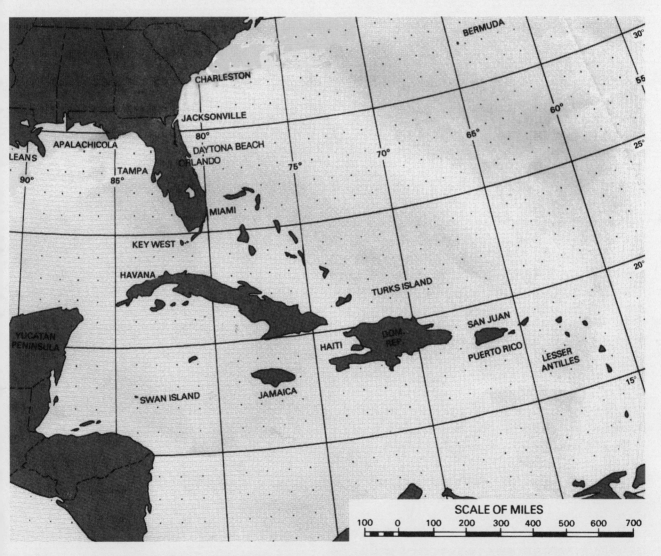

The Hurricane Center finds storms while they are still in the forming stages, and plots their paths on charts. You can plot them, too, on this chart by following the latitude and longitude coordinates given on radio and television when a storm is approaching. Charts are also printed in the newspaper and even on grocery bags.

protect us from many of the ultraviolet rays of the sun that cause sunburn and skin cancers.

Taking care of earth's atmosphere is as important as managing endangered wildlife. Do your part to help Planet Earth remain a good home for all living things, by planting trees and by walking and biking instead of going by car.

Where to learn more

See "The Keys" for more about how hurricanes affect animals.

See "The Panhandle" for more about barrier islands.

See "Water and Wetlands" for more about oxygen and gases.

See "Florida's Seasons" for more about earth movement and latitude and longitude.

See "Directions for the Crew of Spaceship Earth" for more about taking care of Planet Earth.

Do you know these words?

atmosphere	barrier islands
equator	gravity
hurricane	latitude
longitude	meteorologist
Northern Hemisphere	pollution
Southern Hemisphere	storm surge
trade winds	tropics

Chapter 27

Monitoring the Weather

The study of weather has been documented since 300 B.C., when Aristotle's pupil, Theophrastis, wrote *Book of Signs*, describing more than 200 signs of approaching rain, wind, or fair weather. Some signs were rather strange, referring to the behavior of sheep or crawling centipedes. But his book was the weather predictor's reference for the next 2,000 years!

Farmers were among those who most needed to know what tomorrow's weather would bring so they would know whether to cut the hay or wait, for rain would spoil it.

Sailors from the days of sailing ships knew: "Red sky at night, sailor's delight; red sky in the morning, sailors take warning." The description is still reasonably accurate for predicting the next day's weather. Because a red sunset is caused by the sun's rays glancing off dust particles, we infer that there is more dust than moisture in the air; therefore tomorrow will be less likely to bring rain.

But the closest people came in earlier times to scientific measurements was a bucket and ruler to measure rainfall and a weather vane to indicate wind direction.

Finally, in the 17th century, the development of instruments such as the barometer made it possible to make comparative measurements.

Farmers still hope for accurate forecasts to guide them, and many of them are excellent weather predictors, relying on observation, experience, and a few simple instruments.

Reading the clouds

In 1803, English meteorologist Luke Howard gave Latin names to three main cloud formations: cirrus, meaning "curl of hair"; cumulus, meaning "pile"; and stratus, meaning "spread out."

Cirrus (SEER-us) clouds look like wispy, wavy fibers, and are usually 6,000 to 12,000 meters (20,000 to 40,000 feet) above the ground. They are not rain clouds, but sometimes indicate distant storms whose winds are blowing these clouds ahead.

Cumulus (KYEW-mew-lus) clouds are those that pile thickly in the sky, rising from the bottom of the cloud, which may be only 2,400 meters (8,000 feet) above the earth, to the top of the cloud, which may be 13,500 meters (45,000 feet) high. These clouds are among Florida's most beautiful natural phenomena, taking anvil shapes or looking like faces or animals. Cumulus clouds are not rain clouds unless the tops climb extremely high (20,000 meters or 60,000 feet) and develop into clouds called cumulonimbus (KYEW-myew-low-NIM-bus). Tall, dark cumulonimbus clouds are the ones that bring thunderstorms.

Stratus clouds stretch out in long lines. They gather low over the earth, usually below 2,400 meters (8,000 feet). The solid gray cloud cover that often drops drizzly rain is made up of stratus clouds.

These three types have been combined to make cloud families and are divided into three sections by height:

- low clouds below about 3 kilometers (2 miles) called stratus, stratocumulus, and nimbostratus;

- middle clouds from 3 to 8 km (2 to 5 miles) called altocumulus and altostratus;

- high clouds from 8 to 9 km (5 to 6 miles) called cirrus, cirrostratus, and cirrocumulus.

The shapes, height, and movement of these clouds give strong clues to the weather.

Cirrocumulus clouds look like a thin sheet of ripples, called a mackerel sky. These clouds precede a warm front that will thicken as the storm nears. Before dropping rain, cirrocumulus clouds will become cirrostratus clouds, often causing a halo effect around the sun that announces rainfall within 24 hours.

Altocumulus clouds do not rise as high as the cumulus clouds. They are sometimes a sign of rain, especially when some begin to rise higher than others.

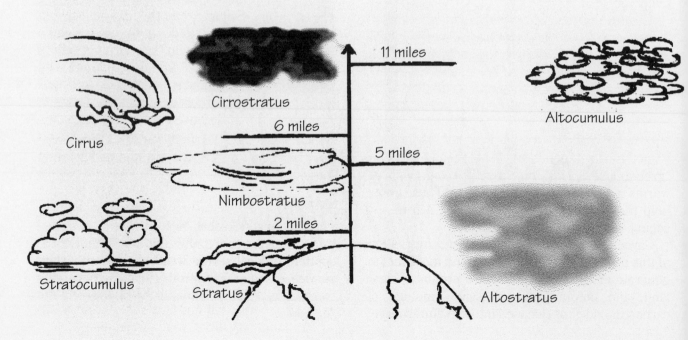

Cirrostratus

Cirrus

11 miles

6 miles

5 miles

Nimbostratus

2 miles

Stratocumulus

Stratus

Altocumulus

Altostratus

Altostratus clouds look like a layer of stratus clouds that is thin enough for the sun to illuminate it. When it increases, it is likely to indicate a long rain.

Nimbostratus clouds are altostratus clouds that have accumulated close to the ground, blotting out the sun and bringing continuous rain.

Stratocumulus clouds hang low in the sky in dark sheets or patches. They may come after a cold front passes through, and usually bring no rain, though rain is possible.

Weather instruments

A barometer is an instrument that measures the pressure of the air. The increase and decrease in the readings of a barometer scale indicate that the weather is going to change. If it increases, the weather will become clearer; if it decreases, there may be a storm approaching.

Being able to read the direction and speed of the wind is also important to predicting the weather. Most weather vanes are designed to show which direction the wind is blowing from, and an anemometer measures the speed of the wind.

A hygrometer measures the humidity (amount of moisture) in the air. Warm air is able to hold more moisture than cooler air without precipitating (raining), so the relative humidity is always related to the temperature.

And, of course, a thermometer indicates the temperature of the air.

The development of more sophisticated instruments has led to environmental discoveries which have caused worldwide interest and concern. You may have heard of some of these, such as global warming and acid rain.

Global warming

Planet Earth depends on a blanketing layer of "greenhouse gases" to keep the atmosphere warm enough for people to live here. These gases help trap the sun's heat, preventing it from escaping back into cold, dark space.

Carbon dioxide is the main gaseous ingredient of this blanket. As we burn more and more fuel to generate electricity, manufacture products, clear land, and power cars, excessive amounts of carbon dioxide are released into the atmosphere, trapping too much heat in the greenhouse blanket.

This process of accelerated warming of the atmosphere is called global warming. Sophisticated computer models input data on global temperatures, carbon dioxide concentrations, and many other complex physical, chemical, and energy interactions to interpret this warming trend.

Many scientists believe that if this warming trend continues, temperatures could increase by as much as 4.4° centigrade (7° F) by early in the next century. This could have disastrous consequences for Florida's environment, as well as its population, because rising sea levels from melting polar ice could flood beachfront property and increase saltwater contamination of the state's underground aquifers.

Acid rain

Acid rain is caused by an abundance of two main pollutants: sulfur dioxide resulting from burning coal, and nitrogen oxide that results from vehicle exhaust.

These pollutants rise high into the air and can be blown by winds to places very far from where they originate. A problem occurs when the pollutants and the moisture in the air combine chemically to form acid that falls to earth in the rain. Acid rain kills aquatic life in lakes and streams and damages forests, vegetable crops, buildings, and human health.

Acidity is measured as a pH reading; pH ranges from 0 through 14 with 7 being neutral. Normal rainfall has a reading of about 5.6. Any reading below 5.6 is acid rain.

In 1990, the National Audubon Society coordinated an acid rain monitoring program in the United States. Participants in Florida included teachers and their students, as well as other citizens. Early results showed that Florida received more acid rain during the months of April and August.

Skywarn

The National Weather Service has a program called Skywarn that trains and uses volunteers as spotters of local severe weather. This important service is something you might enjoy becoming involved in. Find the address for Skywarn in the Appendix.

Florida LakeWatch

If your school is near one of Florida's many lakes or you live near a lake yourself, and you have a boat or canoe you can use, you can help in another way by monitoring a different part of the water cycle.

Some Florida schools are participating in LakeWatch. LakeWatch is a University of Florida program that has created and organized an "early warning" system for lake eutrophication, the "aging" of a lake as organic sediments from decaying aquatic plants build up on the bottom.

Lakewatch volunteers take water samples from their lakes once a month to check on the amount of algae, the nitrogen and phosphorus content, and on how clear the water is. Laboratory tests are run on the samples.

The first sample is tested for algae. Algae are tiny plants that float in water. They are food for many tiny animals, but too much algae can deplete the oxygen level in the lake, causing odor, scum, and sometimes fish kills. You collect water in jugs from different places in your lake (the same places each month), take them to your "home laboratory," and filter them through a paper filter, saving the paper and the algae collected on it. The filters can be frozen until they can be delivered to or picked up by people from the University of Florida to be analyzed.

The second sample is tested for nitrogen and phosphorus, nutrients that fertilize plants, including plants that grow in the water. These nutrients wash into the lake from lawns, shrubs, and agricultural fields that are fertilized, and from detergents in cleaning products. You collect the samples in small bottles and freeze them for later analysis by the University of Florida.

The third test is measuring water clarity with a Frisbee-like disk, called a Secchi (SEH-key) disk, painted black and white and suspended from a rope. You lower the disk over the side of the boat into the water until it barely goes out of sight. Then you record how deep it was at that point according to the measurement on the marked rope. The clearer your lake, the deeper you will be able to see the Secchi disk. Silt, algae, and the natural color of the water all affect clarity.

LakeWatch hopes that information gathered by the volunteers will make it possible to spot changes in the quality of the lakes early enough to manage and protect them.

Florida LakeWatch has a booklet about the program, how to take samples properly, and what the test results will show. For information on how to contact LakeWatch, see the Appendix.

Your backyard weather station

Meteorology—the study of any aspect of the weather—is a complex science, but much of it involves using simple observations and experience to foretell what the weather is going to do next. With a small, backyard weather station, you can try your hand at predicting the weather—and you may learn to do it as well as the meteorologists can.

To monitor the weather you will need a thermometer, a hygrometer, a barometer, a weather vane, and an anemometer.

Begin by noting the temperature. Then, with a hygrometer, check the humidity. If the hygrometer shows an increase in moisture but the temperature remains the same, or if the temperature drops but the humidity remains the same, then rain is possible.

The barometer reads the pressure of the air. The rising and falling of the barometer indicates that the weather is going to change. If it's rising, the weather will probably clear up; if it's falling, the weather will likely become stormier.

Being able to read the direction of the wind with a weather vane and the speed of the wind with an anemometer is also important in predicting the weather. Again, changes in the normal direction and speed of the wind indicate a likely change in the weather.

Weather vane

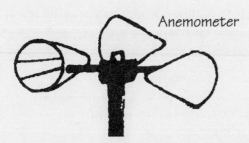

Anemometer

Wind sock

Some of the instruments in your backyard weather station can be made of things you have at home or can buy inexpensively.

Two thermometers, a shoestring, and a small jar, for example, can serve as a hygrometer to measure the moisture in the air. Mount the thermometers on a board so that you can read them side by side. Cut the tips off a shoestring and slip one end over the bulb of one of the thermometers. Put the other end of the shoestring into a jar of water. The thermometer with the wet shoestring on it will read a lower temperature because of the cooling effect of the water evaporation. The difference between the two readings can be compared to a relative humidity chart that tells how saturated the air is. This gives you a clue as to the possibility of rain.

An old method of telling the amount of moisture in the air was to hang a stick on a rope from a beam in the barn. If the rope absorbed moisture from the air, its fibers lengthened and unwound slightly, turning the stick. When the weather cleared, the rope shrank slightly and wound back up again.

You can make a hygrometer by bundling a few of your own hairs together and fastening one end of the bundle to a rod from which the hairs can hang freely. Tie a pointer to the other end. Stand a ruler on end nearby for a scale. When the hairs stretch or shrink with the moisture in the air, the pointer will indicate the change on your scale.

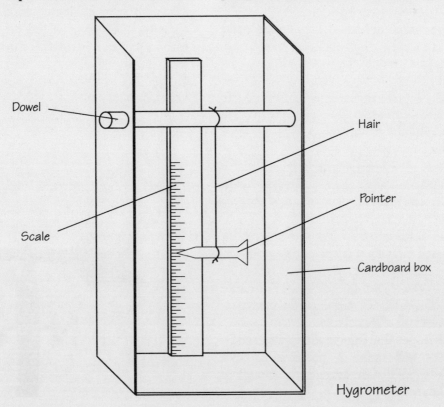

Dowel

Hair

Pointer

Scale

Cardboard box

Hygrometer

What direction the wind is coming from gives clues to the weather that is coming. When you know the prevailing winds in your location, any change in the direction will let you know that the weather will change. A simple weather vane can give you this information. Use a compass to set up your north-south-east-west marker in its proper orientation, and any arrow-shaped vane on a point that allows it to turn easily will point in the direction the wind is coming from.

Gauging the speed of the wind is more difficult. A wind sock, similar to those found at airports, will show you if the wind is still, blowing slightly, or blowing hard. An anemometer is the name of the instrument that measures wind speed. You can make an anemometer with three aluminum kitchen funnels mounted on a wheel that turns freely, such as a roller skate wheel. You can calibrate (determine and mark graduations of) the anemometer by holding it out the car window and counting revolutions while someone drives the car at various speeds.

Where to learn more

See "The Air Around Us" for more on ozone.
See "Prairies—Wet and Dry" for more on eutrophication.

Do you know these words?

acid rain	algae
anemometer	barometer
calibrate	cirrus
cumulus	eutrophication
global warming	humidity
hygrometer	meteorologist
meteorology	pH
pollutant	stratus
weather vane	

Chapter 28

Florida's Seasons

Some of the people who move to Florida from "up north" think that Florida has no change of seasons—only summer all year long. Native Floridians, on the other hand, think that some northern states such as Minnesota and Maine don't have any more seasons than Florida—they have only winter!

Climatic Seasons

Florida does, indeed, have four seasons, though they are more subtle than the striking contrast between snow and flowers. The lengths of the seasons, speaking climatically (related to the climate—sunshine, rain, temperature, etc.) rather than astronomically (related to the movement of the earth and sun), are not equal.

In south Florida, the changing of the seasons is even more subtle than other parts of the state. There, the difference relates more to rainfall than to temperature. It rarely gets as cold—or as hot—as central and northern Florida, but its summer rainy season and winter dry season usually are more pronounced.

Spring Spring comes earlier in Florida than in more northern states, stretching out over February, March, and April. Spring brings a fresh growth of leaves on trees and bushes (even evergreens such as pines and Live Oaks), the promise of no more chance of frost, gradually warmer temperatures, and—though flowers of some species or another bloom every month of the year in Florida—many plants begin blooming early in the year.

And in Florida, spring is "fall"—when new shiny needles and leaves push off the old, dry ones on pines, oaks, and other evergreen trees. The falling leaves of many trees carpet the lawn and woodland floor—in the spring!

Summer Summer is usually hot, rainy, and humid, and may last for nearly six months. Hot summer temperatures may begin as early as mid-March even in central Florida, though the mornings and evenings are usually still comfortable until late May or early June. By midsummer, the temperature rarely drops below 21°C (70°F) at night, and the daytime temperatures rise above 36°C (into the 90s F). Temperatures in cities are often as much as ten degrees higher than less developed areas with trees and bushes or coastal areas with offshore breezes.

The heat, moisture from lakes and sea, and ocean breezes cause cumulus clouds to pile high in the sky nearly every day, and rain falls frequently, often inches in an hour. The proximity of surface water (lakes, rivers, and oceans) provides a cooling influence, but the moisture combined with the heat raises the humidity, making some people uncomfortable because perspiration doesn't evaporate and cool the skin. Songbirds, however, seem to ignore the heat, singing and sometimes raising two or three families a season.

Fall Fall comes between late October, November, and early December. It begins when the days become noticeably shorter and you can tell a difference in the nighttime temperatures. Fall

Astronomical Seasons

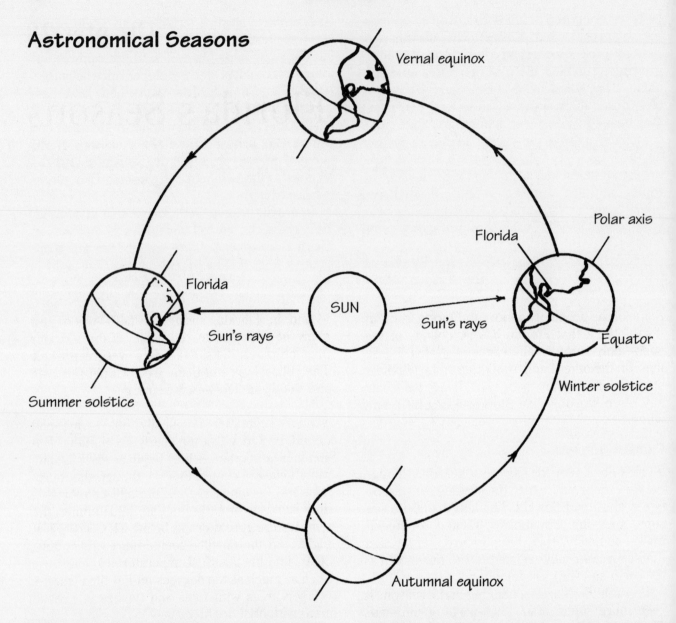

Asters and Goldenrods bloom purple and yellow. The leaves on deciduous trees, such as Wild Cherry, Red Maple, and Bald Cypress, begin to change color to yellows, reds, and browns. Though the fall colors are not as brilliant or as widespread as in the Great Smoky Mountains, they're here all the same, especially in wetland areas where Red Maples and Sweetgum grow thickly.

Fall is the time when migrating warblers and ducks fly through, or come to stay a while.

Winter   Winter in Florida may last only six or eight weeks. Deciduous trees lose their leaves, but buds begin to swell soon after. Chilly weather is short-lived, with cold fronts often lasting only a few days. In south Florida, the temperature may never drop below 15°C (60°F), while in north Florida there may be nights when frost is heavy and the temperature dips several degrees below freezing. Snow flurries cause headlines in north Florida newspapers every few years.

Certain plants bloom in the winter: the exotic Christmas Poinsettia, of course, and the native Carolina Jessamine and some of the beautiful Florida grasses. The berries on the Beauty Berry bushes turn glossy purple and the holly berries turn bright red, and they hang on the branches all winter for birds to eat.

Many plants have a short period of dormancy when they are not actively growing. Tropical species that have been planted too far north may be severely injured or killed by a drop in temperature or a cold wind. Native ferns, shrubs, and grasses look brown and dead, only to begin growing again after the first rain and a little sunshine. The Florida Black Bear and Opossums slow down their activities and sleep more, but they never go into a true hibernation (becoming completely inactive for weeks) as they do farther north.

Migratory ducks stay a short while during the winter months, seeking refuge in sheltered marshes and wetland creeks. It seems a very brief time before they fly back through again, going north.

Keep a section in your journal for a full year on the changes you observe as the seasons roll by.

Astronomical Seasons

So, what causes "seasons" anyway?

Astronomers (uh-STRON-uh-mers) explain that the seasons are caused by the movement of the earth around the sun. Astronomy is the scientific study of the earth's relationship to the sun, the moon, the other planets, the stars, and all celestial bodies, and how they move.

Seasons on earth are caused by the earth's tilt. An imaginary line that runs through the center of the earth from the North Pole to the South Pole is called the polar axis. The earth spins on this axis once every 24 hours, causing one cycle of day and night.

But this axis is not perpendicular to the path of the earth's yearly orbit around the sun. If it were, the sun would be directly above the equator at all times. Instead, the North Pole always points out in space toward the North Star (also called Polaris, or the Pole Star). This causes the earth to have a permanent tilt that makes the sun's rays fall at different angles at different times of the year.

The Solstices The moment when the North Pole is tilting its farthest away from the sun—on or about December 22 every year—is called the winter solstice (*solstice* means "sun-stop"). When the earth is at the opposite side in its orbit around the sun, the North Pole tilts toward the sun, and Florida and the rest of the Northern Hemisphere receive the sun's rays more directly. The moment when the North Pole tilts most toward the sun, which occurs on or about June 22, is called the summer solstice. In Orlando, the noonday sun at the summer solstice strikes at an angle of 85° from the horizontal.

The earth is not its hottest at the summer solstice or its coldest at the winter solstice because it takes a long time for the earth—both land mass and ocean mass—to warm and cool.

(In the Southern Hemisphere, summer and winter are opposite from the Northern Hemisphere. June is the beginning of winter and December is the beginning of summer. Can you visualize why?)

In the illustration, you can see that in summer the rays of the sun fall more directly on the Northern Hemisphere and in winter they are more sharply angled. The energy of heat and light is less intense when the rays are angled, as in winter, than when they are direct, as in summer, when the rays of the sun fall nearly straight toward the earth.

Try this simple experiment. Shine a flashlight onto the wall from a few feet away, aiming the flashlight straight at the wall. You will see a circle of light on the wall perhaps several centimeters (a few inches) in diameter. Now, without changing the distance of the flashlight from the wall, tilt it slowly upward. The same amount of light energy will gradually spread out over a considerably larger area, but it will not be quite as bright as when the flashlight was pointed straight at the wall. The amount of the sun's energy that reaches the earth changes from summer to winter in a similar way.

High angle—concentrated energy

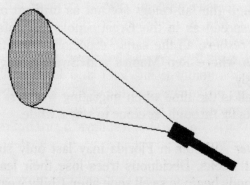

Low angle—spreads out energy

The Equinoxes The seasons of spring and autumn begin when the earth is in a position in its orbit that places the sun directly above the equator at noon. At this time, day and night are exactly equal at the equator, and the event is called the equinox (*equi-* = "equal" and *nox* = "night"). The vernal, or spring, equinox occurs on or about March 21 each year, and the autumnal, or fall, equinox occurs on or about September 23.

Surprisingly, if you count the days between the dates of the seasons, you'll notice that the astronomical seasons are not the same length. This is because the earth does not move at the same speed throughout its orbit because it is not moving in a perfect circle around the sun—almost, but not quite. The orbit is slightly eliptical. The earth slows down as it approaches the aphelion (the part of its orbit farthest from the sun; *helion* means "sun") and speeds up as it approaches the perihelion (the part of its orbit closest to the sun). Therefore, the time interval between the spring equinox and the fall equinox is longer than between the fall equinox and the next spring equinox.

Because of the tilt, the length of daylight changes throughout the year also. Astronomers are able to pinpoint mathematically the exact fraction of a second when these changes occur. The longest day of the year is a single summer day, on or about June 22. But it is only seconds longer than the three or four days before it and the three or four days after it. In Miami, there are eight days with 13 hours and 49 minutes between sunrise and sunset. In Orlando, there are eight days of 14 hours and one minute. In Tallahassee, the longest eight days are 14 hours and nine minutes.

The shortest day of the year occurs on the winter solstice, on or about December 21, when the sun is at its farthest south. In Miami, at the winter solstice, the sun rises at 7:05 a.m. and sets at 5:35 p.m. Eastern Standard Time. Again, there are several "shortest" days on either side of that date, each 10 hours and 30 minutes long, but the sun is actually rising later and later until the middle of January, and the sun is setting its earliest a week or so before December 21.

In Orlando, the shortest days are 10 hours and 18 minutes long. In Tallahassee, the shortest days are 10 hours and 10 minutes long. The shortest days in Minneapolis, Minnesota, however, have only 8 hours and 45 minutes of daylight, while the longest have nearly 15 hours and 30 minutes!

The lengths of the days at the vernal and autumnal equinoxes are 12 hours and seven minutes in Miami, Orlando, and Tallahassee.

Check the information in your newspaper that gives you sunrise and sunset times each day, and pinpoint the date of equal day and night where you live.

Did you know that at the North Pole the longest day lasts for six months? Can you explain why the longest day is longer farther north?

Why Florida is Warm in Winter

In far north latitudes, the sun is never as high in the sky as it is in Florida. The heat from the sun's slanting rays, passing through more of the earth's atmosphere, is absorbed by the atmosphere, causing less of the warmth to reach the earth when the sun is low on the horizon than when it is high overhead. This makes winters colder in places closer to the North and South poles than it ever gets in places closer to the equator, such as Florida. Near the equator, the noonday sun is nearly directly overhead year-round. In Florida and other places along the lower latitudes, the sun is high overhead for part of the year and lower above the horizon at other times, even at midday.

Since oceans make up the biggest part of the earth's mass, they help moderate the temperatures of coastal areas such as Florida, which has much smaller seasonal temperature variations than inland areas.

Another feature of Florida that keeps it warm is its lack of mountains. The warmth we feel is caused by the earth's absorption of the heat from the sun and then its slow release back into the air. Places where the atmosphere is closer to sea level and heavier are warmer than on the tops of high mountains where the air is thinner and holds less heat.

Twilight

Twilight is the time between the setting of the sun and darkness. Because light rays can be bent by the atmosphere, we see the glow from the sun after the sun has gone below the horizon, causing the brief period called twilight.

If you moved to Florida from a northern state, you may be surprised that Florida doesn't have the long twilight that you are used to, for in far north states twilight may last an hour and 50 minutes in the winter to as long as two hours and 45 minutes in the summer.

If you have lived all your life in Florida, you may not even know that "up north" in the summertime the evening often stays light enough for outside activities for nearly three hours after the sun sets. In Florida, twilight lasts about an hour and a half year-round, varying by only 12 minutes from summer to winter.

Speaking astronomically, twilight is the time between sunset and when the sun reaches 18° below the horizon. If you think about the angle of the sun as it falls below the horizon, you can see that in northern latitudes, it would take longer for the sun, descending at a shallow angle, to reach a point 18° below the horizon. In Florida, where the sun descends almost straight, the sun would reach 18° below the horizon more quickly.

Wherever you live in Florida, if you pay attention to where on the horizon the sun rises and sets each day, you will observe that the sun rises farther north on the eastern horizon and sets farther north on the western horizon in the summer; and it rises and sets farther and farther south as the year changes to winter.

The Night Sky

The North Star has been a guiding light for mariners and wilderness hikers for centuries. Its position in the sky relative to any point on earth never changes, for the earth's polar axis always points to the North Star. In Florida, the North Star

Twilight is a good time to see wildlife, for diurnal animals are settling down for the night and nocturnal animals are beginning to stir.

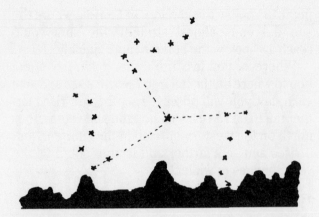

The Big Dipper appears to circle the North Star throughout the night.

is fairly low in the north sky. If you can find the Big Dipper constellation and watch it at different times of the night and year, it will appear to be swinging around the North Star. Sometimes the Big Dipper will be below the horizon. At other times it will be higher in the sky. But always a line connecting the stars on the front of the cup will point to the North Star.

Years ago the stars in the night sky appeared to be much brighter than they seem today. The bright lights of cities cause "light pollution" by filling the sky above them with an artificial brightness that dims the stars.

Many parts of Florida are still dark enough to see the beauty of the night sky, but most people live too near city lights. Even nearby streetlights and lighted billboards will prevent good nighttime viewing. Most light pollution is caused by improperly installed lighting and could be reduced (and energy saved) by aiming outdoor fixtures downward instead of upward, by using reflectors to direct light where people need it, by using electrically efficient lamps such as sodium vapor, and by turning off unneeded lights, such as those on billboards, in the middle of the night.

Why don't you write a letter to your newspaper or your county commissioners suggesting some of these ways to prevent "wasted" light?

If you have the opportunity, be sure to take time to gaze at the marvels of the night sky from a dark place. If you can get 32 kilometers (20 miles) or more away from the glow of city lights, you can see the mass of stars called the Milky Way. When skywatching at night, allow your eyes to adjust to the darkness for about 30 minutes. Using binoculars will make it possible to see many more stars, and leaning back in a lounge chair will make it easier to watch the stars higher in the sky. According to an astronomer, three places with especially good conditions for seeing the stars and planets include the Florida Keys, near Chiefland in north central Florida, and at Lake Kissimmee State Park.

Where to learn more

See "Speaking of Trees" for more about autumn colors.
See "The Everglades" for more on wet and dry seasons.
See "Monitoring the Weather" for more about clouds.

Do you know these words?

aphelion	astronomical
astronomy	atmosphere
celestial	climatic
constellation	cumulus
dormancy	equator
equinox	evaporate
hibernation	horizon
humidity	latitude
migrating	Northern Hemisphere
orbit	perihelion
season	solstice
Southern Hemisphere	twilight

Your Part in Florida's Future

Chapter 29

Environmental Careers

Have you ever been asked, "What do you want to be when you grow up?"

Perhaps you've already given it some thought, and have decided that a career working in an environmental field is for you.

With an increasing awareness and concern for the welfare of animals and the protection of the environment, many people are turning their interests into a rewarding profession (profession: an occupation or vocation, especially one requiring specialized knowledge and sometimes long preparation).

The last few decades have seen a steady increase in career opportunities in environmental protection and wildlife conservation. Because the environment affects almost every aspect of our lives, the list of job possibilities is a long one: environmental attorney, landscape architect, wildlife researcher, forester, environmental writer, wildlife manager, wildlife veterinarian, park ranger, science teacher, camp counselor, public health officer, secretary, artist, and many more.

Some jobs will keep you in an office most of the time, others in a laboratory looking through a microscope, and still other jobs will send you into the fields and swamps. Some jobs allow you to do all of these. Employers can be government agencies, private corporations, or nonprofit organizations.

How do you prepare yourself for an environmental job? Many young people are already gaining valuable experience by volunteering their time to help with conservation programs in their schools and communities. Some are members of conservation groups such as the Audubon Society and Sierra Club, or participate in Scouting and 4-H Clubs. Many of these organizations offer nature walks, camping trips, and other outdoor adventures, and perform conservation service projects. Joining any of these organizations will give you experience in outdoor activities and knowledge of Florida's natural history.

In the summer months, the Florida Division of Forestry and the Florida Game and Fresh Water Fish Commission offer special camps that provide exciting opportunities for nature study, hiking, and boating on state lands. Many churches, garden clubs, and nature centers also offer summer camp programs that specialize in Florida's ecology.

Sometimes participants return in later years as counselors where they share the information they learned about the environment with new campers. These summer experiences can help you find out what interests you the most and the special talents you have, and can help you plan what courses to take during your high school years or in college.

Most jobs involved with conservation work will require you to have one or more college degrees, and for this reason, your academic preparation in high school is very important. A strong background in math and the sciences—biology, chemistry, and physics—as well as computer and communications skills will increase your chances of being accepted by a college or university that offers an environmental program. Many environmental jobs require the ability to write clear, concise reports, so remember the importance of your

English writing courses. Participation in extracurricular activities, such as science and ecology clubs or writing for student newspapers, can help you gain additional experience. And don't forget the importance of good grades.

Occasionally high schools offer opportunities to work with businesses and other groups doing conservation work in your community. Your guidance counselor at school will be able to give you this information and can guide you toward the course work you need.

Here are some of the activities of various scientific professions:

Botanist

Botany is the scientific study of plants, and a botanist is a scientist who studies plants. Botanists look at everything from the vastness of the forest to the tiny parts of plants that can be seen only with a microscope.

Field botanists apply their knowledge in the marshes, flatwoods, and prairies, searching for plants and studying how and where they grow.

Some botanists research old manuscripts to find out what plants were described and named many years ago. Others study prehistoric plants and plant fossils. Some study the parts of plants under a microscope, or make collections of dried, pressed samples for study or for preservation in museums. Others specialize in botanical photography or illustration. Still others specialize in studying trees, wildflowers, or marine plants (plants that grow in the sea), or some other part of the vast field of botany.

Botanists can work in plant nurseries, for park and forest services, for government agencies, and for developers and landscapers. They can become professors in colleges and universities and do research on plants, writing about their discoveries.

Ornithologist

Ornithology is the study of birds, and an ornithologist specializes in birds. Many ornithologists work in the field, counting species and numbers of birds, or numbers of nests of particular species, or watching a single pair of birds to document their behavior from courtship to nest-building to raising their family. Some capture birds, weigh them, check their health, band them with identification tags, and release them, in order to find out more about bird populations and their habitats, and ways to recover endangered and threatened species.

Some ornithologists work in the laboratory, preserving skins of birds that have died. Bird skins include all the feathers and features of the bird, but the internal organs have been removed. The skins make it possible to carefully check small differences between species, such as length and width, coloring and markings. Scientists can check parasites, stomach contents, fat content in the tissues, and other details. Genetic and DNA studies give clues to the relationships between closely related species.

Some ornithologists concentrate on the mysteries of migration, or study fossil birds from archeological finds. High-speed photography makes it possible to stop the motion of birds in flight so ornithologists can study how they take off and land, soar and hover. New techniques for recording sounds enable ornithologists to study bird vocalizations and "languages."

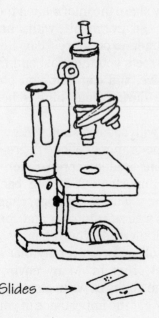

Slides →

Meteorologist

Meteorology is the scientific study of the weather, and a meteorologist is a scientist who studies the weather. The "weatherman" on TV is not the only job for a meteorologist. Meteorology is a scientific field that still has more questions than answers. Research is ongoing and will be for a long time.

Those in basic research look for answers to the age-old questions about weather, climate, the atmosphere, and prediction, using new technologies such as meteorological satellites and Doppler radar.

Those in applied research take the basic data and fit it to a specific application, such as communications, airplane design, conservation of water resources, city planning, and many other fields.

Operational meteorologists use the results of applied research to benefit clients, including farmers, utility industries, governments, and aviation.

Engineering meteorologists apply knowledge to buildings, highways, or bridges in an effort to make them withstand the atmospheric environment.

Other environmental careers:

Biologist: studies all living organisms.

Ecologist: studies the interrelationships between plants and animals, and their habitats.

Entomologist: studies the biology of insects.

Geologist: studies the rock and soil formations of the earth.

Herpetologist: studies the biology of reptiles and amphibians.

Marine biologist: studies both plants and animals in the sea.

Zoologist: studies the biology of animals (birds, reptiles, mammals, insects, etc.).

Where to learn more

See "Insects are not just 'Bugs'!" for more on entomology.

See "Alligators, Snakes, and Other Reptiles" for more on herpetology.

Do you know these words?

Can you list them in alphabetical order?

environment	profession
conservation	species
subspecies	biology
ornithology	herpetology
zoology	marine biology
entomology	geology
ecology	botany
meteorology	prehistoric

Chapter 30

Directions for the Crew of Spaceship Earth

A central Florida student, who was a sixth grader when she wrote a letter to the Florida Audubon Society, said, "I am concerned about the problems our earth is facing every day! . . . Many things need to be done in the near future, but the biggest thing that needs to be done is for everyone to do their part by not littering our earth. . . . I never realized that pollution was such a severe problem. I think we could improve the problem if everyone did their part by recycling and placing all their other trash in the garbage. With everyone's help and support we can make our world a cleaner, more beautiful place to live."

We all wonder how we can ever do enough to pick up all the litter, save all the wildlife, and make all our lakes and rivers and oceans clean again. When you learn in school or see programs on television about all the problems—the hole in the ozone layer in our atmosphere, the tangled fishing lines and lost hooks that injure birds, the pollution of lakes that we used to swim in, the forests that are being cut down—you wonder how just one person can possibly do enough to be of any use.

But if two million Florida students do something, think how much can be accomplished! Set yourself a goal of doing at least one new conservation project each month, until you and your family have made a habit of doing all of these, and more.

Recycle

One of the most important single things you can do is recycle as many things as possible. Your grandparents, who probably lived through World War II, may remember the slogan from that era: "Fix it up, use it over, wear it out." In those war days, children washed steel ("tin") food cans, peeling off the labels, cutting out the ends, and stamping them flat for recycling. They made many things serve longer, composted their vegetable garbage, and used paper and clothing many times, instead of throwing them in the landfill.

You can do it, too, at school and at home.

- Recycle aluminum and steel cans, glass and plastic bottles, newspapers and school papers, and telephone books.

- When you help with yard work, leave the grass clippings on the lawn, or put them around plants to enrich the soil and hold in moisture (instead of buying chopped-up cypress trees for mulch). Or put them in a compost pile along with vegetable scraps from the kitchen to turn into soil that can be used

around flowers and shrubs, or for house plants.

- Instead of throwing away broken toys, books you've read, games you don't play with any more, or your old bike, share them with other kids by taking them to the Salvation Army or Goodwill Industries where they will be repaired and reused.

Don't litter

- Don't throw even a chewing gum wrapper (or your chewed gum) on the ground. If your parents smoke, try to convince them to not throw their cigarette butts on the ground.

- If you go fishing, never leave behind your tangled fishing line. Birds, fish, and other animals can accidentally get caught in it, and suffer terribly when no one can help them.

- Other plastic items, such as six-pack rings, harm wildlife, too. Even if you throw them away properly, be sure every loop is cut so that no animal at the landfill can get caught in it.

- Polystyrene foam cups and "peanut" or "popcorn" packaging never decay in the natural environment. Sea turtles and birds eat them, thinking they're food. Avoid using them any

time, anywhere, and talk to those who use them at club meetings or public places to see if you can convince them to use mugs and cups made of glass, china, or pottery.

- Balloons filled with helium and released at parties and festivals are another hazard to wildlife. Don't participate in any balloon release, and tell people that balloons and their strings can hurt animals. Remember that Florida passed a law prohibiting the release of ten or more helium-filled balloons at a time.

- Use cloth clean-up rags, napkins, and handkerchiefs that can be washed and used over and over again instead of paper towels, paper napkins, and tissues. Thousands of trees are cut down every year to make these paper products that end up in the landfill after one use.

What else can you add to this list?

Shopping

- Take a cloth bag with you when you go shopping with your folks. If you use paper and plastic bags, recycle them as garbage bags in your own kitchen, or take them back to the store to bring home your new order of groceries or for recycling.

- You can buy notebook paper made from recycled paper. It is important to buy and use products made from the items we recycle.

- Reuse your lunchbags, or buy a lunchbox that you can use over and over again. Plastic baggies and aluminum foil can be washed and used again to hold sandwiches and cookies. Use a thermos to hold your drink instead of buying individual juice cartons that cannot be recycled.

- Buy a pen and pencil set that can be refilled instead of thrown away when the ink or lead runs out.

- Try to find crayons that are made from beeswax, and buy water-based paints and markers instead of those made from petroleum products.

What else can you add to this list?

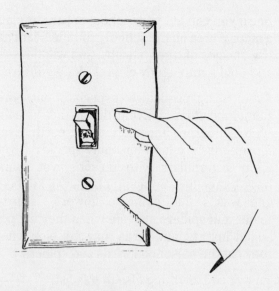

Energy conservation

Making electrical power is a process that pollutes both air and water. The less electrical power we use in our homes and schools, the less power companies have to produce. You can save power in many ways, and—though each little bit may seem too small to make any difference—the total is large.

- Don't hold the refrigerator door open to "look over" the contents.

- Turn off the lights and TV when not in use.

- Open doors and windows when the outside temperature is comfortable instead of using the air conditioner, but be sure to keep doors closed when the heater or the air conditioner is running.

- Shut off unused rooms from heat or AC.

- Walk or ride your bike instead of asking someone to drive you in a car.

- Plant a tree that will shade your house.

- Don't waste hot water. Hot water heaters use lots of power.

- Sit by a window to read, using natural light instead of electric light.

- Even batteries pollute when thrown away. Buy a battery charger and rechargeable batteries for your flashlights, radios, and clocks.

What else can you add to this list?

Water conservation

The change in Florida's rain cycle has caused an ongoing drought that has lowered lake levels and reduced the amount of water in the state's underground aquifers. With more and more people moving to Florida and needing their portion of the state's supply of drinking water, water conservation needs to become an important part of everyone's thinking.

Saving water is just as simple as saving power.

- Tell your parents if you know of any drippy faucets in your house that need fixing. An amazing amount of water is wasted when faucets drip.

- Don't stand under the shower longer than needed to get clean.

- Water the lawn only when it begins to wilt, and never during the hot part of the day when the water evaporates more rapidly. Many towns in Florida have water conservation measures that require people to water only during cooler hours on certain days. Check the newspaper or call the water company or your Water Management District to find out what rules apply to your house. Make sure your lawn sprinkler waters the grass, not the street.

- When you're asked to wash the car, do it on the grass so the water helps the lawn instead of going into the gutter and down the storm drain. Wet the car with the hose, then turn the hose off while you wash the car with soapy water from a bucket. Then rinse it with the hose.

- Don't let the water run when brushing your teeth.

Simple, isn't it? What else can you add to this list?

Helping wildlife

Did you know that the best thing you can do for wildlife is to leave it alone? Young birds leave the nest when they get big enough to grow flight feathers. They often hop around in the bushes and on the ground for a few days, but they are not lost or abandoned. The parents are nearby, caring for them and feeding them and sheltering them

from rain and nighttime chill. Don't try to rescue them unless you know that the parents are dead.

- If a storm blows down a nest of tiny, unfeathered birds, you can replace the nest in the tree and put the baby birds back in it. The parents will find them by their chirping. If the nest is destroyed, you can put its pieces or some shredded newspaper in a berry basket or small box. Put the babies in the box and tie the box back in the tree close to where the nest was found. The parent birds will not reject their babies if you have touched them, but handle them as little as possible because you can easily injure them.

- You can help all kinds of wildlife by leaving part of your yard less "neat." Don't plant it with grass or mow it. Plant it with native plant species, or let it grow back to weeds. If a tree in your yard should die, encourage your parents to leave it standing for woodpeckers and make this your wildlife area. The dead tree can be tied up to a nearby sturdy tree with a rope to keep it from falling. Put a small pile of sticks or short logs in your wild area for lizards and beetles to live under. Put up a birdhouse, a bird feeder, and a birdbath. What fun you'll have watching your wildlife patch!

- See if you can get your school to save or plant a natural area on the school grounds. Plant native species of trees, shrubs, and wildflowers, and hold nature study classes along your trail.

- Avoid using pesticides, especially outdoors. Remember that all living things, not just the "cute" ones, are important to the earth. Even mosquitoes are food for many species. If you spray caterpillars with poisons, you won't have butterflies. Spraying plants will kill bees and wasps that pollinate flowers. Lizards, toads, and spiders may die when they eat poisoned insects, and birds may get sick when they eat the poisoned lizards and spiders.

Can you add anything else to this list?

Pets

Pets are great fun, but they are also a responsibility. The best kind are domesticated animals such as dogs and cats, not exotic animals such as parrots and snakes.

Never take wild animals for pets. Wild animals belong in their natural homes. Besides, they are often difficult to care for and can become dangerous. In Florida, capturing a wild animal for a pet is against the law.

Cats and dogs should be neutered to prevent unwanted kittens and puppies. If your cat roams outside, put a bell on its collar so birds can be warned in time to fly away. Train your dog to come when it's called and to take care of its needs in the same place every day in your own yard. Prevent your pet from chasing birds or other animals.

Even though these suggestions seem like little things, each one is important. They don't sound too hard, do they? You just need to remember to do them often enough so that they become a habit.

Where to learn more

See "Speaking of Trees" for more about cypress mulch.

See "The Fun of Watching Birds" for more on helping birds.

See "Florida's Native Plants" for more on making a wildlife patch.

Do you know these words?

aquifer	atmosphere
compost	conservation
drought	exotic
flight feathers	mulch
ozone	pollinate
pollution	

A great Englishman named Edmund Burke once said, "Nobody made a greater mistake than he who did nothing because he could only do a little."

The authors hope that reading this book about the nature of Florida will encourage you to help preserve and protect its special places, plants, and animals.

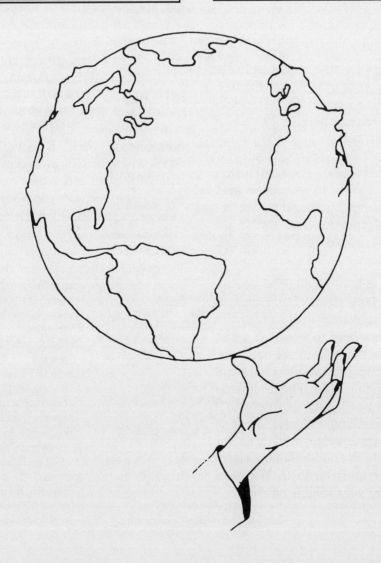

Glossary

A

acid rain—an airborne mixture of sulphur dioxide from burning coal and other fossil fuels and moisture, which results in sulphuric acid, or acid rain.

adapt—change to fit into new conditions. (adapted)

agate—a stone composed of layers of quartz of different colors.

agatize—to change into agate as when silica (sand) replaces coral. (agatized)

aigrettes (A-grets)—the wispy feathers that grow on herons and egrets during breeding season.

algae (AL-jee; this is the plural; the singular is alga, pronounced AL-guh)—a group of usually green plants, some of them microscopic, such as seaweeds and pond scum that often grow in water.

amateur—one who engages in a science or pursuit as a hobby or pastime, not as a professional.

amphibian (am-FIB-ee-un)—an animal such as a toad or frog that begins life in fresh water, then changes into an animal that can live on land.

anemometer (an-uh-MOM-uh-ter)—an instrument for measuring wind speed.

animal—a member of the Animal Kingdom; mammals, birds, insects, reptiles, etc.

annual—a plant that lives for only one year, or one growing season.

aphelion (a-FEEL-yun)—the point in a planet's orbit when it is farthest from the sun.

aquatic (uh-KWAT-ik)—pertaining to water.

aquifer (AK-wif-er)—a underground layer of rock that holds water.

arboreal (ar-BOR-ee-ul)—describes a species that climbs trees.

astronomy (uh-STRON-uh-me)—the study of celestial bodies, including the earth and sun. (astronomist)

atlas—a book of maps.

atmosphere (AT-mus-feer)—the blanket of air surrounding the earth, which is held in by gravity.

B

barometer (bar-OM-uh-ter)—an instrument for measuring air pressure; changes in air pressure indicate a coming change in the weather.

barrier island—a sand bar off the coast of Florida or other coastlines that protects the mainland from waves and storms.

biennial (by-EN-ee-ul)—a plant that grows for two years before putting out seeds and dying.

binocular vision—the ability to look at something with both eyes.

binomial (by-NOME-ee-ul)—the two Latin or Greek words, or words given Latin endings, that identify a species.

biodiversity (by-oh-duh-VER-sit-ee or by-oh-dye-VER-sit-ee)—the total variety of biological organisms on earth.

biology (by-ALL-uh-jee)—the scientific study of living things. (biologist)

bird of prey—a raptor; a bird with strong talons and hooked beak for capturing and tearing live animals to eat.

birdbanding—a scientific method of identifying birds by attaching metal bands around their legs.

birder (birders)—a serious, amateur bird watcher.

birdwatching—the study of birds seen in their natural habitat, usually by amateurs.

blight—a plant disease causing discoloration, wilting, and death.

boot (boots)—the stub of a broken frond on a palm tree, particularly the Sabal Palm.

botany—the scientific study of plants. (botanical, botanist)

brackish—slightly salty water.

breeding plumage—the special, often colorful, feathers that grow on birds when they are ready to attract a mate.

bromeliad (bro-MEE-lee-ad)—a family of plants that often live attached to other plants, including Spanish moss and the pineapple.

C

calibrate—to mark with graduations on a measuring device.

calyx (KAY-lix)—the outermost whorl of flower parts; the sepals.

camouflage—coloring or markings that make it possible for an animal to blend with its surroundings.

canopy—the highest level of foliage in a forest.

carapace (KARE-uh-pase)—the top part of the shell of a turtle.

carnivore—a flesh-eating animal.

carrion (KARE-ee-un)—dead animals, which may be used as food by other animals.

caterpillar—the larval stage in the life cycle of a butterfly or moth.

cavity—a hole or hollow place. (cavities)

celestial (suh-LES-chul)—pertaining to the sky.

chitin (KYE-tin)—a material similar to fingernails that forms the outer covering of many insects.

chrysalis (KRIS-uh-lis)—the case enclosing the stage in a butterfly's life when it metamorphoses (changes) from larva to adult.

circum-Gulf—around the Gulf of Mexico, referring to bird migration.

cirrus (SEER-us)—referring to clouds that look like wispy, wavy fibers.

Class—part of the scientific system of naming things, below Subphylum.

climatic—pertaining to the climate, or weather conditions, of an area.

cocoon—the silky outer wrapping of an insect larva in the pupa stage.

cold-blooded—describing an animal such as a reptile whose body temperature is regulated by the temperature of the air and soil around it.

cold front—the forward edge of a moving mass of cold air.

community—the variety of plants and animals occupying an area.

compost—a mixture of decaying vegetation used for fertilizer.

compound—describing a leaf that is made up of two or more leaflets.

conservation—preserving (natural resources) from loss, harm, or waste.

constellation—a group of stars that have been given a name, such as Big Dipper.

controls—natural or manmade forces that reduce the severity of other natural forces.

coral—the limestone skeletal deposits of polyps.

coral polyp—an animal that secretes a skeletal cup in which it lives.

coral reef—a natural community of millions of coral polyps growing together.

corolla—all of the petals of a flower.

crest—a raised tuft of feathers on top of a bird's head.

crown—the mass of foliage at the top of a tree.

crustacean (krus-TAY-shun)—an aquatic animal with an exoskeleton, such as a shrimp.

cumulus (KYEW-mew-lus)—referring to clouds that pile thickly, rising high in the sky.

cyclone (SI-klone)—a tornado.

D

debris (duh-BREE)—an accumulation of plant, animal, or rock fragments.

decay—the slow decomposition of vegetation.

deciduous (dee-SID-yew-us)—referring to a plant that sheds its leaves each year.

detritus (duh-TRY-tus)—particles of decaying animals and vegetation; plant fragments or loose bits of rock, caused by wearing away.

dewlap—the colorful skin under the chin of anole lizards that is stretched out during courting display.

diurnal (dye-URN-ul)—describes animals that are active and hunt during the daytime.

diversity—variety; containing many different species.

dome—a stand of trees with taller trees in the center and shorter trees near the edge, giving the stand a dome shape.

domestic—living near the habitations of humans, such as farm animals or pets; not wild.

dormancy—a state of being asleep, or inactive.

drainage basin—the entire area surrounding a water body from which surface water flows toward the water body.

drought—an extended period of dry weather; lack of rain.

dune—the ridge of sand at the ocean's edge that is piled up by wind and waves.

E

ebbs—flows backward toward the sea.

ecology (ee-KALL-uh-jee)—the study of the relationships between living things and their environment. (ecologist)

ecosystem (EE-ko-sis-tum)—a community of plants and animals that naturally grow and live together in harmony.

endangered—threatened with extinction; when the number of individuals in a species of plant or animal are so few that they can no longer reproduce young faster than the old individuals die.

endemic (en-DEM-ik)—living only in a particular locality or region.

entire—describing a leaf that has smooth edges.

entomology (EN-tuh-MALL-uh-jee)—a branch of zoology that studies insects. (entomologist)

environment (en-VYE-run-mint)—the physical, chemical, and biological factors that affect living things within a natural community.

enzyme (en-zime)—an organic substance in a cell that produces chemical changes.

epiphyte (EP-uh-fite)—an air plant whose nourishment comes from moisture and dust in the air; a plant that grows on another plant without harming the plant on which it grows.

equator (ee-KWAY-ter)—the imaginary dividing line around the earth, equally distant from the North and South poles, that divides the earth into the Northern Hemisphere and the Southern Hemisphere.

equinox (EE-kwi-noks)—the time when the sun crosses the earth's equator, making day and night equal at the equator.

erosion (ee-ROE-zhun)—the wearing away of the surface of sloping ground.

estuary (ES-chew-air-ee)—the watery area where a river meets the sea, where river flow meets tide, and fresh water meets salt water.

eutrophication (YEW-truh-fuh-KAY-shun)—the "aging" process that causes a lake to become shallower from increased nutrients that cause excessive plant growth, and therefore increase organic sediment.

evaporation (ee-VAP-uh-RAY-shun)—the process of changing from liquid to vapor; a part of the hydrologic cycle.

evapotranspiration (ee-VAP-oh-trans-per-AY-shun)—the transfer of water from the earth to the atmosphere through the evaporation of surface water from lakes, wetlands, etc., and through the transpiration of water from plants.

evergreen—referring to a plant that does not shed its leaves all at once.

exoskeleton (EK-so-SKEL-uh-tin)—the shell on the outside of the soft parts of an insect's body.

exotic (egg-ZOT-ik)—not native to the place where found; introduced from another area.

exterminate (eks-TERM-in-ate)—to eliminate organisms by killing individuals of the species.

extinction (eks-TINK-shun)—the death of an entire population of a species so that it can never exist again.

F

Family—part of the scientific system of naming things, below Order; the Family name of animals always ends with "-idae"; the Family name of plants always ends with "-aceae" or "-ae."

fauna—animal life, including mammals, birds, reptiles, insects, and so forth, especially the animals in a particular habitat.

field guide—a book arranged especially for identifying plants or animals.

field mark—an easily seen identifying feature on a wild animal.

fledglings—young birds just learning to fly.

flight feathers—the large stiff feathers on a bird's wings and tail necessary for flying.

floodplain—the area alongside a river that is flooded when seasonal heavy rains or melting snows cause the river to overflow its normal banks.

flora—plant life, especially the plants in a particular habitat.

florets—tiny flowers that make up the flower head of certain plants.

Floridan aquifer—Florida's largest underground water supply, underlying all but the southernmost part of the state.

flyway—one of the major routes for migrating birds.

foliage (FOE-lee-uj)—all of the leaves of a plant or cluster of plants.

food chain—the arrangement of organisms in an ecological system according to what they eat.

forage (FOR-uj)—noun, food for animals; verb, to search for food.

frond—the large leaf of a palm tree or a fern.

fungus—plants that are not green, such as mushrooms, molds, rust, etc.

G

genetics—the study of heredity; the passing on of characteristics to offspring.

genus—a kind, sort, or class; the first word in a scientific name.

germination—the sprouting of a seed.

glabrous—without hairs, sometimes referring to leaves, stems, or other parts of plants.

global warming—a trend toward higher temperatures over all the earth, thought to be caused by the release of too much carbon dioxide from the burning of wood, oil, and coal, which causes depletion of the protective ozone layer in the upper atmosphere.

gravity—the force that holds everything on Planet Earth.

ground water—water in the aquifer; water deep underground.

H

habitat—the place where a plant or animal naturally grows or lives.

hammock—an area of higher or lower ground that supports a community of plants different from the surrounding area.

head—a stand of trees growing in a depression.

herb (erb)—an annual, biennial, or perennial plant that does not develop woody stems.

herbaceous (er-BAY-shus)—describing plants or parts of plants that are soft, not woody.

herpetology (HERP-uh-TALL-uh-jee)—the scientific study of reptiles and amphibians. (herpetologist)

hibernate—to sleep or rest for an extended period of time in the winter; to be dormant.

horizon (hor-EYE-zun)—the line where earth and sky appear to meet.

humidity—the moisture in the air.

hurricane—a huge, doughnut-shaped storm that forms usually in the Atlantic Ocean during warm months and which can cause great destruction. Also called typhoon and tropical cyclone.

hydrologic cycle (HYE-druh-LAW-jik SYE-kul)—the process that recycles all water on earth through clouds, rain, transpiration, and evaporation.

hygrometer (hi-GROM-uh-ter)—an instrument that measures moisture in the air.

I

icthyology (IK-thee-ALL-uh-jee)—the scientific study of fishes. (icthyologist)

impoundment—an area surrounded by a dike for the purpose of making the land either all wet or all dry, sometimes to discourage mosquito breeding.

incubation period (IN-kew-BAY-shun)—the length of time it takes for eggs to hatch.

insecticide (in-SEK-tuh-side)—a chemical poison that kills insects.

insectivorous (in-sek-TIV-uh-rus)—referring to plants or animals that eat insects.

insolate (IN-so-late)—to warm by exposure to the sun's rays or a warm surface.

instinct—an animal's inner, unlearned impulse to respond to its natural environment. (instinctive)

intertidal zone—the area on a beach where the surf breaks.

introduced—describes a species that is not native to an area, but has been brought in from another location.

invertebrate (in-VERT-uh-brate)—an animal without a backbone, such as an insect.

K

key—little island, from the Spanish word *cayo.*

Kingdom—the highest classification in the scientific system of naming things. There are three: Animal Kingdom, Vegetable Kingdom, and Mineral Kingdom.

L

lagoon—a shallow water body partly surrounded by land that shelters it from the sea.

lanceolate (LANCE-ee-OH-late)—shaped like a lance-head; long, wide at the base and tapering to a point at the other end; commonly used to describe the shape of a leaf.

latitude (LAT-uh-tood)—one of a series of imaginary reference lines on the earth running parallel to the equator.

larva—(LARV-uh; the plural is larvae, pronounced LARV-eye) the juvenile, often wormlike, form of an insect.

leach—to dissolve out in water and trickle through.

lichen (LI-kin)—a plant consisting of a fungus in symbiotic relation with an alga, often found growing on rocks or trees.

life list—a recorded list of species of birds or other organisms seen throughout one's life.

linear—long and narrow; commonly used to describe the shape of a leaf.

longitude (LON-juh-tood)—one of a series of imaginary reference lines on the earth running from North Pole to South Pole.

M

mammal—one of a Class of animals with a backbone (vertebrates) that includes humans and all other animals with skin that have hair and that nourish their young with milk from mammary glands. (mammalogist)

mandibles (MAN-duh-bulls)—the upper and lower parts of a bird's bill. Also the lower jaw of other animals, and mouthparts of insects.

marine—pertaining to the sea.

marl—soil containing limestone.

metamorphosis (MET-uh-MORE-fuh-sis)—the extreme change in size, appearance, and behavior of certain insects such as butterflies during part of their life cycles.

meteorology (MEE-tee-yore-ALL-uh-jee)—the study of the atmosphere and weather. (meteorologist)

microclimate (MYE-krow-KLI-mut)—a small, special atmosphere, caused by a natural enclosure of space, such as in a sinkhole or cave.

microscopic—too small to be seen by the unaided eye.

midden—a mound of shells and bones, left by early Indians.

migrate (MI-grate)—to travel seasonally from one place to another; often applied to the journey of birds south in winter and north in summer. (migration)

molt—the shedding of feathers in preparation for growing new ones.

mulch—a covering of leaves or other vegetative material placed around plants to help retain moisture or reduce weeds.

N

nape—on a bird, back of the head.

native—living or growing naturally in a certain place.

naturalized—to become established as if native.

nocturnal (nok-TURN-ul)—describes animals that move about and hunt during the nighttime.

Northern Hemisphere (HEM-us-feer)—the half of the earth between the equator and the North Pole.

nursery—an area where the young of a species live for the early part of their lives.

nutrient—food; something that promotes growth and provides energy to an organism.

O

obovate (OB-oh-vate)—broader above the middle and rounded at both ends, often describing the shape of a leaf or fruit.

old-growth—describing an unlogged area with very old trees.

orbit—the path of the earth around the sun, or any celestial body around another celestial body.

Order—part of the scientific system of naming things, below Class; the Order name always ends with "-iformes."

organic—made up of living (or formerly living) things.

organism—a living thing; any form of plant or animal life.

ornithology (OR-nith-ALL-uh-jee)—the scientific study of birds. (ornithologist)

ozone—a natural layer in the upper atmosphere caused by solar ultraviolet radiation reacting with oxygen.

P

paleontology (PAY-lee-un-TALL-uh-jee)—the study of past geologic periods from bone fossils. (paleontologist)

palmate—shaped like the palm of the hand; used to describe the shape of a leaf.

panhandle—a long, narrow, projecting part of an area or state that is not a peninsula.

peat—rich soil made up of compressed decomposed plants.

pelagic zone (puh-LAJ-ik)—the area of deep ocean waters.

peninsula—a body of land almost surrounded by water.

perennials (purr-EN-ee-uls)—plants that live for three or more years.

perihelion (pare-uh-HEEL-yun)—the point in a planet's orbit when it is nearest to the sun.

periphyton (pare-uh-FIE-tin)—a type of algae and one-celled animals found growing together in clumps or mats, seen frequently in the Everglades.

petal—one of the segments of the corolla of a flower.

petiole—the stalk of a leaf.

pH—letters that give an indication of chemical acidity on a scale of 0 to 14; 7 is neutral, below 7 is acidic, and above 7 is alkaline.

photosynthesis (FO-toe-SIN-thuh-sis)—the process by which plants change energy from the sun, water, and nutrients in the soil into sugar, oxygen, and water the plant needs to grow.

Phylum (FIE-lum)—part of the scientific system of naming things, below Kingdom; a "race" of related living things; the Phylum name always ends with "-ata."

pistil—the part of a flower that contains the seeds.

plastron (PLAS-trun)—the bottom part of the shell of a turtle.

plumage (PLOO-mij)—the entire covering of feathers on a bird.

pneumatophores (new-MAT-uh-fors)—plant parts of the Black Mangrove tree that grow up out of the mud and aid in transpiration.

pollen (PALL-in)—the fertilizing dust of a flower that must be blown or carried to another flower of the same kind of plant in order to produce seeds. (pollinate)

pollution (puh-LOO-shun)—human-caused waste that contaminates the environment. (pollute, pollutant)

polyp (POLL-lip)—see coral polyp.

predator (PRED-uh-ter)—an animal whose food is other animals, rather than plants.

preen—the action a bird does with its bill to smooth, oil, and comb its feathers.

prehistoric—before written history.

prescribed burn—a carefully controlled fire purposely set to remove vegetation.

prey—the food of a meat-eating animal.

profession—an occupation or calling, especially one requiring extended or special learning.

propagate (PROP-uh-gate)—to increase and multiply an organism.

pubescent (pew-BESS-int)—with hairs, sometimes referring to leaves, stems, or other parts of a plant.

pupa—the stage of a metamorphic insect that is encased in a chrysalis or cocoon.

R

raceme (ray-SEEM)—a type of flower cluster in which each flower has its own stem on a longer stem.

raptors—birds of prey, such as eagles, hawks, and owls, with special beaks and claws for capturing live animals for food.

refuge—a place set aside for protection of plants and animals; same as sanctuary.

relict—a plant or animal that is a surviving remnant of an otherwise extinct organism.

reproduce—to produce new individuals of the same kind by seeds, eggs, birth, etc. (reproductive) reptile—an animal that is cold-blooded, that crawls on its belly such as a snake, or on small, short legs such as a lizard or turtle, and that usually is covered with scales or bony plates.

roost—a place where birds rest, often together.

S

salinity (suh-LIN-uh-tee)—saltiness; the amount of salt in water, usually about 35 parts per thousand in the ocean. (saline)

salt tolerant—able to live in or near saline or brackish water.

sanctuary—a place set aside for protection of plants and animals; same as refuge.

saturated—soaked; full of moisture.

scavenger—an animal that feeds on carrion or garbage.

SCUBA—an acronym using the first letters of the words Self-Contained Underwater Breathing Apparatus.

season—one of the four periods of the solar year.

seepage—the slow oozing or dripping of water.

sepals—the leaflike, outermost parts of a flower.

serrate—saw-toothed, as a leaf edge.

silviculture—tree farming; the care of forests, usually planted rather than natural forests.

simple—pertaining to a leaf that is undivided.

snag—a dead tree that has not fallen.

snorkel—a tube for breathing when your face is underwater.

solstice—"sun-stop"; the two periods in the year when the sun is farthest from the equator, on or about June 22 and December 22.

Southern Hemisphere (HEM-us-feer)—the half of the earth between the equator and the South Pole.

spatulate (SPAT-yoo-late)—spoon-shaped; birds' bills and leaves on plants can be spatulate.

species (SPEE-shees; this word is both singular and plural)—kinds or sorts of animals or plants.

Species of Special Concern—describes a species of plant or animal whose populations in Florida are not yet threatened or endangered, but are showing signs of being in trouble.

spike—a type of flower cluster in which flowers grow close together on a stem.

stalactites (stuh-LAK-tites)—formations in caves that hang down from the cave ceiling.

stalagmites (stuh-LAG-mites)—formations in caves that build up from the cave floor.

stamen—the part of a flower that bears the pollen.

steephead—a type of ravine such as those found along the Apalachicola River in the Panhandle of Florida.

storm surge—the increased height of the ocean along a coast caused by a hurricane.

stratus clouds—clouds that stretch out in long lines close to earth.

Subphylum (SUB-fye-lum)—part of the scientific system of naming things, below Phylum; the Subphylum name always ends with "-ata."

subspecies—a subdivision of a species; one that may be isolated from others of its species.

surface water—water on the surface of the ground, such as lakes, rivers, and water in the soil near the top of the ground.

symbiosis (SIM-bee-OH-sis)—different organisms living together in a close association that benefits each species. (symbiotic)

symbol—something that stands for something else.

systematics (SIS-tuh-MAT-iks)—the system of naming all plants, animals, and minerals with a binomial; taxonomy.

T

talon—the sharp, curved claw of a bird of prey.

taxonomy (tax-ON-uh-mee)—the system of naming all plants, animals, and minerals with a binomial; systematics.

tentacle (TENT-uh-kul)—a slender, flexible feeler, usually on an animal's head.

terrestrial (tuh-RES-tree-ul)—pertaining to land.

thermal—a rising column of warm air.

thorax—the middle section of the three parts of an insect.

threatened—describes a species of plant or animal whose populations are not yet endangered, but are showing signs of being in severe trouble.

topsoil—surface soil, in which most plants have their roots.

tornado—a narrow, whirling, funnel-shaped wind that can cause great destruction. Also called cyclone and twister.

trade winds—winds that blow almost constantly in one direction.

trans-Gulf—across the Gulf of Mexico, referring to bird migration.

transpiration (TRANS-per-AY-shun)—the transfer of water from the earth to the atmosphere through the leaves of plants.

tropical—relating to or occurring in the tropics, the zones on either side of the equator.

U

umbel—a flower cluster that is flat or rounded like an umbrella.

understory—the shrubs, herbs, and grasses that grow under the canopy of trees in a forest.

V

vertebrate (VERT-uh-brate)—an animal with a backbone, such as a bird, fish, or mammal.

W

water table—the level of the surface water in the soil.

wetland—an area that is often saturated with water, but is not a lake or river.

wildlife—living things that are not human, nor domesticated or cultivated by humans.

weather vane (or wind vane, or vane)—an instrument that indicates the direction the wind is blowing; the arrow usually points toward the compass point from which the wind is blowing.

X

xeric (ZEER-ik)—dry; often used to describe plants that need little water to survive, or to describe landscaping that uses plants that thrive in the moisture naturally present in the soil.

Z

zoology (zo-ALL-uh-jee)—the scientific study of the entire Animal Kingdom. (zo-ALL-uh-jist)

zygomorphic (ZYE-guh-MOR-fik)—a type of flower that is symmetrical from side to side, but not top to bottom.

Artists

These artists have contributed their talents to one or more of the chapters in this book, most of them when the chapter first appeared in The Florida Naturalist. *The authors are grateful for their generosity. We have made a great effort to notify each of them, but we were unable to contact a few of the original artists.*

Richard Daniel Adams was Senior Artist for Walt Disney World for several years, and is now a landscape and wildlife artist. He won the design contests for both the "Challenger" license plates and the official Orange County flag. ("John James Audubon in Florida")

Daniel "Butch" Ambrose is a native Floridian and a self-taught artist who lives along the Tomoka River. He spends many mornings sketching nature from his canoe. He has studied with several master wildlife artists, has displayed his art in many festivals and shows, and has been featured in several publications. ("Exotics–More than Just a Nuisance")

Dick Ayre is from Michigan, attended the Cooper School of Art in Cleveland, Ohio, and has pursued a full-time art career in Sarasota since 1986. His work is displayed in galleries, gift shops, and art festivals, and has been published in *The Florida Naturalist* and other magazines. ("The Big Scrub")

Jeanne L. Barnes is a free-lance illustrator and commercial artist in Gainesville. She especially enjoys wildlife illustration. ("Discovering the Beach")

Marcy Bartlett is a central Florida free-lance artist. An example of her artwork is in the Smithsonian Institute. She says her favorite things to draw are butterflies and other insects. ("Insects Are Not Just 'Bugs'!")

Jon Bortles is a graduate of the Ringling School of Art in Sarasota and a free-lance artist in the central Florida area. ("The Keys")

Betty Caldwell of Orlando paints and draws as a hobby. ("Keeping a Nature Journal")

Mitzi Chilton is a free-lance artist whose paintings and lithographs have been displayed at the Arts Center in St. Petersburg and at shows in the Tampa Bay area. ("Florida's Native Plants")

Dave Dickson has been a graphic artist in the Orlando area, and is now a free-lance wildlife artist. ("The Mysteries of Bird Migration" and "Alligators, Snakes, and Other Reptiles")

Ellen Doughty is a free-lance artist in the central Florida area. She has worked on designs for Walt Disney World Co., Universal Studios, The Marketplace, Church Street Station, and Tupperware. ("Extinction Is Forever")

Janet English was an artist for Walt Disney's prize-winning animated films, "The Little Mermaid" and "Rollercoaster Rabbit." She does painting and sculpture and now lives in Washington State. ("Directions for the Crew of Spaceship Earth")

Joyce Estes lives near the Apalachicola River in Florida's Panhandle. Her illustrations were first published in *Portrait of an Estuary* by Verle Barnes. ("The Panhandle")

Vicki Ferguson, Ph.D., research entomologist and consultant, is a self-taught wildlife artist. ("The Fun of Watching Birds")

Valerie Gohlke is an environmental educator with the Florida Audubon Society. ("Monitoring the Weather")

Julia Damon Hanway lives in northwest Florida and has worked as a commercial artist in the Tallahassee area for many years. ("Speaking of Trees")

Mary Justice of Orlando has done drawings and paintings that have been shown in Jacksonville and Sarasota art galleries. ("A Little Botany Lesson")

Daniel Lindvig is a self-taught artist living in central Florida. He has been drawing seriously for several years, especially portraiture and wildlife art. ("Florida's Seasons")

Lowell Lotspeich is an architect and artist in the central Florida area. ("Pine Flatwoods" and "Prairies— Wet and Dry")

Heather McElroy received a Bachelor of Fine Arts from Cornell, and worked at the Artists Foundation Art Gallery in Boston, Massachusetts before traveling to Czechoslovakia. ("The Air Around Us" and "Monitoring the Weather")

Ann McKinney is a mixed media artist and a fifth-generation Floridian. She was serving as a conservation intern at Florida Audubon headquarters when she did the artwork for *Young Naturalists.* ("Florida's Symbols")

Katie O'Brien of DeLand has a science background, but is now an artist. ("Springs, Sinkholes, and Caves")

Diane Pierce, a graduate of the Cleveland Institute of Art, is a free-lance artist and illustrator of wild birds. She provided 34 color plates for the *National Geographic Society Field Guide to the Birds of North America.* She lives in Lake Wales. (Cover art, "Prairies—Wet and Dry," "Pine Flatwoods," "What's in a Name?" "What Is a Bird of Prey?")

Elizabeth Smith paints in watercolor and draws in pen and ink. Her art, including watercolors of native plants and butterflies, has been displayed in local galleries. She has illustrated several books, and her art has appeared on magazine covers. ("The Everglades" and "Water and Wetlands")

Laura Dunn Stoia is a self-taught, free-lance artist working primarily in pen and ink. She has illustrated a field guide for the Florida Department of Environmental Protection, and her art has been displayed in a Naples gallery. She also works for the *Naples Daily News.* ("The Salt Marshes")

Mary Ruth Webb of Ormond Beach has her own graphics design studio and did the artwork for a coral reef poster for the National Oceanic and Atmospheric Administration. ("Underwater Treasures: Coral Reefs")

Appendix

Addresses

Archbold Biological Station
  813/465-2571
  P.O. Box 2057
  Lake Placid, FL 33852

Florida Audubon Society
  407/260-8300
  460 Hwy. 436, Suite 200
  Casselberry, FL 32707

Florida Native Plant Society
  407/299-1472
  P.O. Box 680008
  Orlando, FL 32868

The Nature Conservancy
  Florida Chapter
  407/628-5887
  2699 Lee Rd., Suite 500
  Winter Park, FL 32789

Florida LakeWatch Program
  904/392-9613
  7922 N.W. 71st Street
  Gainesville, FL 32606

Skywarn, National Weather Service
  Rockville, Maryland 20852

Center for Marine Conservation
  813/895-2188
  One Beach Dr. S.E., Suite 304
  St. Petersburg, FL 33701

Bird Banding Laboratory
  U.S. Fish and Wildlife Service
  Laurel, Maryland, 20798
  or: Washington, D.C. (no zip code is
  needed)

The Environmental Careers
  Organization
  813/886-4330
  4902 Eisenhower Blvd., Suite 217
  Tampa, FL 33634-6324

Florida's Water Management Districts
  (WMD):

  St. Johns River WMD,
  P.O. Box 1429
  Palatka, FL 32178-1429

  South Florida WMD,
  P.O. Box 24680
  West Palm Beach, FL 33416-4680

  Southwest Florida WMD,
  2379 Broad St.
  Brooksville, FL 34609-6899

  Suwannee River WMD,
  Rt. 3, Box 94
  Live Oak, FL 32060

  Northwest Florida WMD,
  Rt. 1, Box 3100
  Havana, FL 32333-9700

Florida Game & Fresh Water Fish
  Commission
  Nongame Wildlife Program
  904-488-1960
  620 S. Meridian St., Tallahassee, FL
  32399
  (Official List of Endangered and
  Potentially Endangered Flora and
  Fauna in Florida, published
  periodically by Florida Game and
  Fresh Water Fish Commission, is
  free on request).

Florida Department of Environmental
  Protection
  3900 Commonwealth Blvd., #304
  Tallahassee, FL 32303

Florida Books for More Reading and Reference

(Besides using the library and your
local bookstores, field guides may be
ordered through the Florida
Audubon Society. Books about
Florida or by Florida authors can be
ordered from Mickler's Floridiana, in
Oviedo, Florida. Books may also be
ordered directly from the publisher.)

Guides to Plants:

The Trees of Florida, Nelson, Pineapple
  Press
The Guide to Florida Wildflowers,
  Taylor, Taylor Publishing
*Florida Wild Flowers and Roadside
  Plants*, Bell and Taylor, Laurel Hill
  Press

*Native Trees and Shrubs of the Florida
  Keys*, Scurlock, Laurel Press
*Seashore Plants of South Florida and
  the Caribbean*, Nellis, Pineapple
  Press

Bird Guides:

Florida's Birds, Kale and Maehr,
  Pineapple Press

Guides to Reptiles:

*Handbook of Reptiles and Amphibians
  of Florida, Part I, Snakes*, Ashton,
  Windward Publishing
*Handbook of Reptiles and Amphibians
  of Florida, Part II, Lizards, Turtles,
  and Crocodilians*, Ashton, Windward
  Publishing
*Handbook of Reptiles and Amphibians
  of Florida, Part III, Amphibians*,
  Ashton, Windward Publishing

Other books:

The Climate and Weather of Florida,
  Henry, Pineapple Press
The Springs of Florida, Stamm,
  Pineapple Press
Florida Rocks, Minerals and Fossils,
  Comfort, Pineapple Press
*Protecting Paradise, 300 Ways to
  Protect Florida's Environment*,
  Cavanaugh and Spontak, Pineapple
  Press
The Nature of Things on Sanibel,
  Campbell, Pineapple Press
The Rivers of Florida, Marth, Pineapple
  Press
Florida's Butterflies and Other Insects,
  Stiling, Pineapple Press
*Exploring Wild South Florida, A Guide
  to Finding the Natural Areas of the
  Everglades and Florida Keys*, Jewell,
  Pineapple Press
The Gulf of Mexico, Gore, Pineapple
  Press
Coral Reefs of Florida, Voss, Pineapple
  Press

Rare and Endangered Biota of Florida
    Series:
    Fishes
    Mammals
    Amphibians and Reptiles
    Plants
    Birds
    Insects
    Published by University Press of
    Florida.
Water Resources Atlas of Florida,
    Fernald & Patton, Ed., Florida State
    University Press
Forest in the Sand, Marjory Bartlett
    Sanger, Atheneum

World of the Great White Heron,
    Marjory Bartlett Sanger, Devin-Adair
The Yearling, Marjorie Kinnan
    Rawlings, Scribners
Cross Creek, Marjorie Kinnan
    Rawlings, Scribners
The Everglades, River of Grass, Marjory
    Stoneman Douglas, Pineapple Press
Marjory Stoneman Douglas: Voice of
    the River, An Autobiography, with
    Rothchild, Pineapple Press
Audubon in Florida, Kathryn Hall
    Proby, University of Miami Press
Bartram in Florida, Edited by Helen
    Cruickshank, Florida Garden Clubs

Index

(Italic page numbers indicate illustrations.)